HOLY BOLDNESS

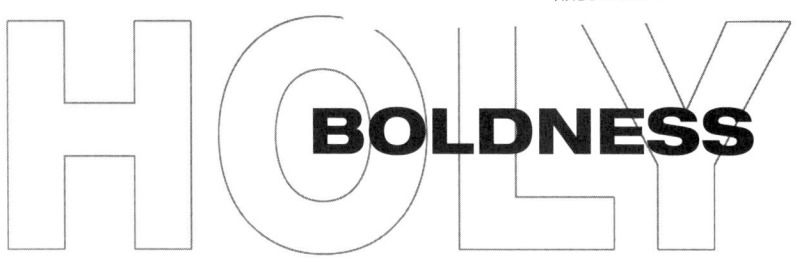

Practices of an Evangelistic Lifestyle

PAUL R. DEKAR

SMYTH&HELWYS
PUBLISHING, INCORPORATED   MACON, GEORGIA

Smyth & Helwys Publishing, Inc.
6316 Peake Road
Macon, Georgia 31210-3960
1-800-747-3016
©2004 by Smyth & Helwys Publishing
All rights reserved.
Printed in the United States of America.

The paper used in this publication meets the minimum requirements of
American National Standard for Information Sciences—
Permanence of Paper for Printed Library Materials.
ANSI Z39.48–1984. (alk. paper)

Library of Congress Cataloging-in-Publication Data

Dekar, Paul R.
Holy boldness : practices of an evangelistic lifestyle / by Paul Dekar.
p. cm.
ISBN 1-57312-385-4 (pbk. : alk. paper)

1. Evangelistic work.
2. Christian life.
I. Title.
BV3795 .D45 2003
269'.2—dc22

2003017051

Table of Contents

Foreword..v
Words of Dedication..viii
Introduction...1

Part I: Practices of Humility

Introduction..14
Holy Prayer...18
Holy Sabbath..28
Holy Play...38
Holy Discernment..48

Part II: Practices of Loving-kindness

Introduction..58
Practices of Love..63
Practices of Listening...72
Practices of Compassion...84
Practices of Testimony...97

Part III: Practices of Just Living

Introduction..108
Practices of Reconciliation..112
Practices of Jubilee..124
Practices of Dialogue...136
Practices of Servant Leadership...147

Part IV: Seasonal Practices

Introduction..160
Practices of Thanksgiving..163
Practices of Advent, Christmas and Epiphany..............................173
Practices of an Easter People...184

Appendix...194

For Gordon Kurtz, Bob Yanke, Chris Page, and Nancy Sehested

*I thank my God every time I remember you,
constantly praying with joy in every one of my prayers for all of you,
because of your sharing in the gospel* (Phil 1:3-5).

Foreword

I'll be honest. Humility, compassion, peace, and justice were not the first words that came to mind when I read the subtitle of this book, "Practices of an Evangelistic Lifestyle."

That's unfortunate. It's also understandable. For many prodigal Christians like me, words such as evangelical and evangelistic long ago had the salt and light stomped and shouted out of them by pulpit-pounding, big-haired Bible-wavers who told us about heaven and condemned us to hell but not before reminding us that Jesus needed our money.

Over the years, want-to-believers like me had too many Elmer Gantrys grab our wallet or our girl and too few Billy Grahams grab our heart. We heard too many Pat Robertsons tell us about the gospel of self-preservation and too few Ron Siders tell us about the gospel of the kingdom. We knew too much about the Jim Bakkers of the world, not enough about evangelists like Tony Campolo, Will Campbell, or Paul Dekar.

What a shame. When we confused evangelism with televangelism and the Sermon on the Mount with sermons on amounts, the good news seemed like bad news. We believed, but we were overcome with unbelief, or maybe disbelief. So we threw the baby out with the "specially-anointed" baptismal water. We let a few mischievous messengers kill the message.

If only we'd found out sooner that the evangelical tradition predates PTL and the 700 Club. If only we'd learned earlier that *evangelize* is the verb form of the noun *gospel*, and thus, *to evangelize* simply means to share the gospel. If only we'd been told on day one in Sunday school that preaching isn't the only way in which to share the gospel. If only we'd known from the beginning that the first evangelist wasn't Jimmy or Jerry. The first evangelist was Jesus.

"Jesus, surely, is the best illustration of how to communicate the Good News," evangelical author and teacher Ronald J. Sider wrote in *Good News and Good Works*. "If anything is clear in Jesus, it is that he announces the kingdom by word and deed. God Incarnate shared the Good News by verbal proclamation and visible demonstration."

Jesus didn't simply preach and teach. He prayed and listened and forgave and healed and, above all, loved. Jesus practiced what he preached. The practices of Jesus of Nazareth, as recorded in the four Gospels, are the "Practices of an Evangelistic Lifestyle." In other words, contrary to the misperceptions of recovering Christian cynics such as myself, the evangelical tradition isn't all talk. It isn't merely invitational; it's also instructional, inspirational, and incarnational. True evangelicals talk the talk *and* walk the walk.

"Remember, we are calling people not merely to accept a set of beliefs about Jesus that will somehow trip the divine lever and get them into heaven when they die. Oh, no!" evangelical author and teacher Richard J. Foster wrote about the evangelical tradition in *Streams of Living Water*. "We are inviting people to believe in Jesus by becoming his disciples, and as his disciples (or apprentices) to enroll in his school of living. Thus, people become trained in the Way, increasingly taking into themselves Jesus' hopes, dreams, longings, habits and abilities."

Or, as Paul Dekar puts it in his introduction to this book, "Christian beliefs must be put into practice." Why? Not to get into the kingdom of heaven, but to model the kingdom on earth as in heaven. Although this may come as a revelation to each of us at some point, it is not an original evangelistic thought. Benedict gave us rules, Ignatius exercises, Thomas à Kempis imitations, and Wesley methods. Not all of us are monastics, ascetics, or prophets, however. The rest of us could use something a bit more modern, accessible, and doable than the Rule of Benedict.

That's what we get in *Holy Boldness: Practices of an Evangelistic Lifestyle*. It's a contemplative "how-to," a manual for the whole gospel. Dekar takes a wide assortment of spiritual disciplines from various Christian traditions and shows us how and why all the pieces fit together. For example, modern evangelism often gets reduced in pulpit and pew to something known as "testifying." But, as Dekar shows, sharing the gospel also means sharing our stories, listening and dialoguing. Dekar's explications are even more encouraging than they are enlightening. The more you read, the more you realize that we already know "how to," that the evangelistic lifestyle doesn't require a seminary degree, a television audience, or questionable financial practices, but such simple (though not simplistic) practices as kindness, fairness, and boldness.

How refreshing also to recover an evangelical tradition defined not by Sinclair Lewis but by Clive Staples Lewis. Dekar's evangelistic heritage dates back to St. Peter and includes true evangelicals such as Jerome, Dominic, Luther, Calvin, Wesley, and Finney. For this book, Dekar drew insight and inspiration from an even wider assortment of Judeo-Christian spiritual mentors, from Buber and Heschel to Thurman and King. That's the true value of Dekar's work here. In a time when evangelicalism unfortunately is seen as a narrow, dogmatic denominationalism, Dekar is a bold, evangelical ecumenist.

Raised and mentored by a Russian Orthodox father and a mother with Jewish roots, Dekar found God for himself through adult baptism in the Baptist tradition. Like Dr. Martin Luther King Jr., Dekar is a Baptist in the truest religious liberty and soul competency senses of the word. Since the late 1960s, he has been deeply involved in sharing the gospel of peace and justice through such organizations as the Fellowship of Reconciliation, the Baptist Peace Fellowship, and Amnesty International. Dekar and his wife Nancy have cultivated and shared their evangelistic lifestyles in missions and ministries from Chad to Cameroon and even to Canada, where Dekar taught theology at McMaster University. In 1995, he came to Memphis to teach at Memphis Theological Seminary. Here, in the city where C. H. Mason lived in prayerful humility, Carroll Dozier served in loving-kindness, and Martin Luther King Jr. struggled for just living, Paul Dekar works in holy boldness, preaching, teaching, and healing in the name of Jesus, the boldest holy man ever.

David Waters
"Faith Matters" columnist for *The Commercial Appeal*

Words of Dedication

Authors often nod to the long-suffering family then recognize scholars who inspired a particular book. In my case, this is neither descriptive nor good-mannered. I could not have brought this project to completion without my family. I owe a great debt to Nancy Rose Dekar, Nathaniel Paul Dekar, his wife Jacqueline Jennifer Miller Dekar, and Matthew Paul Dekar. They encourage me. As I err, they forgive me. At times when I am on the road or preoccupied, they patiently reassure me of the worth of this project. When I am discouraged by real-life challenges, they refocus me on Martin Luther King Jr.'s dream of the Beloved Community, his phrase for the future new heaven and new earth (Rev 21:1).[1]

Daily, Nancy leans into the vision of the Beloved Community. My life companion on the journey, she makes tangible words of a poster: when you have a dream, don't let anything dim it; keep hoping, keep trying. The sky is the limit.

The themes of this book arise from my engagement with religious communities. The Russian Orthodox Church and Judaism shaped my early religious experience. From the latter tradition, I absorbed an inspirational and moralistic story derived from the account of Abraham interceding on behalf of Sodom and Gomorrah. Abraham bartered. What if ten righteous are there? God answered, *For the sake of ten I will not destroy it* (Gen 18:32).

Hasidic legends tell of the *Lamed Vov,* the Thirty-six Just. The righteous ones are equal in dignity to Abraham and Sarah, Isaac and Rebekah, Jacob and Rachel. These upright individuals are unaware that their prayer and service support the earth and prevent its destruction. We should always be mindful that a neighbor could be one of the hidden just.[2]

If the legend of the *Lamed Vov* bears any truth, I have surely met some of them. Among them, I celebrate the ministries of three pastors whose bold witness ultimately inspired this book. Gordon Kurtz, pastor of South Avenue Baptist Church in Rochester, New York, from 1957–1969, is now retired. He lives in Bayfield, Ontario, Canada, with his wife Melisse. Bob Yanke, pastor at MacNeill Baptist in Hamilton, Ontario, Canada, from 1968–1990, is also retired. He lives in Dundas, Ontario, with his wife Doris. Chris Page was Bob Yanke's associate for three years and succeeded Bob as pastor of MacNeill Baptist Church from 1990–1995. He now lives in Melbourne, Victoria, Australia where he serves as pastor of East Doncaster Baptist Church. Nancy Sehested, pastor of Prescott Baptist in Memphis, Tennessee, from 1987–1995, serves as pastor and prison chaplain in North Carolina. She lives in Asheville, North Carolina, with her husband Ken.

Gordon, Bob, and Nancy are three of the righteous ones. Their prayer and service are the foundation of the universe. In their woundedness, they are transparent. In the manner Paul affirmed of coworkers in Christ Jesus, they are risk-takers (Rom 16:4). In life-giving ways, they are Christ to me. I think of them as companions on the journey to the Beloved Community.

Whether explicit or not, writing is autobiographical. One's story influences one's writing. As well as family and pastors, other significant individuals have shaped my journey.

In the household of my childhood and teen years, my family never restricted religion to the sphere of one's private life. Caring parents Paul and Ariadne Dekar and my siblings Marguerite and George challenged me to do justice, love kindness, and walk humbly with God.

Around 1959, Alan Smith, a high school friend, invited me to accompany him to the Cow Palace in San Francisco where Billy Graham was conducting a crusade. I recall being turned off initially. Prior training had not prepared me for what I experienced, especially the emotionalism. I left the gathering at the earliest possible moment. As we drove from the parking lot, I felt God's call. I returned to the auditorium, went forward, and committed my life to God.

That night, Paul Lindholm counseled me. Subsequently, he guided me in my newfound faith. Mel Pekrul administered baptism at Valley Baptist Church. Several youth leaders challenged me to live out my faith amid the pain of the world. Now Shell Ridge Community Church of Walnut Creek, California, this congregation continues to care for my extended family.

At university, Lou Lucky cooked for the Christian house where I lived. One day she invited me to her Missionary Baptist congregation. I attended. I started sharing in street preaching and community organizing. From Lou and from her congregation I learned that the economic, political, and social events touching my life were not separate from religion.

On 2 July 1964, Lou and I were in the basement of an inner city congregation. As President Lyndon Johnson signed the Civil Rights Act, a solemn, not jubilant mood pervaded the room. A sense of realism tempered temptation to overstate the significance of this legislative gain. A storm cloud, almost palpable, seemed to gather. Would Southern states implement provisions for desegregated public accommodation? What would be the impact of the impending candidacy of Barry Goldwater, likely to be crowned the next week in San Francisco as Republican Party nominee for the United States presidency? How would the possibility of increased United States military involvement in Vietnam impact civil rights gains? Were we any closer to realizing the Beloved Community? "We've crossed a river. There's a mountain ahead. We've got to keep on walking," summarized Lou.

Despite this air of uncertainty, we knew there was no way to turn back. Working together, ordinary people could perform extraordinary deeds. As words of a song we sang that night suggest, there is no easy walk to freedom. We had to keep walking, together journeying a little further toward the Beloved Community. "For those who walk there is no road; the road is made by walking."[3]

Lou introduced me to writings of Howard Thurman (1900–1981). Thurman was among those who cultivated the ground for the transformation of race in the United States. "Even though he would never put himself in this category, [Thurman's] work provided the foundation for a great deal of what we call liberation theology and black theology. But it was for him Jesus theology."[4]

Thurman was neither a civil rights movement activist nor a systematic theologian. Rather, he was a spiritual guide for thousands of people of every race, creed, and ethnicity grappling with all the pain and confusion experienced in the world at the time. Not by chance, Martin Luther King Jr. was among those Thurman inspired. Thurman was a family friend and teacher. King carried a copy of Thurman's *Jesus and the Disinherited* in his briefcase.[5]

Thurman provides a role model par excellence of a ministry of pastoral care, preaching, teaching, and writing. One of his meditations shapes my theology of evangelism:

When the song of the angels is still,
When the star in the sky is gone,
When the kings and princes are home,
When the shepherds are back with their sheep,
The work of Christmas begins:
To find the lost,
To heal the broken,
To feed the hungry,
To release the prisoner,
To rebuild the nations,
To bring peace among people,
To make music in the heart.[6]

Since 1975, I have taught in university and seminary settings at undergraduate and graduate levels in Australia, Canada, and the United States. Many criticize the intellectual world as an ivory tower. This has not been my experience. The academic context has stimulated growth of mind and spirit. The craft of teaching has allowed me to touch the lives of people genuinely and feel their aches and joys. Material in this book arose from courses at Memphis Theological Seminary, my professional community since 1995. Students have helped render my grasp of practices of an evangelistic lifestyle concretely. Jane Williamson and others on the library staff have given crucial help. Among those who read and commented on draft material, the Reverend Dr. Steven Mosley, the Reverend Eyleen Farmer, and my Sunday morning seminar class at Prescott Baptist have offered keen insights.

In early 1996, at Memphis Theological Seminary, I delivered the Bowen Lectures on the practice of reconciliation. Feedback I received stimulated me in 1998 to devote six months to the topic. During that period, the Japan Presbytery of the Cumberland Presbyterian Church, the China Graduate School of Theology in Hong Kong, and Whitley College and the School of World Mission at the University of Melbourne in Australia offered hospitality, stimulation, and critique. Twice, in 1998 and 2002, Whitley College students helped deepen my understanding of the practice of reconciliation in Australia as well as in several Asian and South Pacific contexts.

In July 1998, I delivered the Rattan Lectures with the Reverend Graham Paulson, the first ordained Baptist Aboriginal pastor. I benefited from his incisive presentations and from the wisdom of his family. During intense conversations in 1999, 2000, and 2002, I continued to learn from the Paulson family. For me it has been a fruitful pilgrimage to journey into the world of Aboriginal spirituality. When we who are from younger cultures encounter ancient wisdom, we open ourselves to find our truest selfhood.

Since I began teaching in 1975, I have identified with two small-membership Baptist congregations and with numerically modest movements such as the School of Servant Leadership in Memphis, Tennessee. Members of peace-and-justice groups and of the historic peace churches (Mennonites, Brethren, and Religious Society of Friends) have been my companions amid the pain of the world. This has often been a source of anguish, but I have come to appreciate the power of small circles working in quiet ways to affect healing and transformation. With Adrienne Rich, "My heart is moved by all I cannot save; so much has been destroyed, I have to cast my lot with those who age after age, perversely, with no extraordinary power, reconstitute the world."

---

[1] *New Revised Standard Version* (Grand Rapids: Zondervan, 1989). I endeavor to use inclusive language. This is not mere convention. Through words we express our most basic commitments.

[2] See André Schwarz-Bart, *The Last of the Just*, trans. Stephen Becker (New York: Bantam, 1960); Gershom Scholem, "The Tradition of the Thirty-Six Hidden Just Men," *The Messianic Idea in Judaism and Other Essays on Jewish Spirituality* (New York: Schocken, 1971), 251-56; Elie Wiesel, *Legends of Our Time* (New York: Schocken, 1982), 125-29.

[3] "Caminante, no hay camino. Se hace el camino al andar." By these words, the Spanish poet Antonio Machado y Ruiz emphasizes the image of a journey. Also see Athol Gill, *Life on the Road: The Gospel Basis for a Messianic Lifestyle* (Scottdale: Herald Press, 1992).

[4] Vincent Harding in *Sojourners* 22/10 (December 1993): 16. Also see chapter 13 of my *For the Healing of the Nations: Baptist Peacemakers* (Macon: Smyth & Helwys, 1993).

[5] Vincent Harding, "Foreword," *Jesus and the Disinherited* (Boston: Beacon Press, 1996).

[6] Baptist Peace Fellowship of North America, *PeaceWork* (November-December 1987).

Introduction

What does the LORD *require of you but to do justice, and to love kindness, and to walk humbly with your God?* (Micah 6:8)

A legend recounts the return of Jesus to glory after his time on earth. Even in heaven he bears the marks of his earthly life with its cruel cross and shameful death. The angel Gabriel approaches Jesus, saying, "Master, you must have suffered terribly for your people down there."

"I did," Jesus replied.

"And do they know all about how you loved them and what you did for them?" continued Gabriel.

"Oh, no," said Jesus, "not yet. Right now only a handful of people in Palestine know."

"Then what have you done to let everyone know of your love for them?" persisted Gabriel.

"I've asked Peter, James, John, and a few more friends to tell others about me. Those who are told will in turn tell still other people about me, and my story will spread to the farthest reaches of the globe. Ultimately, all will have heard about my life and what I have done."

Knowing of what poor stuff people are made, Gabriel frowned. "Yes, but what if Peter and James and John grow weary? What if the people who come after them forget? What if at the end of the twentieth century people are not telling others about you? Haven't you made any other plans?"

Jesus answered, "I haven't made any other plans. I'm counting on them."[1]

Jesus is counting on us. This truth is the central theme of this book.

Just as Jesus' confidence in his disciples and subsequent generations of his followers elicited skepticism on the part of Gabriel, some readers may already be on edge. For many, evangelism is considered a dirty word. Some are embarrassed by spiritual frauds who pose as evangelists, especially those who use such dubious means as posturing or lying to promote Christianity. Others equate evangelism with proselytizing.

There are other, understandable reasons why people are reluctant to evangelize. Some individual lives are too empty or busy for the overflow that constitutes evangelism. Some feel vulnerable or lack the confidence to share the gospel with family members or friends. Others are content to let the pastor evangelize. Some are content with congregations that adopt a maintenance mentality. By this, I mean that they fail to enlist members for the work of evangelism and seal themselves and their congregations off from the wider world.[2]

Still, many Christians do look for ways to practice evangelism. Commonly, situations such as declining or aging membership inspire concern for evangelism by a congregation. One response has been to render evangelism an office of the church or a professional duty. The idea is to form a committee or preach on the theme. Pastors and laypeople go to workshops, take courses, or participate in retreats. By doing so they manifest an implicit assumption that there is a formula to achieve congregational renewal or numerical growth.

An alternative approach suggests evangelism is what ordinary people do daily in ordinary ways. Christians come alive with boldness in the day-to-day world. They discover their greatest joy is to share Jesus with the world, serve as agents of God's reconciling love, invite people to become part of God's family, and nurture them in their newborn lives. From this perspective, evangelism is natural, essential, and intentional as God empowers Christians to participate in God's mission.

In English, the words "evangelism" and "to evangelize" derive from the Greek *euangelion* and *euangelizomai*. Biblical translators characteristically express these words as "gospel" or "good news" and "to proclaim" or "to tell the good news." In the *Theological Dictionary of the New Testament*, Gerhard Friedrich mentions many of the uses in the Hebrew Bible and non-canonical literature of the word evangelism and its cognates.[3] The people of ancient Israel encountered and announced the saving works of God. Thus, while the language of evangelism is more distinct and common in the New Testament, evangelism in the general sense of proclaiming God's way of salvation is not unique to the early Christian community. To comprehend New Testament belief in God's coming reign, the theme of the dawning of a new age is significant. *How beautiful upon the mountains are the feet of the messenger who announces peace, who brings the good news, who announces salvation, who says to Zion, "Your God Reigns"* (Isa 52:7).

Even when the people Israel focused on their exacting status as God's elect, they held their self-understanding as God's chosen people in tension with their conviction that they were instruments through whom God extended the covenants and saving power to the nations. From ancient times, Jews have sought to discover ways of balancing this tension by realizing the universal thrust of Judaism without abandoning the intense particularism of the tradition.

Over a hundred New Testament passages use evangelism and cognate words. Writers focus on the good news of the dawning of salvation, the coming of Jesus to earth, his announcement of God's coming reign, and his message of peace. The life, death, resurrection, and glorification of Jesus make visible Israel's messianic hope. Evangelism is about sharing this.

Sharing is something we do all the time quite naturally and unintentionally. To cite several examples, we usually warn others where danger exists or when something is to be avoided. Or, when we see a good movie or play, we call friends and loved ones and urge them to see the film or production. Typically, we may even accompany them. So too when we learn of a good product or of the availability of favorable prices, we let family or friends know. They reciprocate by letting us know of a movie that communicates moral qualities. They help us out in matters of personal finances. Whether or not the movie is good, whether or not we take advantage of the discounts, we take care to respond with expressions of gratefulness.

Sharing the gospel, the good news of Jesus Christ, is comparable to letting somebody know about a movie or sale, only more important. It is offering to others the gift of salvation, a better life on earth, and the promise of eternal salvation. Evangelism is a sharing that invites response and aims at transformation. Many factors inspire us to share the good news of Jesus with others. For example, we have gratitude that God has touched our lives or a deep sense that what gives us wholeness and the promise of eternal life with God are gifts that God offers all or the conviction that people need Christ to combat sin and evil. These are powerful motivations. Evangelist Daniel Thambyrajah Niles (1908–1970) of Sri Lanka characterized such evangelism as a beggar telling other beggars where to find bread.

Evangelism is the specific manner by which we embark upon God's transforming work. Following Jesus in the footsteps of countless disciples, martyrs, saints, clergy, and laypeople, we are God's own people called to proclaim the mighty acts of him who called us out of darkness into his marvelous light (1 Pet 2:9). If, in these words of Peter, we are called to proclaim the mighty acts of Jesus, the giver of salvation, how are we to fulfill this responsibility?

First, we must acknowledge always and without exception and in humility that the Holy Spirit is the crucial actor in the activities of evangelism. As we serve as agents of God's love and reconciliation, we do so under power of the Holy Spirit. This effects the transformation of personal lives and of society through these transformed individuals.

We continue by noting that apart from any specific evangelistic activity we may undertake, evangelism is something we live out daily. As followers of Jesus, we become signs and symbols of God's grace in our ordinary relationships with others.

In bold words, the evangelist John affirmed that Jesus the Word became flesh and lived among us. In Jesus, we beheld God's glory (John 1:14). In his first letter, John explained that Jesus came to us to show us God and God's love. *See what love the Father has given us, that we should be called children of God; and that is what we are. . . . Beloved, we are God's children now* (1 John 3:1-2). John's claim was that in Jesus we find our true identity as daughters and sons of God. Furthermore, John witnessed that those who abide in love abide in God and God abides in them. *Love has been perfected among us in this: that we may have boldness on the day of judgment, because as he is, so are we in the world* (1 John 4:17).

In a world that devalues the human, this is a remarkable assertion. As Jesus was, so are we in the world. Astonishing! As God's beloved children, we point others to Jesus. Jesus manifested the Holy One and showed his disciples an incarnational way of living. The disciples were with Jesus as he offered a spring of water welling up for eternal life to a sinful Samaritan woman (John 4:1-42). The disciples accompanied him when they entered a home where Simon's mother-in-law was in bed with a fever, and Jesus cared for her (Mark 1:29-31, parallels). The disciples heard him teach in synagogues and proclaim good news of God's realm (Matt 9:35-37, parallels). They were with him when Jesus healed a foreigner, the daughter of a Canaanite woman (Matt 15:21-28).

For three years, the disciples lived with Jesus. They became a new community of God's people. As Jesus forgave, healed, and taught, they became aware of what Jesus expected of them. They no longer controlled what happened in their lives. His mission became theirs.

The disciples in turn modeled practices of an evangelistic lifestyle for us. The book of Acts and the writings of John, Paul, and Peter record their example. From these biblical texts, we learn that to practice an evangelistic lifestyle is a natural, essential, and inevitable outgrowth of the experience of saving grace. Of course, it is much simpler to write these words than to live them.

Too often, we think of evangelism solely as leading people to belief in Christ or bringing people to church. So it can be. But while evangelism can be invitational, it must be seen primarily as living the Jesus way. Evangelists must be prepared to do more than simply invite people to a feast. They must be prepared to set the table, sup together, and do the cleanup work. To engage in evangelism is to offer oneself to help people along the way. As people enter God's realm and allow God to transform their lives, we must nurture them in their new ways of living and accompany them in the practices of prayer, Bible study, corporate worship, and service. We must practice patience. We must be forgiving and self-forgiving.

At its best, evangelism liberates in two ways. People are liberated *from* bondage, and people are liberated *to* self-fulfillment as God's beloved children. Evangelism awakens people to awareness of the debilitating effects of *personal* and *social* sin in their lives and of the difference Jesus can make for good in individual lives and through people.

God invites people to follow Jesus, their true love. God sends the Holy Spirit to restore to people the fullness of the image and likeness of God. God recruits people to help save others from their worst selves, sins, and entanglements. Called, we respond with gratitude and communicate good news of God's love to others so they too may understand the message. They in turn place their trust in God and live into the reality that they too are God's beloved children.

As evangelists, we become agents awakening all creation to its freedom. A person does not need to go overseas as a missionary to see the presence of the evil one in the lives of other people. One does not need to go overseas as a missionary to engage Muslims, Hindus, or happy hedonists with claims of Jesus. One does not need to go overseas as a missionary to see the impact of scarcity for those living in poverty amid the glitter of abundance. That 25 percent of North America's population live below the poverty line is offensive to the gospel of Jesus Christ.

This is why it is so important to be aware of what is happening in our own circumstances and in the state of affairs of those individuals God places in our lives daily. Most of us are not in a position to do anything to overcome the obstacles that challenge Christian witness. For example, that 80 percent of the world is not Christian, that religious intolerance is on the rise around the world, or that two-thirds of the world is poor are abstractions and not life-determining realities.

However, awareness of the need for Jesus in the lives of our families, friends, and neighbors can be a powerful motivation to do something. In the name of Jesus we can act on the awareness of the need to befriend a non-Christian in our neighborhood. In the name of Jesus we can act on awareness of the need for food, clothing, or shelter on the part of the marginalized in our locality.

Lifestyle evangelism manifests Jesus to people concretely. In the name of Jesus, we offer a cup of cold water to all in need (Matt 10:42). In so doing, we invite them to embrace the gospel, allowing it to transform their lives and others' lives. Along the way, we see the face of God.

This book highlights three ideas: holiness, boldness, and practices. The first is holiness. Holiness concerns living in Christlike ways. Reconciled to God in Christ, we are to live holy and blameless and irreproachable lives (Col 1:22). Each of us, seeing God's glory as though reflected in a mirror, are being transformed into the same image from one degree of glory to another; for this comes from the Lord, the Spirit (2 Cor 3:18).

Certain feelings come over me when approaching the idea of holiness. Sometimes, pious people turn me off. Sometimes, the demands of the Christian walk intimidate me. I am much like Gandhi in a story told of him. A troubled mother approached Gandhi with her daughter. The mother explained her daughter was in the habit of eating far more sweet food than was good for her. Would Gandhi please speak to the girl and persuade her to give up this harmful habit? Gandhi sat for a while in silence and then said, "Bring your daughter back in three week's time. I will speak to her then." They went away and returned three weeks later. This time Gandhi quietly took the daughter aside. In a few simple words he pointed out the harm of indulging in sweet food. He urged her to abandon the habit. Thanking Gandhi for giving her daughter such good advice, the mother then said to him in a puzzled voice, "Still, I would like to know why you did not just say those words to my daughter three weeks ago when I first brought her to you?" Gandhi replied, "Three weeks ago I myself was still addicted to eating sweet foods!"

I share this story because, in all honesty, I am trying to write about holiness as part of my own walk with God. In good measure I write for myself, for I am aware of my own unholy condition. I struggle with temptation. I fail to claim my identity in Christ as God's beloved. John declares I am God's beloved child, but I do not live into this unconditional divine love (1 John 3:1).

This is who I am and this is who you are: God's beloved child. I am aware of the warning not to practice one's piety before others (Matt 6:1). Yet we are called to live holy lives as participants in the divine nature, as those who bear the image and likeness of God restored by Christ (2 Pet 1:4).

Boldness, the second theme, has to do with being courageous and trusting as we seek to live into holiness (Josh 1:7). When faced with any challenge, one's adrenaline starts to flow. This can lead a person to want to hide, but there is another possible reaction to the situation. A story told in Numbers 13–14 and Deuteronomy 13 exemplifies the options. The story concerns the challenge the ancient Israelites faced as they prepared to enter the promised land after a period of wandering through wilderness lands. They faced two competing readings of evidence before them.

Years after their escape from captivity in Egypt, the Israelites neared the time and place where they were to go. God told Moses to send men to spy out the land of Canaan. He did so. After forty days, the spies returned. The majority of them reported that the people who lived in the land of Canaan were strong, their towns fortified, and their lineage imposing. In the face of these obstacles, many murmured, *Would that we had died in the land of Egypt . . . let us go back to Egypt* (Num 14:2, 4).

Caleb quieted the people before Moses. He offered an alternative viewpoint. *Let us go up at once and occupy [the land], for we are well able to overcome it* (Num 13:30). On the journey to the promised land, Caleb acknowledged that obstacles were opportunities. With boldness, he challenged the people to overcome the obstacles and claim God's promises.

Another example of what I mean by holy boldness comes from the ancient sage Jesus Ben Sirach. He urged people to give a means of livelihood to the unemployed, food to the hungry, consolation to the despairing, a home to orphans, and justice to the oppressed. He called for living lives of radical, holy boldness:

Take circumstances into account and beware of evil and have no cause to be ashamed of yourself...
Do not refrain from speaking when it will do good...
Fight to the death for truth, and the Lord God will war on your side.
Do not be bold of tongue, yet idle and slack in deed;
Do not be like a lion at home, or cowardly towards your servants.
Do not let your hands be outstretched to receive, yet tight-fisted when the time comes to give back. (Sir 4: 20-31)

The final key concept is that of practices. In this book I explore fifteen practices of an evangelistic lifestyle.[4] Why call activities such as prayer, play, and testimony practices rather than use phrases such as disciplines of the Christian life or ordering the lives of Christian believers? Practices are what we do as a matter of course. Since the first century, Christians have learned forms of daily living that are appropriate to their culture and that they assimilate into their being. In medieval times, there were the four cardinal virtues of justice, prudence, temperance, and courage. Modern Christians focus on the Pauline virtues of faith, hope, and love. However summarized, Christians have generally understood that faith entails more than a set of doctrines or convictions. Christian beliefs must be put into practice.

I have in mind the image of training. The author of Hebrews writes, *let us run with perseverance the race that is set before us, looking to Jesus the pioneer and perfecter of our faith, who for the sake of the joy that was set before him endured the cross, disregarding its shame, and has taken his seat at the right hand of the throne of God* (Heb 12:1b-2).

A musician preparing for a concert or an athlete gearing up for competition seeks correction, fine-tuning, and even the perfecting of her or his mental, physical, spiritual, and technical state of readiness. As musicians and athletes require a goal and determination to persist to the end, so do Christians. Many are seeking some basic direction regarding ways by which they might strengthen their discipleship through practicing an evangelistic lifestyle.

The Christian life is a disciplined life. For two thousand years, Christians have practiced such classical disciplines as prayer, worship, and service as ways to deepen one's spiritual life. For some, the disciplined life has entailed life under a rule of faith such as the *Conferences* of Cassian (5th century), the *Rule* of Benedict (6th century), or the *Rules* of Francis and Clare (13th century). But we should not be led to believe that such rules are only for monks and nuns. The monastic orders have had an influence disproportionate to their numbers. This is true in North America at this time. Though professions have declined, numbers of retreatants at monasteries and convents are at an all-time high. Perhaps one reason is that their principles for living together and serving Christ continue to prove relevant to ordinary people.

A characteristic of this time in North America is the need for formation in the spiritual disciplines. They are like signposts pointing beyond us toward God. A comment by Michael Ramsey, formerly Archbishop of Canterbury of the Church of England, illustrates the way in which we discipline ourselves to be open to an encounter with God. When asked how long he spent each day in private prayer, he replied "One minute. But it takes me half an hour in silence to get to that one minute."

The greatly loved former bishop of Chicago Joseph Cardinal Bernadin admitted toward the end of his life (he died November 1996) that what was important, yet what had proved most difficult throughout his life, was prayer. He got distracted. He daydreamed. Sometimes, as he bore the illness that ultimately took his life, he lay in bed unable to get up and incapable even of prayer. He was a prophetic figure who wrote on nuclear war and the economy and a man who spent most of his life in active ministry. Yet he acknowledged he had a hard time praying. Even at the end, he needed to strengthen this practice.

With awareness of all that is involved in discipline, training, and related concepts, I prefer to use the word *practice*. *Practices of an Evangelistic Lifestyle* follows a two-thousand-year tradition through which spiritual masters have acknowledged the necessity of adopting certain daily routines within a rule of faith. The book takes in the idea of training that corrects or molds one's mental, physical, and spiritual being and yet is forgiving, for God gives strength for the journey.

There is no magical number of practices. This book explores fifteen. Micah 6:8 provides structure for their organization. Regarded by biblical scholars as a summary of prophetic faith, the text states, *What does the* LORD *require of you but to do justice, and to love kindness, and to walk humbly with your God?* Around each of these three expectations are clustered four practices. In a fourth, concluding section, I will explore ways in which our seasonal practices enable us to live into God's coming realm or commonwealth of justice and peace.

Lifestyle evangelism arises from an overflow of experiencing God's love. A starting point is to humble ourselves before God or to walk humbly with God. Prayer, Sabbath-observance, holy play, and discernment of God's call on our lives are practices by which we focus on God and humble ourselves before God.

While we first explore practices arising from the last clause of Micah 6:8, we should be ever mindful of the earlier phrases. Knowing God and knowing ourselves to be God's children, we are empowered by God's Spirit to practice loving-kindness through loving, listening, compassion, and giving testimony. We practice just living through lives of reconciliation, jubilee, and dialogue. As servant leaders, we order our economic lives in godly ways.

A final section explores specific moments when many Christians experience intensely the frustration of practicing the faith. By our seasonal practices during the Thanksgiving, Christmas, and Easter cycles, we can give recognition to God as the bedrock of our lives.

The practices are interrelated. While doing one, you find yourself observing another. We cannot uncouple earth-centered practices of just living and loving-kindness from walking humbly yet boldly with God. Unequivocally, with bold faith we may have confidence in God. Words of a praise chorus express, "Be bold, be strong, for the Lord, your God, is with you. . . . Come on and walk in faith and victory, for the Lord, your God is with you."[5]

Our daily lives are tangled up with what God is doing in the world. In plain English, I seek to provide insights for people who hope to address fundamental human needs and conditions by our Christian living. Each chapter concludes with a prayer, questions for reflection, and conversation and sources. You may think of other practices that would be part of a finished tapestry. Focusing on even a single practice can lead you into a new way of life.

[1] Joseph Aldrich, *Life-Style Evangelism: Crossing Traditional Boundaries to Reach the Unbelieving* (Portland: Multnomah, 1978), 15-16.

[2] Michael Green, *Evangelism through the Local Church* (Nashville: Thomas Nelson, 1992).

[3] Ed. Gerhard Kittel, trans. Geoffrey W. Bromley (Grand Rapids: Eerdmans, 1964), 707-37.

[4] Inevitably in a book that delves into following Jesus, the practices overlap with themes in other books. One widely read title is Dorothy C. Bass, ed., *Practicing Our Faith: A Way of Life for a Searching People* (San Francisco: Jossey-Bass, 1997). Fourteen essays explore a biblical matrix out of which people can practice a way of life that comes pretty close to a biblical vision of how things are supposed to be. Rather than examining a Christian way of life as a whole, the authors survey twelve of the most important activities of the Christian life: honoring the body, hospitality, household economics, saying yes and saying no, keeping the Sabbath, testimony, discernment, shaping communities, forgiveness, healing, dying well, and singing God's praise. Other titles include Richard J. Foster, *Celebration of Discipline: The Path to Spiritual Growth* (rev. ed., San Francisco: Harper & Row, 1988) and Ronald J. Sider, *Genuine Christianity: Essentials for Living Your Faith* (Grand Rapids: Zondervan, 1996).

[5] Song by Morris Chapman, *Maranatha Music "Praise" Chorus Book*, 3rd ed., citing Joshua 1:9 and Hebrews 13:6 (San Clemente: Maranatha Music, 1991). Originally published in London by Word Music (1983).

Practices of Humility

Introduction

*What does the L*ORD *require of you but . . . to walk humbly with your God?* (Micah 6:8)

In this section, we explore four practices that ground us in a humble walk with God. The words *humble* and *humbly* derive from the Latin *humus*, the brown or black soil resulting from partial decomposition of plant or animal matter. Anyone who gardens knows the value of humus. Even though I have lived most of my life in cities, I marvel that something as unassuming as the organic matter of soil is in fact the stuff from which things grow.

Humble people remind me of humus in at least three respects. First, they are grounded. There is no room for pie-in-the-sky spirituality among the humble! Second, they are deeply rooted. Just as humus works beneath surface soil, the roots of the humble become intertwined with the roots of everything around them. Third, they point to the source of life beyond themselves. God transforms them and affects their growth.

In biblical cultures, the social value of humility did not suggest self-diminishment but rather acceptance of one's place in life. Humble people did not claim more for themselves than life circumstances allotted them. Humble people did not threaten the rights of others or challenge cultural norms.[1] Biblical authors describe God as favoring those who humble themselves and punishing those who do not. For example, in Deuteronomy 8:2, we read of God's leading the people into the wilderness for forty years to humble and test them. Would the people be able to keep God's commandments? Would they acknowledge God as the source through which their daily needs were satisfied?

God humbles those who do not follow God's ways and do not fear God (Ps 55:19). In Isaiah 57:14-21, the One who inhabits eternity, whose name is Holy, is with those who are *contrite and humble in spirit*. God revives the spirit of the humble and revives the heart of the contrite. Even when they turn back to their own ways, God heals them and leads them on the right path. This passage also warns that God is enraged by the covetousness of the wicked. The implication is that God will put down those who strive for fame, who seek to better themselves at the expense of others, or who strive to acquire more power, prestige, and wealth than others.

In the New Testament, Matthew insists Jesus was not haughty *but gentle and humble in heart* (Matt 11:29). He records Jesus' entry into Jerusalem as fulfilling words of the prophet Zechariah, *Tell the daughter of Zion, Look your king is coming to you, humble, and mounted on a donkey, and on a colt, the foal of a donkey* (Matt 21:5, citing Zech 9:9). In Jerusalem, Jesus denounced the self-assured religious authorities of the day. They were not humble. Yet Jesus urged his followers not to challenge the honor of others: *The greatest among you will be your servant. All who exalt themselves will be humbled; and all who humble themselves will be exalted* (Matt 23:11-12; Luke 18:14 is a parallel text).

In yet another reversal of cultural values, Jesus emphasizes that to enter God's realm, one must serve God and God alone. To this end, Jesus exhorts his followers to become humble like children. *Whoever becomes humble like this child is the greatest in the kingdom* (Matt 18:4; Mark 9:37 and Luke 9:48 are parallel texts). Jesus himself depends on God. In the passion narratives, Jesus is reported to have used *Abba* as a term of intimacy. *Abba, Father, for you all things are possible; remove this cup from me; yet, not what I want, but what you want* (Mark 14:36). Here we see Jesus himself submitting to the parental authority, care, and grace of God.

The positive valuation of humility in biblical times is not congruent with modern North American ideals. Our culture encourages and rewards competition and achievement; it admires publicizing one's successes and profiting from them. In the face of these cultural values, Jesus tells his followers to be mindful of God's call to practice humility intentionally. The Apostle Paul tells us to imitate Jesus. *Let the same mind be in you that was in Christ Jesus, who . . . humbled himself and became obedient to the point of death—even death on a cross* (Phil 2:5, 8). James advises that we humble ourselves before God so that we might be blessed (Jas 4:10; see also 1 Pet 5:6).

How are we to take up these challenges? How are we to respond to Micah's call that we walk humbly with our God?

In ancient Israel, fidelity to God was not simply an abstraction. It was manifested in lives lived out within the covenant framework. Traditional forms of humbling the self included fasting, the rending of garments, weeping, lamenting, and confessing one's sins. By these practices, people accorded the respect due to God. But observing them entailed more: doing justice and loving kindness.

> *Is such the fast that I choose, a day to humble oneself? Is it to bow down the head like a bulrush, and to lie in sackcloth and ashes? Will you call this a fast, a day acceptable to the* Lord? *Is not this the fast that I choose: to loose the bonds of injustice, to undo the thongs of the yoke, to let the oppressed go free, and to break every yoke? Is it not to share your bread with the hungry, and bring the homeless poor into your house; when you see the naked, to cover them, and not to hide yourself from your own kin? Then your light shall break forth like the dawn, and your healing shall spring up quickly; your vindicator shall go before you, the glory of the* Lord *shall be your rear guard. Then you shall call, and the* Lord *will answer; you shall cry for help, and he will say, Here I am.* (Isa 58:5-9a)

Four roads to humility are prayer, Sabbath-observance, play, and discernment of God's call. Certainly there is no one way to travel any of these. Even the attempt to practice these disciplines requires boldness, for each demands self-control and will bring us into conflict with norms of the dominant North American culture. According to Christian educator Thomas Groome,

> To form ourselves and others in . . . a faith that is embodied in living for and by God's reign is a most difficult task in our present social ethos. If our commodity culture makes it difficult for us to know who our God is, it makes it equally difficult for us to live as God's people. The basic operating principle of our social and political structures is competition rather than cooperation, individualism instead of solidarity, self-sufficiency instead of interdependence. To live our identity as God's people calls us to be counter-cultural, to swim against the tide of our ethos and transform it.[2]

Each practice can be done individually, but we need the support and encouragement of a group of people. This is because each practice is potentially risky, calling believers to swim against cultural givens of our time. As we learn to walk humbly with God, we discover deeper ways of faithful living. We find that God provides companions for the journey. This communal dimension of friendship was a characteristic of early Christianity. So it is today. We grow into Christlikeness by journeying together with Jesus and with the companions of Jesus.

---

[1] Bruce J. Malina, "Humility," in *Biblical Social Values and Their Meaning: A Handbook*, ed. John J. Pilch and Bruce J. Malina (Peabody: Hendrickson, 1993), 107-108. John J. Pilch, *HEAR THE WORD!*, vol. 2 of *Introducing the Cultural Context of the New Testament* (Mahwah: Paulist, 1991), is another helpful resource that bridges the gap between the culture of New Testament authors and our own understandings.

[2] Thomas H. Groome, "Walking Humbly with Our God," *To Act Justly, Love Tenderly, Walk Humbly: An Agenda for Ministers*, ed. Walter Brueggemann, Sharon Parks, Thomas H. Groome (Mahwah: Paulist Press, 1986), 56.

Holy Prayer

Lord, teach us to pray. (Luke 11:1)

As we seek to be formed in the practices of humility, we do well to begin with Jesus.[1] In passage after passage, Matthew, Mark, Luke, and John describe prayer as essential to Jesus' life. Jesus thus becomes our teacher and exemplar along the journey to holiness.

It was natural for Jesus to pray. Through the intimacy of prayer, Jesus centered himself in and poured himself out to God. At the start of his public ministry, Jesus established a practice of withdrawing in the morning to deserted places where he prayed (Mark 1:35 and Luke 4:42).

At crucial moments in his life, Jesus withdrew to pray. After being baptized, Jesus was led to the desert where he prayed (Luke 4:1). After revealing to his disciples the cost of following him, Jesus climbed the mount of transfiguration where he prayed (Luke 9:28). Immediately after celebrating the Passover with his friends, Jesus went to the Mount of Olives to pray (Luke 22:39-46). Having revealed to his disciples that difficult days lay ahead of them, Jesus prayed for them (John 17). Jesus talked of the need of his followers to pray always and not lose heart (Luke 18:1). It was natural then that the disciples turned to Jesus for instruction in prayer. Jesus offered what we call the Lord's Prayer.

He began and ended his model prayer by acknowledging the holiness of God. He offered God adoration and prayed that God's realm be established on earth as in heaven. Jesus then petitioned God to nourish, to forgive, to protect from temptation, and to deliver from evil. In a few brief phrases, Jesus made a crucial point. Prayer did not insulate him from the world. He wanted people to know that, as they responded to the gracious call to follow him, prayer should shape their spirituality for life in this world, as well as the realm to come. God reigns on earth as also in heaven.[2]

Prayer was a means by which Jesus centered his life in God and the coming reign of God. Prayer led Jesus into service in the world. By modeling a balanced life of prayer and action, Jesus taught the disciples to engage in both prayer and action as one common path to wholeness and holiness. For Jesus and his disciples, action was a mark of holy prayer.

Not all prayer is holy. Guides to contemplation, meditation, prayer, and other spiritual practices flood the market. Recently when a group of editors of the religious press sought an explanation of this phenomenon, they discovered their readership of how-to books on spirituality comes almost entirely from the upper income bracket of society. Their readers had virtually no interest in social justice.[3]

The model prayer of Jesus connects followers of Jesus more with doing justice and loving-kindness than with popular notions of spirituality. True prayer, holy prayer, is an antidote to an individualized, otherworldly spirituality. Seekers looking for practical tips might bear in mind that one truly holy person is worth more than any number of books or articles about holiness. Contact with gifted and exemplary human beings inevitably leads one into the pain of the world.

Thomas Merton was one of the best-known spiritual writers and contemplatives of recent times. A Trappist monk of the Abbey of Gethsemani near Bardsville in central Kentucky, Merton wrote that solitude and interior prayer were closely linked with the awakening of love and compassion. He allowed no divide between spirituality and social responsibility. Reflecting on the occasion when Jesus visited Martha and Mary and when Jesus affirmed Mary's service of adoration (Luke 10:38-42), Merton observed that prayer and action are not mutually exclusive. "The contrast between [prayer and active work] should not be exaggerated; they're really doing pretty much the same thing and they should feel that they are sisters to one another like Martha and Mary . . . no community would be a full . . . community if there were not Marthas and Marys together. They are both needed, and the real community is a synthesis of these two."[4]

Jesus is our model in prayer. Jesus is also our friend. Friends spend time together. If we are to claim Jesus as our friend, we must spend time with him. Prayer is one way to do so.

Jesus is only one of a long history of spiritual masters who insist that prayer is essential to living. Through the centuries, spiritual writers have affirmed prayer as a spiritual discipline and an innate, God-given, psychological drive. Sometimes I sense an overwhelming impulse to pray. Sometimes, though my need to pray is not diminished, I find it hard to pray. In his fourth-century autobiography, *The Confessions*, Augustine expressed this as a homing instinct: ". . . you made us for yourself and our hearts find no peace until they rest in you."[5]

Though prayer is a universal phenomenon, many in our society have forgotten how to pray. There are many possible reasons for this. Essentially, I believe it is because we no longer live in a continual state of intimacy with God. We tend to limit experience of God to what happens one hour a week in congregational buildings. Too often, we give perfunctory attention to joys and concerns but are not mindful of the impact of worldly attachments on our lives. By contrast, the insight of New Testament writers is that we are called by God to life in Christ: *he chose us in Christ . . . to be holy and blameless before him in love* (Eph 1:4).

How then do we recover silent, fervent, believing prayer, which is at the root of personal, corporate, and social holiness? Each person must find her or his best way to pray. Some close their eyes. Toyohiko Kagawa (1888–1960) preferred eyes wide open. A Presbyterian pastor and prolific writer, Kagawa focused on the redemptive love of God in Christ. Known in the United States as a social reformer, Kagawa is remembered in Japan primarily as an evangelist.

Some set aside specific periods of time for prayer. Frank Charles Laubach preferred living so that to see anybody or hear anything will be to pray. He developed what he called flash prayers. By this he meant moments of prayer prompted by a sunset, a few good lines in a book, a person, or an event. He understood that each stimulus is God-infused. God enters the experience of every believer and brings each to fullness of life in Christ.[6]

Some sense God uniquely in prayer. Others experience dryness in prayer. The Russian Orthodox spiritual guide, Anthony Bloom, tells of a pious woman who came to him for counsel on how to pray. For years she had prayed the Jesus Prayer. This prayer consists in repeating "Lord Jesus Christ have mercy on me." She had never sensed the presence of God. "What shall I do?" she pleaded. Bloom suggested she sit in a comfortable place, relax, knit, and try to enjoy the peace of her room. "I forbid you to say one word of prayer," he told her. The woman did not think this very good advice, but she followed the directions of her spiritual advisor. As she "knit before the face of God," she became more and more aware of the silence. "Then I perceived that this silence was not simply an absence of noise . . . . All of a sudden I perceived that the silence was a presence. At the heart of the silence there was Him who is all stillness, all peace, all poise."[7]

In his advice to this devout Christian, Bloom acknowledged that God comes to us in a variety of ways. To pray is to receive God in all the richness that characterizes the Holy One. To see prayer as a learning process saves one from dismissing any particular form of prayer as wrong.

The ways Christians pray are extremely varied. Many use a daily devotional book of meditations on the Bible. Others have a spiritual guide or director. If either is your pattern, let yourself be steered to a passage of Scripture. It may be one that has somehow lost its power through familiarity or lack of attention. Read the passage afresh. Meditate upon certain verses. God's Spirit will enable you to discover new insights. Praying Scripture is a means of transforming our hearts and loving God more fully. Through a spiritual reading of the Bible, we are awakened to God, to others, and to the world.

The Psalms are an especially rich source of prayer. Due to their centrality in monastic life, praying the Psalms has been a popular form of meditation. Written some three thousand years ago, the Psalms continue to have amazing authenticity and contemporary relevance. By their expression of a full range of human emotions including anguish, elation, rage, and praise, the Psalms enable us to find a voice for our journey to God.[8]

Another practice is to take advantage of external aids. The intent is to turn the minds and hearts of believers toward the light of God's holiness. Prominent among Catholics or Orthodox Christians is the use of *icons*, a Greek word for images. In my Russian Orthodox upbringing, my father taught me to establish an icon corner in each room of the house. This should be a place where an icon is positioned and a place toward which anyone entering the room almost automatically turns.[9] Even a reproduction of a painting can serve as a visible sign directing one to God's holiness.[10] External aids figure in not only the interior of one's home, but also in churches or gardens. For example, some congregations have developed the labyrinth as a path of prayer. Those familiar with Roman Catholic practice know the Stations of the Cross.

Centering prayer is another widely used contemporary prayer form. This practice has a long lineage. For example, in the Middle Ages, a little volume called *The Cloud of Unknowing* offered Christians instructions on entering into centering prayer.[11] The anonymous author suggested three movements of centering prayer. First, settle into a place of solitude and quiet. It can be anywhere. Virtually every home has a place where no one will disturb you. For myself, I have a corner in a room that I have set aside for meditation. I also like to pray outside.

A second movement of centering prayer is to calm the body. Whether one sits on the floor, in a comfortable chair, outside on the grass, or somewhere else, or prays in some other posture, it is important to unwind and center your mind. Sitting in whatever position one chooses, one enters by faith into a period of intentional reflection on the presence of God. Generally, I find it easiest to sit in a comfortable chair with uncrossed legs, hands on my lap, and eyes closed. Sometimes, however, I focus on an image or a lit candle. I find it helpful to begin with a breathing exercise. I inhale and exhale slowly. Consciously, I relax all of my body.

The third movement of centering prayer involves asking God to give you a single, simple phrase that expresses a response to God. The medieval author suggests one-syllable words such as *God, joy, love,* or *peace.* The word should reflect God in all the divine fullness to you. Simply let this word and nothing else represent the fullness of God's presence during this time of prayer. Let nothing else hold sway in your mind or heart.

What about distractions? Whenever in the course of prayer you become aware of anything else, gently return to the prayer word. To follow these instructions, it may be psychologically helpful to set a place apart where no one will disturb you. As you settle down and move in faith to an awareness of God's presence, you may encounter interruptions. When the time determined for prayer is completed, stop using the prayer word. Pray as you will. Enjoy the silence. Acknowledge God's presence. Pray spontaneously in your own words. Use words such as the Lord's Prayer. A lifetime is required to learn the Lord's Prayer. The disciples' words become our words: *Lord, teach us to pray* (Luke 11:1). Spiritual writers stress that repeating the Lord's Prayer can lead to change taking place in our lives. One option is to give the fullest possible attention to each word. We may stop at a particular word or phrase and dwell on it. Alternatively, we may write a prayer based on the Lord's Prayer or use a modern paraphrase.

We have already noted the essential elements of the Lord's Prayer. They are adoration and petition. By these forms of prayer, we acknowledge the holiness of God and our dependence on God. Of course, God already knows we need daily bread, forgiveness, and strength to endure the trials of life. By giving voice to our need in these essential areas of life, we express our desire to walk a path of humility, holiness, and boldness with our God.

What about falling asleep during our time of prayer? There is no harm in this. Fatigue may indicate that God is telling you that you are tired or that you need to change your time to pray. Alternatively, the period of drowsiness before you sleep may be a suitable time to pray. I have benefited, for example, from the prayer of examination, a mode of prayer characteristic of Jesuit spiritual direction. Each evening as I lie in bed, I visualize the events of the day, confess sins of commission or omission, pray for God's forgiveness, and drift off to sleep resting in God's grace.

Another model for private prayer is to write out prayers. This may be coupled with keeping a journal. Journal-keeping is like storytelling except that, apart from God and self, there is no audience. Journal-keeping allows us to relate to the events of life and to discern how God is present to us. Journal-keeping is appropriate for complaint and for lament. I keep a journal. The most important aspect of this practice is that there is no one way to do it right. The journal is personal. It is impossible to go wrong in journal-keeping.

For what and for whom shall we pray? We all have needs. We all are part of a needy world. We all participate in wider networks or communities where there are needs. Praying for ourselves, for the world, and for others is called intercessory prayer. Before we pray, God already knows our needs and the needs of others. Intercessory prayer does not intend to influence God. Yet by bringing our petitions before God, we offer ourselves to God and hold those on whose behalf we pray in the light of God's love and compassion. Our prayers become means by which, in cooperation with God, we attune ourselves to God's power and release to God the burdens of our hearts. Studies show that those for whom prayers are offered to God do fare better.[12]

However, we must not expect God to respond to our petitions in the same manner that we expect a vending machine or slot machine to respond to our putting coins into an opening. We pray to express dependence on God. We pray trusting God to respond in God's time and in God's way. Jesus teaches, *Ask, and it will be given you; search, and you will find; knock, and the door will be opened for you. For everyone who asks receives, and everyone who searches finds, and for everyone who knocks, the door will be opened* (Matt 7:7-8).

One does well to remember that our need to pray changes over time and in relation to life circumstances. The prayers of a child are not likely to be the same as the prayers of someone in the later years of life. Sometimes one prays out of need. Other times one prays out of rejoicing. Often in services of worship, a moving experience takes place before a time corporate prayer. Congregants share joys and concerns. By voicing the deep concerns of their lives, they invite the praying community to unite with them.

A word for pastors and other leaders in church life may be appropriate. Over the years, I have attended many workshops and retreats of pastoral agents. I have found many to be worn out, unable to pray, and in great need of spiritual direction. Many have written books that are a cry of the heart.[13] It is difficult to serve when we are empty. We do well to remember our humanity. We experience much of what our parishioners experience. We need to pray, to be prayed for, and to be renewed through prayer in our love of God and of neighbor.

In whatever shape it takes, prayer runs the entire gamut of human experience. Everything is appropriate subject matter. Each manner of praying helps us find the Divine Center. Prayer forms us in Jesus Christ and leads us to the desert, to the Mount of Transfiguration, and even to the cross where Jesus thirsted and cried out his feeling of abandonment. Each helps us remember whose we are and whose purposes we serve.

Prayer also fuels mission. One can cite many examples. In the fourth century, Monica prayed for the conversion of her son Augustine. A self-confessed sinner, Augustine became a great figure in the expansion of Christianity. During the eighteenth century, a group that included John Newton and William Wilberforce prayed at Clapham, England, igniting an evangelical crusade against slavery. In the mid-nineteenth century, business groups prayed and engendered waves of revivals throughout North America. Early in the twentieth century, the prayers of students sparked an explosion of missionary activity by which Christianity became truly global.

To pray is to live in Christ. Paul repeatedly used the phrase "in Christ." Christ lives and lives in us. *It is no longer I who live, but it is Christ who lives in me* (Gal 2:20). *For me, living is Christ and dying is gain* (Phil 1:21.) Living in Christ is another way of describing holiness. This is why prayer is so important. Life requires nourishment. Life in Christ requires nourishment. Prayer nourishes the living of our days and guides us in humble ways before the living Lord. Prayer becomes a way of seeing, thinking, and ordering life in the light of God's presence. An evangelistic lifestyle begins with a life given to God in prayer.

Let me close with a paraphrase of the Lord's Prayer. It is filled with God's love. Praying this or our own prayer directs us to God. Let us call upon God:

Eternal Spirit,
Earth-maker, Pain-bearer, Life-giver,
Source of all that is and that shall be,
Father and Mother of us all,
Loving God, in whom is heaven:
The hallowing of your name echo through the universe!
The way of your justice be followed by the peoples of the world!
Your heavenly will be done by all created beings!
Your commonwealth of peace and freedom sustain our hope and come on
    earth.
With the bread we need for today, feed us.
In the hurts we absorb from one another, forgive us.
In times of temptation and test, strengthen us.
From trials too great to endure, spare us.
From the grip of all that is evil, free us.
For you reign in the glory of the power that is love, now and for ever.
    Amen.[14]

---

[1] Excellent studies of Jesus stress this point. See, for example, Athol Gill, *Life on the Road: The Gospel Basis for a Messianic Lifestyle* (Scottdale: Herald, 1992), esp. ch. 7.

[2] Jesus' prayer parallels one then in general use: "May Thy Kingdom and Thy lordship come speedily, and be acknowledged by all the world, that Thy Name may be praised in all eternity . . . . For Thine is the greatness and the power and the dominion, the victory and the majesty, yea, all in Heaven and on earth. Thine is the Kingdom and Thou art lord of all beings for ever. Amen" (I. Abrahams, *Studies in Pharisaism and the Gospels* [New York: Ktav, 1967], 98-99).

[3] Donald Nicholl, *Holiness* (London: Darton, Longman and Todd, 1981 [1987]), 6.

[4] Thomas Merton, *Contemplation in a World of Action* (New York: Doubleday, 1973), 387.

[5] Augustine, *Confessions 1.1*, trans. R. S. Pine-Coffin (New York: Penguin, 1961), 21

[6] "We Christians must learn to flash *hundreds of instantaneous prayers* at people near and far, knowing that many prayers may show no visible results, but that at least some of them will hit their mark" (Frank C. Laubach, *Prayer: The Mightiest Force in the World* [Old Tappan: Fleming H. Revell, 1959], 25). Laubach (1884–1970) was a Congregational missionary to the Philippines. In fifty-six books, Laubach promoted prayer and literacy based on a highly successful technique of teaching the illiterate to read. Developed in the 1930s, the method is still in use.

[7] Anthony Bloom, *Beginning to Pray* (New York: Paulist Press, 1970), 60-61.

[8] Walter Brueggemann, *Praying the Psalms* (Winona: Saint Mary's Press, 1986). Joan Chittister, *The Psalms: Meditations for Every Day of the Year* (New York: Crossroad, 1996) offers daily meditations inspired by the Psalms. Nan C. Merrill, *Psalms for Praying: An*

Invitation to Wholeness (New York: Continuum, 1997) reworks the Psalms in contemporary language as a resource for individual prayer and liturgical usage. Nancy Schreck and Maureen Leach, *Psalms Anew in Inclusive Language* (Winona: Saint Mary's Press, 1986) and Eugene H. Peterson, *Praying with the Psalms: A Year of Daily Prayers and Reflections on the Words of David* (San Francisco: Harper, 1993) are resources for public worship.

[9] Jews fix a *mezuzah*, a container with a biblical verse, to the doorpost of houses. See Deuteronomy 6:1-4. See also James H. Forest, *Praying with Icons* (Maryknoll: Orbis, 1991).

[10] Like literary works of art, the visual arts serve as beacons to those who would make a 180-degree turn and walk humbly with God. For example, in his *Return of the Prodigal Son: A Story of Homecoming* (New York: Continuum, 1995), devotional writer Henri J. M. Nouwen describes the inspiration of a painting by Rembrandt. It is based on Luke 15:11-32. In her *Walking on Water: Reflections on Faith and Art* (New York: North Point Press, 1980), Christian writer Madeleine L'Engle refers three times to inspiration she received in the Prado in Madrid, Spain, from viewing a painting by El Greco of St. Andrew and St. Francis.

[11] Several modern translations are available, including one edited by James Walsh in the Classics of Western Spirituality series (New York: Paulist, 1981). M. Basil Pennington, "Centering Prayer," *Finding Grace at the Center*, ed. Thomas Keating (Petersham: St. Bedes, 1978) is a good introduction to this traditional form of prayer.

[12] "Prayed-for Patients Fare Better," *Memphis Commercial Appeal,* 26 October 1999.

[13] In *A Crying Shepherd: A Therapy of Tears* (Winter Park FL: FOUR-G Publishers, 1993), Fred Lofton shares his grief-filled prayers during the period of his wife's illness and death. In *Conversations with God: Two Centuries of Prayers by African Americans* (New York: Harper, 1994), James Melvin Washington offers an anthology of prayers, many of which are by the oppressed. His death in 1997 is a great loss to family, friends, academy, and church.

[14] *A New Zealand Prayer Book* (San Francisco: Harper, 1997), 181. For another example of a paraphrase, see Dorothee Soelle, *Revolutionary Patience*, trans. Rita and Robert Kimber (Maryknoll: Orbis, 1977), 24-26.

For Reflection and Conversation

- How does Jesus speak to you of prayer? Can you let his practices shape your own?

- Write your own paraphrase of the Lord's Prayer. Can you share it with your family or friends?

- Bring all your life before God, identifying what you like in yourself and a couple areas of difficulty.

- Who are you holding in the light of God's love and forgiveness?

- What is the relationship between prayer and evangelism?

Holy Sabbath

Observe the sabbath day and keep it holy. (Deuteronomy 5:12)

In 1982 I was living with my family at Tantur, a study center located on the road between Jerusalem and Bethlehem. Each morning I went to the rooftop. The view was beautiful. Scanning the landscape to the west, I could see the hills outside Old Jerusalem some five miles away and a road that winds down to the Mediterranean Sea. To the north immediately beyond the institute's enclosure, a lane twisted its way through olive groves. Palestinian Christian friends told us it was the path along which Joseph and Mary walked for the census decreed by Emperor Augustus. To the east stretched the Judean desert. If conditions were just right, I could see the waters of the Dead Sea through a gap between the barren hills. Eastward, I could see the Herodian, the volcano-like mound within which Herod built his palace, and ruins of a water system and other engineering marvels built during his reign. To the south, I could make out the Shepherds' Fields at Beit Sahour where an angel first announced, *Do not be afraid; for see—I am bringing you good news of great joy for all the people* (Luke 2:10). I could also see the Church of the Nativity in Bethlehem where the heavenly host praised God, saying, *Glory to God in the highest heaven, and on earth peace among those whom he favors* (Luke 2:14).

This land called Holy is a small, resource-poor land. It is a land scorched by passion. The peoples of the land seem to contain a force. They are as explosive particles; they seem always ready to erupt with passion.

As each week's end approached, something truly awesome and irresistible happened. Each week for a few hours, all that produced noise in a modern city fell silent. All the divisions of modern Israeli politics dissolved. All the tensions between Israelis and Palestinians dissipated.

Each Friday noon, I heard the piercing call of a muezzin inviting faithful Muslims to pray. The pace quickened as Jews prepared to greet the Sabbath or *Shabbat*. As Friday afternoon gave way to evening, I often heard the words *shabbat shalom*, a blessing in Hebrew that means Sabbath peace. If I was in West Jerusalem, I had to return to Tantur by sundown after which time most public transportation ceased to run. Sometimes I was fortunate to have been invited to the home of observant Jews to share in the lighting of candles, readings, blessings, and a special meal.

On one occasion, my son Nathaniel and I walked to Jerusalem. It was Yom Kippur, the Jewish Day of the Atonement. All vehicular traffic stopped. Nothing was open. Israeli radio and television were silent. With hundreds of other pilgrims and tourists, we merged into a great throng of people moving to the Temple Mount. As they have for centuries, Jews from around the world gathered at the Western or Wailing Wall to lament the destruction of the temple in the first century and, during this holiest day in the Jewish calendar, to join in a time of penitence. Overwhelmed by the diverse multitude, I felt the whole of humanity advancing up the pavement in a single body. We heard no sound except the whispers of the faithful at prayer. Time past and time present seemed to merge with time eternal. Part of a great mingling of humanity, we participated in the timeless Sabbath or *Shabbat* of God.[1]

Jews, Christians, and Muslims, spiritual descendants of Abraham, have organized time in a cycle of seven days. For Christians, Sunday is the week's climax. For Muslims, it is Friday noon. For Jews, Sabbath goes from Friday dusk until Saturday eve. Friday, Saturday, or Sunday, Sabbath time is the highlight of each week. This has been true from classical times to the present.

The Sabbath in Judaism

Jews observe the Sabbath as a special expression of divine grace for the people Israel. According to Jewish scholar Abraham Joshua Heschel, one of the most distinguished words in the Bible is the Hebrew *qadosh*, holy. More than any other, the word is representative of the divine. In his book *The Sabbath: Its Meaning for Modern Man*, Heschel suggests that when we become aware afresh of God, we are able to share in the holiness of silent rest and endless peace. According to Jewish tradition, this is the beginning of what eternity means. Heschel writes, "There are few ideas in the world of thought which contain so much spiritual power as the idea of the Sabbath.

Aeons hence, when of many of our cherished theories only shreds will remain, that cosmic tapestry will continue to shine. Eternity utters a day."[2]

For Jews, Sabbath is a way of organizing time around a pattern of six days of work followed by one of rest. The full rhythm of the week dramatizes key themes of Judaism: creation, revelation, redemption, and the centrality of Torah.[3] Six days a week, we work under strain and are beset with worries that are enmeshed in our busy lives. Then comes a day when all work is brought to a standstill. We lay our worries before God and desist from our other preoccupations.

God's act of creation was the precedent. God worked six days. God rested. God blessed this seventh day as holy. *Thus the heavens and the earth were finished, and all their multitude. And on the seventh day God finished the work that he had done, and he rested on the seventh day from all the work that he had done. So God blessed the seventh day and hallowed it, because on it God rested from all the work that he had done in creation* (Gen 2:1-3).

In a modern midrash, Jewish scholar Julius Lester playfully expresses the idea of rest as a time of refreshment and renewal.

> With the joining of Adam and the Woman, creation was complete.
>
> Quietly, God returned to the ribbon shape and wafted back to heaven.
> "Welcome home," Sara greeted him.
> "Thanks. Well, I'm done, Sara. My world is almost complete."
> "It's a beautiful world, God."
> "Yes. It is, isn't it?"
> "So, what else do you need to create?"
> "Shabbat. The day of rest."
>
> And so God rested from all the work he had done and he contemplated himself and the infinite universe and he was refreshed and renewed.[4]

The Bible commands Sabbath observance as one of the Ten Commandments: *Remember the sabbath day, and keep it holy. Six days you shall labor and do all your work. But the seventh day is a sabbath to the L*ORD *your God; you shall not do any work—you, your son or your daughter, your male or female slave, your livestock, or the alien resident in your towns. For in six days the* L*ORD made heaven and earth, the sea, and all that is in them, but rested the seventh day; therefore the* L*ORD blessed the sabbath day and consecrated it* (Exod 20:8-11). This text reveals God's purpose that not only Jews observe the Sabbath, but also slaves, aliens, animals, and indeed the whole of creation.

By giving Sabbath to humanity, God expressed universal intentions. Sabbath was for all. In an ancient text, "On the Creation of the World," Philo Judaeus reinforced this point: "But after the whole world had been completed according to the perfect nature of the number of six, God hallowed the day following, the seventh, praising it, and calling it holy. For that day is the festival, not of one city or one country, but of all the earth; a day which alone it is right to call the day of festival for all people, and the birthday of the world."[5] This passage marks the special holiness of the Sabbath day as a day of festivity and joy. What does it mean to practice Sabbath? If we imitate God by setting aside one day in seven on which to refrain from work and to rest, what in our day constitutes work? What comprises rest?

In the Bible, several passages detailed what Jews could or could not do. Nonetheless, in the biblical period Sabbath observance was not yet universal. What to practice was sometimes debated. As an example, a passage in 1 Maccabees 2:29-48 recorded differences of opinion about self-defense on the Sabbath. Flavius Josephus gave an account of Jews defending themselves on the Sabbath in his history of the *Wars of the Jews*.

From the sixth century BC onward, what generally distinguished the Sabbath from the other six days of the week were weekly assemblies for worship in local synagogues. After the destruction of the temple in AD 70, synagogue Sabbath worship became the central ritual institution of Judaism.

Today, each of the differing streams of modern Judaism has its own emphases regarding Sabbath observance. Despite some differences, Jews are one in the accepting of the Sabbath as the climax and highlight of the week. In the State of Israel where the Orthodox stream predominates, rabbis have recently accepted some farming work on the Sabbath as acceptable. This constitutes an adaptation of ancient teaching to modern conditions.[6]

A pious Jew, Jesus recognized the Sabbath as a day of joy, renewal, and holiness. It was his custom to be in synagogue on the Sabbath (Luke 4:16). Sabbath practices probably also took place in his home. Yet according to the four Gospels Jesus violated certain Sabbath restrictions. When he did not interfere with his disciples as they gathered grain on the Sabbath, Jesus replied to queries saying, *The sabbath was made for humankind, and not humankind for the sabbath* (Mark 3:27; parallels: Matt 12:1-8; Luke 6:1-5). When he healed on the Sabbath, Jesus insisted this was God's work (John 5:1-18). Other times, Jesus stressed the life-giving spirit of Sabbath laws (Luke 13:10-17; 14:1-6). New Testament scholar Mitzi Minor summarizes:

> [Jesus] made the Sabbath a day filled with health, celebration, and the full possibilities of life in the *basileia* of God. Through his release of the life-giving power of God, the Lord of the Sabbath (2:28) made the Sabbath serve humanity as it was meant to do (2:27). Thus observing the Sabbath in ways that meet human needs is an authentic response to God's gift of Sabbath rest. Furthermore, doing good and saving life are also authentic responses to God's gifts of both Sabbath rest and life-giving power. Doing evil and killing life are the obviously inauthentic responses. Doing nothing in the face of human need is equally inauthentic.[7]

The earliest Christians were Jews who continued to honor Jewish Sabbath practices. As the number of non-Jews increased, Christians came to highlight Sunday, the day of Resurrection. By the fourth century, Sunday had become the central day for Christian worship. It has so remained except for a few Christian groups that observe Saturday Sabbath worship.

Sunday is not the same as the Sabbath. Sunday commemorates Jesus' resurrection the third day after he died. On Sundays, Christians remember Christ's victory over death and celebrate Easter triumph. Each Sunday is Sabbath-like, however, as it is the climax of the week. Just as Jews remember their liberation from their enslavement in Egypt and entry into covenant with God at Sinai, Christians remember their liberation from enslavement to sin and their entry into the New Covenant through which God has reconciled Gentiles to God's self.

As Jews by their Sabbath observance mark a day of armistice in the struggles of economic survival and conquest of nature, Christians by their Sunday practice pause, break routine, and keep the commandment to remember the Sabbath day and to keep it holy. For Christians and Jews, Sabbath time affirms a special relationship to the Holy One and permits rest, play, worship, and connection with family and friends.

What is good to do on Sunday? What is not? For Christians as well as for Jews, one good thing is the worship of God. There are many avenues into worship, and all times are holy with God. However, there are benefits of setting aside time weekly to worship God. Joining other Christians for common worship is a way not only to take a day off, but also to acknowledge and thank God. For many Christians, the highlight of Sunday worship is the celebration of the Eucharist, the Greek word for thanksgiving. Eucharist is an act of remembering the Last Supper. Words were no pious convention but a real prayer that his music would bless God.

In addition to worship, North Americans need Sabbath time to liberate them from busy schedules. Who does not need time for rest and recreation, time to enjoy art, nature, sports, family, and friends? Everyone in fact needs a common weekly day to pause, to break from the hectic patterns so characteristic of early twenty-first-century life. In *The Overworked American: The Unexpected Decline of Leisure,* Harvard economist Juliet B. Schor highlights the extent to which many people in the United States feel squeezed for time. She points out that through much of this country's history, reduction of worktime was one of the nation's most pressing social needs. In the face of increasing pressure on people's time, setting aside a common pause day remains an urgent social issue.[8] This should alert congregations not to devour Sundays by scheduling too many events or creating endless meetings. Ironically, Christian bodies often encroach on Sabbath time!

For people whose professional lives do not require Sunday work, Sunday is a natural day to set aside for play, creative endeavors, and staying connected with family and friends. Such ordinary activities are a blessing. They engender joy, renewal, and holiness. For this reason, Johann Sebastian Bach could inscribe the words "Soli Deo Gloria" (to God alone be the glory) on all his working manuscripts, even those we now call secular.

Holy Sabbath and the Practices of an Evangelistic Lifestyle

In the first century AD, Christianity burst into the world with great and unexpected suddenness. Despite Jesus' efforts to prepare them for his death and resurrection, the disciples were not ready for what happened. Perhaps this is because early followers of Jesus were not distinguished. They were not well educated, nor did they have influential backing.

So it is with most of us. Most of us are not particularly distinguished. Most of us do not have great educational qualifications, nor do we have powerful allies. What we have is a story to tell to the nations. Like the post-resurrection disciples, we have good news to share, which we can do with authenticity, enthusiasm, and courage. Belief that God has transformed the apparent defeat of Good Friday into the supreme victory of Easter Day spills over into every aspect of our lives.

Keeping Sabbath time bears witness to our conviction that God has done and continues to do great things. It is not a practice we undertake to gain God's grace. Rather, we acknowledge the need to order our lives in accord with the rhythm of God's creative work, rest, redemption, and creative nurture. Keeping Sabbath time is a great way to create space in which we can invite people to see themselves as they already are, children of God, loved with the same unconditional love that Jesus described in the parable of the lost son and his brother (Luke 15:11-32). Evangelization is inviting another person to respond to God's acceptance in and through the Beloved. We may share this reality by word and deed in natural, loving ways through the power of the Holy Spirit.

Special Sabbaths

Some congregations, denominations, and organizations call upon people of faith, both Christian and non-Christian, to observe specific Sabbaths or Sundays with a particular focus. One widely carried out in the United States is the national observance of the Children's Sabbath. Seeking to discern how best to help children and strengthen families, the Children's Defense Fund (CDF) first called God's people to observe a Children's Sabbath in 1992. Congregations were invited to celebrate the gift of children and to help nurture, protect, and seek justice for children. Subsequently, congregations from many denominations and faiths focus every October on a central theme.[9]

In 2000 the CDF sounded the call for joining hearts, hands, and voices to leave no child behind in terms of opportunity. In addition to the CDF, many supporting organizations distributed informational kits showing that countless children in the United States are being left out of the present economic good times. The kits also provided materials that enabled participating congregations to develop each of five themes: children need a healthy start, a head start, a fair start, a safe start, and a moral start.

- A healthy start would mean children would have healthy bodies and minds. There would be a comprehensive health system that provided preventive care when they are well and treatment when they are ill.
- A head start would mean children have strong parents who are supported by communities that truly value families. It would also mean children would get the early foundation they need to get ready for school and attend high-quality schools that inspire, respect, and support them.
- A fair start would mean children grow up where parents have jobs that pay livable wages and that children are protected from poverty, hunger, and homelessness when parents cannot adequately provide.

- A safe start would mean that children are safe and secure in their homes, neighborhoods, and schools. In particular, CDF materials stress the need to protect children from guns.
- A moral start would mean parents, caring adults, and congregations recognize and communicate every child's intrinsic worth and guide by example. Children need to know they are beloved by God. They need loving limits, discipline, and attention in order to navigate the paths to adulthood successfully. They need to learn to give their opinions and act within their capabilities.

By drawing attention to the Children's Sabbath, I am suggesting one way to capture the essence of Sabbath time in contemporary worship. Other special days, such as Martin Luther King Jr.'s birthday or Reformation Sunday, can also be developed for Sunday worship. When we see Sunday as a day of joy and festivity, intergenerational participation tends to work well. I have even included elements of clowning and dancing in services I have organized over the years. Sabbath time is not an anachronism!

For those who teach or participate in other professions, an adaptation of the practice of Sabbath is the Sabbatical Year. It too has roots in biblical practice. Despite the modern pressure upon academics and other professionals to be productive, for example by writing books, we need to keep in mind the religious origins of the Sabbatical Year. It is a time of spiritual renewal and even resistance to some extent to professional pressure. Thomas Merton's comment to Ron Seitz, a friend and poet who teaches in a university, is pertinent. "Glad to hear of your sabbatical! Too bad you have to think you must produce. One does more when there is no obligation to do anything."[10]

According to Mary Pipher, who comments on contemporary social trends in the United States, we are in an elusive crisis, a crisis of meaning, with emotional, spiritual, and social aspects. She observes, "We hunger for values, community and something greater than ourselves to dedicate our lives to. We wake in the night sorry for ourselves and our planet."[11]

Observing Sabbath can make a great deal of difference in the renewal of values, community, and meaning. As a practice of an evangelistic life, Sabbath observance attempts to foster the vision of life as a pilgrimage to the seventh day when God rested. The Sabbath seeks to displace the coveting of things with the coveting of God. Saying yes to God in the company of others week after week, we anchor our lives in a rhythm of work and rest. The real test, of course, is how we live our lives the rest of the week.

Prayer
God who created the world and all that is, we praise you.
God who rested after creating the world, we bless you.
God who willed that we too should set aside a special day, we thank you.
God who raised Jesus on the third day, you are the source of joy. Sin forgiven, death conquered, may our hearts overflow with joy.
May the whole universe be filled with joy. We pray in the power of your Spirit and the name of Jesus who brought us joy. Amen.

---

[1] Donald Nicholl, *The Testing of Hearts: A Pilgrim's Journal* (London: Lamp, 1989).

[2] Abraham Joshua Heschel, *The Sabbath: Its Meaning for Modern Man* (New York: Farrar, Straus and Giroux, 1951 [1981]), 101.

[3] The Torah refers to instruction, specifically the first five books of the Bible and the entire range of Jewish teachings. Jews read and study the Torah during the Sabbath evening service, recited in the synagogue or at home. For Jewish practice, see Abraham E. Millgram, *Sabbath: The Day of Delight* (Philadelphia: Jewish Publication Society of America, 1956); Michael A. Fishbane, *Judaism: Revelation and Traditions* (San Francisco: Harper, 1987).

[4] Julius Lester, *When the Beginning Began: Stories about God, the Creatures, and Us* (San Diego: Silver Whistle, Harcourt Brace & Company, 1999), 72. A midrash is an imaginative or interpretive rendering of a sacred text.

[5] Philo Judaeus, "On the Creation of the World," cited by Millgram, *Sabbath: The Day of Delight*, pp. 213-14.

[6] "Farmers get break from field sabbath, beating challenge by hard-line rabbi," *Memphis Commercial Appeal*, 30 September 2000.

[7] Mitzi Minor, *The Spirituality of Mark: Responding to God* (Louisville: Westminster John Knox Press, 1996), 39.

[8] Juliet B. Schor, *The Overworked American: The Unexpected Decline of Leisure* (New York: BasicBooks, 1992).

[9] The Children's Defense Fund is headquartered at 25 E Street NW, Washington, District of Columbia 20001, United States of America.

[10] Thomas Merton, quoted in Ron Seitz, *Song for Nobody: A Memory Vision of Thomas Merton* (Ligouri: Triumph Books, 1993), 68. See also J. Morgenstern, "Sabbatical Year," *Interpreter's Dictionary of the Bible* (Nashville: Abingdon, 1962), 4:141-44; B. Z. Wacholder, "Sabbatical Year," *Interpreter's Dictionary of the Bible, Supplementary Volume*, pp. 762-63.

[11] Mary Pipher, *The Shelter of Each Other: Rebuilding Our Families* (New York: Ballantine, 1996), 81.

For Reflection and Conversation

- Is Sabbath a meaningful concept for you? If so, how? If not, why not?

- Can you celebrate Sabbath time as gift? As climax and highlight of the week?

- In Judaism, Sabbath is an important time for family and friends. Is this true for you?

- Where is it most important for you to observe Sabbath time: in your home? at your congregation? in other places you set aside for quietness?

- Are there special themes especially appropriate to Sabbath observance?

- What is the relationship between Sabbath and evangelism?

Holy Play

As the ark of the LORD *came into the city of David, Michal daughter of Saul looked out of the window, and saw King David leaping and dancing before the* LORD *. . . .* (2 Samuel 6:16)

Why Pay Attention to Play?

You can journey to holiness anytime and anywhere. The journey is wide-ranging and includes even those parts of one's life that seem humdrum. The ancient rabbis asked why God appeared to Moses in a scrub bush. They concluded that God wanted to show that there is no place where God is not. God intends to use every single aspect of life to draw us closer to the Holy One. Everything we do can serve as a spiritual practice of holiness.

Jesus described God's realm by pointing to a mustard seed. The smallest of all seeds, it grows into a great shrub or tree and becomes a place to which the birds of the air come and make nests in its branches (Matt 13:31). Elsewhere, he pointed to a grain of wheat, which though it dies bears much fruit (John 12:24). Jesus called upon his followers to be salt of the earth and light of the world (Matt 5:13-14). By such illustrations, Jesus taught that there is no unbridgeable gulf between even the most ordinary aspect of creation and the Holy One.

Australian poet Les A. Murray picks up on these images when he wrote of Christians not living as though a spiritual elite, but as baking soda in the loaf of life. Murray urges Christians to meet Jesus of Nazareth in the stuff of life, the rock concerts, sporting events, and political rallies where we have to expect to get some splinters in our hands. Murray recognizes that Jesus met people in every walk of life. By giving his life for the sake of the world, Jesus models self-transcendence and shows us how to live genuine human existence. We too may live into Christ-likeness.

Murray is less interested in nostalgia for a past that never existed (in our context let us call it the myth of a Christian North America) than in finding God in the ordinary places where life is lived, in "the face we saw near the sportswear shop in which mouth-watering and tears couldn't be distinguished." Murray continued, "Whatever its variants of meat-cuisine, worship, divorce, human order has at heart an equanimity . . . a place where the churchman's not defensive . . . the farmer has done enough struggling-to-survive for one day, and the artist rests from theory—where all are, in short, off the high comparative horse of their identity . . . . Christ spoke to people most often on this level . . . all holiness speaks from it."[1]

The practices of praying and observing Sabbath time considered in the first two chapters of this book are understandable aspects of walking humbly with God. The link between holiness and other aspects of our lives may be less evident, for example, our play, work, and sexual conduct. We should be open to the possibility of discovering ever more abundant riches of holiness in all aspects of our daily lives: what we do with our bodies, what we put into them, how we treat them, and what use we make of them. These are spiritual tasks that we carry out in the name of holiness.[2]

By holy play, I mean play that takes us to the realms of creativity, ecstasy, joyous celebration, and make-believe. Holy play encompasses the arts and festivity. In such forms as competition and ritual, holy play can be organized. More commonly, however, holy play entails freedom and spontaneity. Holy play wells up from the depths of our being.

Scholarship highlights the enormous range and power of play. Religious educator Jerome W. Berryman writes of "Godly Play" by which he means something common to all play: the pleasure of it comes from the activity itself. Anthropologist Clifford Geertz writes of "Deep Play," by which he means play in which the stakes are so high that, by contemporary cultural standards of winning and making a buck, it makes no sense at all for people to participate in it.[3]

Holiness may speak from our playing. The inconsequential pursuits we often associate with play are not necessarily holy, but all play can be life-giving and holy. Holy play honors God and enables people to experience the Holy One. Holy play is one of the means by which we live into God's blessings. Holy play offers a true vision of the holy life and can be a witness to others. By our holy play, we enable other people to discern godly ways for living their own lives. A story told of Francis of Assisi by Celano, an early biographer, makes this point.

Francis radiated joy in every aspect of life, as his hymn *All Creatures of Our God and King* attests. He humbled himself before God, his superiors, and common people. One day as Francis passed through a field, a peasant happened to be working there. The peasant ran over to him and asked if he were Brother Francis. Francis acknowledged that he was. The peasant said, "Try to be as good as you are said to be by all men, for many put their trust in you. Therefore I admonish you never to be other than you are expected to be." In humility, Francis embraced the peasant and thanked him for this admonition.[4]

Toward a Recovery of Holy Play

To be human is to play, although not only humans play. Animals also play in much the same way as children play or as couples woo or prepare for coitus. However, humans extend play beyond the doings of even the most intelligent animals: dolphins and chimpanzees.

According to Dutch scholar Johan Huizinga, play is older than culture and is constitutive of culture. The main characteristics of play are freedom and a stepping out of real life into a temporary sphere of activity that has its own rules and sacral characteristics. Religion and ethics are play. Huizinga cites Plato: "What, then, is the right way of living? Life must be lived as play, playing certain games, making sacrifices, singing and dancing, and then a man will be able to propitiate the gods, and defend himself against his enemies and win in the contest."[5] Play takes humans out of ordinary life. Play takes place at moments when people act and feel in ways that are altogether different than what occurs normally in our lives.

People have special locales where they play. The place may be a stage where one acts, a room where one plays an instrument, a workbench in a garage, or a path in the woods. It may be a church or a temple or a clearing in the woods. These are adult versions of the child's playhouse or playground.

People have special times when they play. These intervals break our daily routines. Birthdays, weddings, and other life passages are natural occasions for play. This is also true on days in our secular or sacred calendars: New Year's Eve, national holidays, and the high holy days. Days off from work or special events must be pre-arranged. We organize a vacation or buy a ticket for a concert or a show. We prepare special meals or activities for the special holy days.

Finally, people play in accord with a pattern. In games, there are rules and, often, more than one player. When people play together, they share a common goal that may be attained collaboratively or competitively. Huizinga writes perceptively that play "creates order, *is* order. Into an imperfect world and into the confusion of life it brings a temporary, a limited perfection . . . . The profound affinity between play and order is perhaps the reason why play . . . seems to lie to such a large extent in the field of aesthetics. Play has a tendency to be beautiful."[6]

Typically in North America, we think of play as leisure time. Play is time not spent at work. We associate the words *play* and *leisure* with games, frolic at the beach, swinging in hammocks, and rocking in an easy chair. The list can be expanded virtually without limits.

In the United States, multi-billion-dollar industries such as gambling, sports, and travel dominate the culture. Advertising and the media encourage people to fill their leisure time with hustle and bustle: attending arts or sporting events, entertaining children, and getting away. All of this activity requires organizing, coordinating transportation for various family members, shopping, and other time-intensive labor. Everything easily fuels our feeling overwhelmed.

In two recent books, Juliet B. Schor, senior lecturer and Director of Women Studies at Harvard University, links the pressure people feel to live up to cultural expectations regarding leisure with the loss of community and the loss of meaning in work. To summarize her analysis, play in the United States contributes to the hectic life rather than to holiness.[7]

Historically, the ancient Greeks associated play with leisure and the root of the English word school, *skole*. Free time entailed creativity, dreaming and imagination, seeking truth, and becoming more fully alive. Though only a certain class enjoyed the leisure to learn, play had a significant social function. The arts, science, wisdom, and religion itself were all rooted in the primeval soil of play.[8]

Biblical writers do not address play as such. In biblical cultures, however, there seems to have been plenty of dancing, playing of instruments, singing, feasting, and partying. The Sabbath, a sacred time set apart for God, clearly marked a period of the week intended for rest and restoration of equilibrium in relation to God. The holiness of play extended the possibility of recreation to the whole week.

Practices of Holy Play

Holy play is a gift from God, part of growing into Christ-likeness and our journey to holiness. What practices should govern a modern spirituality of play? Let me suggest four.[9]

Doing Nothing

We should cherish doing nothing. Genesis 2:3 records that at the climax of creation God rested. God blesses the seventh day and hallows it. God enjoys all that has come to be, but God does nothing as such except to invite humans to set aside time for rest, recreation, and worship.

As stated in chapter 2, Sabbath time is essential to the rhythm of life. Acknowledging that it is good to allow time to lie fallow in the rhythm of our lives, we value doing nothing. Doing nothing frees us to discover beauty, goodness, and truth in the silences and hidden places without doing anything in particular, without going anywhere in particular, and without spending lots of money. We can commune with nature, meditate, or talk with family. We can simply be.

A variant of doing nothing is sedentary activity such as going to a movie, reading a book, or watching television. If the choices we make regarding what we see or read reflect such values as harmony, justice, simplicity, and wholeness, our passive activity can enhance the quality of our living and can have benefits, especially for our health and growth in the spiritual and aesthetic realms. I would argue that watching a Bill Moyers special on public television, reading a Booker- or Pulitzer-prize-winning novel, and attending an arts event can contribute to growth and well-being more than watching situation comedies, reading pulp fiction, or going to a mall.

Resisting

While holy play does have benefits, it should not be quantified in terms of costs, benefits, and productivity. The choices we make in the arena of play potentially bring us into conflict with the commodification and commercialization of leisure in North America. The moguls of our play industries in North America make a false equation between what we pay and how much fun we have. It is true that we play hard, and that play can require a great deal of money. This was underscored recently when the Seattle Mariners' free-agent shortstop Alex Rodriguez signed a ten-year contract with the Texas Rangers for $252,000,000.[10]

We can resist the commodification and commercialization of leisure. Sitting with friends; walking through a park; participating in a congregational picnic are examples of activities that do not require much money. Everyone can create her or his own list of activities that are freeing.

Can we liberate ourselves from reliance on material things as we play? One way to do so is through the practice of simplicity, a current that runs deep in the Christian tradition. Contemporary movements call people to "voluntary simplicity."[11] Voluntary simplicity means an ordering and guiding of our energy and our desires with partial restraint in some directions in order to secure greater abundance of life in others. We practice simplicity when we make changes in the way we live. We can change our seasonal practices (see Part IV). We can give priority to our spiritual, physical, mental, and intellectual health. We can practice the five R's of environmental ethics: reduce, reuse, recycle, restore, and respond. We can be in touch with nature. We can slow down.

Voluntary simplicity is a shorthand label for an idea contained in a song composed before 1850 and sung to a tune immortalized in 1944 with the premiere performance of Aaron Copland's *Appalachian Spring*: "'Tis the gift to be simple, 'tis the gift to be free, 'tis the gift to come down where we ought to be, and when we find ourselves in a place just right, 'twill be in the valley of love and delight. When true simplicity is gained, to bow and to bend we shan't be ashamed, to turn, turn will be our delight 'til by turning, turning, we come round right."[12]

Putting Children First

Another practice of holy play is playing with children. We must make the care of children a priority. Whether or not we are parents, we can help children come to the fullness of their humanity. We can support families in their efforts to care for children. Marian Wright Edelman, president of the Children's Defense Fund, states, "Given the crises faced today by all children, especially poor and black children, many of whom are struggling to beat insurmountable odds, it is time for our society to look at what we can do to make parents' jobs easier and how we can change some of the things we are doing that are making it more difficult than necessary to raise children."[13]

What are some of the things we can do to address this crisis? We can play with children. It costs little to play with children! We can listen to children. Again, this costs very little. We can mentor children. We can help filter out the most poisonous vehicles of popular culture, especially the sex and violence on television, video games, and the Internet. We can help children become fully human. In *The Prophet*, Kahlil Gibran writes that children are not our own but "life's longing for itself."[14]

Giving children time is a precious gift. Employers, government, and the community at large can help parents find time for their children. Among needed steps are paid parenting leave, creating family-friendly workplaces through such measures as flexible hours, compressed work weeks, part-time work with benefits, job sharing, and improved day care facilities.

Congregations can play a major role if we make the care and formation of children a priority. Through our communities of faith, we can help our children to know Jesus personally. We can help children develop a sense of wonder. We can help children play noncompetitively. A specific tool is the family pledge of nonviolence: to respect self and others, to communicate better, to listen, to forgive, to respect nature, to play creatively, and to be courageous.[15]

Recovering Community

A number of scholars have chronicled the loss of community and compassion that have been seen as the heart of civic culture in North America ever since Alexis de Tocqueville's *Democracy in America* in the 1830s. In a recent study, Harvard sociologist Robert D. Putnam chronicled the extent to which individualism, consumerism, and materialism have supplanted any sense of the common good. As a symbol of the decline of a sense of connection and of a willingness to associate with others, Putnam documented the growth of people bowling alone. More people are bowling than ever before, but league bowling has plummeted in the last ten to fifteen years. From 1980 to 1993, the total number of bowlers in the United States increased by 10 percent, while league bowling decreased by 40 percent. This is not trivial. In the United States, eighty million people went bowling at least once in 1993, nearly a third more than voted in the 1994 congressional elections and roughly the same number as those who claimed to attend church regularly.[16]

Within the span of a generation, positive values such as freedom, the individual, and material good have been transformed into ideologies. The positive blessings of computers and other technologies have exacerbated our compulsive independence and adulation of the market economy.

Holy play challenges these trends by promoting wholesome play and voluntarism. Do-nots (do not dance, do not drink, do not have sex except to produce children), historically highlighted by Protestantism, give way to clowning, dancing, laughing, and festivity. As we make our places of worship places of joy and celebration, we can also let our joy bubble over into the public arena.

In sum, holy play is life lived in God's presence. Holy play calls us to be mindful of how we live as bearers of the divine image. God can transform everything we do. We witness to God in everything we do, including our play.

Prayer
As David danced before God, may my dancing be bright.
As the psalmist sang new songs to God, may my words be beautiful.
As our Lord enjoyed a party, may my play be filled with happiness.
And may the Holy Spirit, whose presence is liberty, grant me freedom that
    will not hold back my joy in living, loving, and worshiping you.
Grant that this prayer be joined by the praises of the ever-dancing, ever-
    singing, ever-playing hosts of heaven. Amen.

---

[1] Les A. Murray, "Equanimity," in *The Shape of Belief: Christianity in Australia Today*, ed. Dorothy Harris (Homebush West, New South Wales: Lancer, 1982), 27-28.

[2] Donald Nicholl, *Holiness* (London: Darton, Longman and Todd, 1981 [1987]), 52. Several authors in *Practicing Our Faith: A Way of Life for a Searching People* (San Francisco: Jossey-Bass, 1997) consider other aspects of daily living, including our praise of God in song, how we treat our bodies, and our economic practices.

[3] Jerome W. Berryman, *Godly Play: An Imaginative Approach to Religious Education* (Minneapolis: Augsburg, 1991); Clifford Geertz, "Deep Play: Notes on the Balinese Cockfight," in *The Interpretation of Cultures: Selected Essays* (New York: Basic Books, 1973). See also Diane Ackerman, *Deep Play* (New York: Vintage Books, 1999).

[4] Celano records this story in his second life of Francis (c. 1182–1226): *Writings and Early Biographies: English Omnibus of the Sources for the Life of St. Francis*, ed. Marion A. Habig (Chicago: Franciscan Herald Press, 1983), 477 and 1922-23 for the *Canticle of the Creatures*. In most hymnals, this song is called *All Creatures of Our God and King*.

[5] *Laws*, vii, 796, cited by J. Huizinga, *Homo Ludens: A Study of the Play-Element in Culture* (Boston: Beacon, 1955), 19.

[6] Huizinga, *Homo Ludens*, 10.

[7] Juliet B. Schor, *The Overspent American: Upscaling, Downshifting, and the New Consumer* (New York: Harper, 1998) and *The Overworked American: The Unexpected Decline of Leisure* (New York: BasicBooks, 1991).

[8] Huizinga, *Homo Ludens*, 5.

[9] Jim Rice, "Why Play?" *Sojourners* 29/1 (January–February 1997): 24-27.

[10] Robert Sullivan, "Big Bucks and Baseball," *Time* (25 December 2000–1 January 2001), 144.

[11] Richard J. Foster, "Simplicity," ch. 6 of *Celebration of Discipline: The Path to Spiritual Growth* (rev. ed., San Francisco: Harper and Row, 1988); Duane Elgin, *Voluntary Simplicity: Toward a Way of Life that is Outwardly Simple, Inwardly Rich* (New York: Quill, 1993). Alternatives for Simple Living produced a useful resource in *Simple Living 101*. The Baptist Peace Fellowship of North America, 4800 Wedgewood Drive, Charlotte NC 28210 USA distributes the booklet.

[12] "'Tis the Gift to Be Simple (Simple Gifts)," *Voices United* (Etobicoke: United Church Publishing House, 1996), 353.

[13] Sylvia Ann Hewlett and Cornel West, *The War Against Parents: What We Can Do for America's Beleaguered Moms and Dads* (Boston: Houghton Mifflin, 1998), dust jacket. Sweet Honey in the Rock sets lines to music from Kahlil Gibran, *The Prophet* (New York: Alfred A. Knopf, 1970), 18.

[14] Gibran, *The Prophet*, 18. The group Sweet Honey in the Rock has put these words to music.

[15] Jim McGinnis, Ken and Gretchen Lovingood, and Jim Vogt, *Families Creating a Circle of Peace* (St. Louis: Parenting for Peace and Justice Network, 1996), inside front cover.

[16] Robert D. Putnam, *Bowling Alone: The Collapse and Revival of American Community* (New York: Simon and Schuster, 2000), 111-12. See Harvey Cox, *The Feast of Fools* (New York: Harper, 1969); Parker Palmer, *The Company of Strangers: Christians and the Renewal of America's Public Life* (New York: Crossroad, 1981); Robert Bellah et. al, *Habits of the Heart, Individualism and Commitment in American Life* (New York: Harper and Row, 1985); and Charles Taylor, *The Malaise of Modernity* (Toronto: Anansi, 1991).

For Reflection and Conversation

- Why is play a practice of holiness?

- What associations do the words *play* and *leisure* conjure up?

- Are there play and leisure activities in which you participate that are means of walking humbly with God?

- What are some specific play practices that are good and contribute to godly living?

- What is the relationship between play and evangelism?

Holy Discernment

Do not be conformed to this world, but be transformed by the renewing of your minds, so that you may discern what is the will of God—what is good and acceptable and perfect. (Romans 12:2)

What Is Holy Discernment?

Many years ago, I left a career that had been for me the realization of dreams, years of education, and four successful years on the job. The decision was difficult and held no guarantees for the future. I knew my choice was right. It has proved to be so, but how did I know then? God, my family, and my community of faith at the time lent a hand.

God was involved in my life, giving it meaning and purpose. I had the support of my wife. Nancy helped make the decision, backed me in it, and supported me as we bore the economic effects. In terms of the community of faith, Nancy and I were active with the Church of the Saviour in Washington, DC. A small group met at the Potter's House, a storefront café and center for the creative arts, worship, and discussion of issues of contemporary significance. Group members helped me discern God's call on my life.

The English *discernment* derives from the Greek *diakrisis* (to test in crisis) and the Latin *discernere* (to separate). When we face difficult choices such as whether or not to pursue or change a vocation or the decision to enter or leave a relationship, we often feel that we are facing the decision alone and that we are the first person ever to learn how to sort out the issues.

This is rarely the case. However, we sometimes act on the basis of our own assessment of what is necessary. Though God may be guiding the course of action, we customarily go through a process of weighing the pros and cons and coming to a decision. In my case, I was not alone. God, loved ones, and a community of faith helped me recognize my own truth, claim my belovedness, and see myself from a perspective different than that of the culture at large.

Discernment is something we do all the time. We are always acting on the basis of choices we make. Sometimes, but not in every decision, there is a call from God. Holy discernment is an intentional practice by which an individual or a community seeks, recognizes, and intentionally acts on the basis of help received from God. The process entails looking at oneself through spiritual eyes. Holy discernment is the spiritual way by which we endeavor to look at our circumstances from God's vantage point. God helps us discover God's will for our lives. "Our decisions and our search for guidance take place in the active presence of a God who intimately cares about our life situations and who invites us to participate in the divine activities of healing and transformation."[1]

Holy discernment is a biblical process. The Hebrew and Greek words translated as discernment equate the process with deciding and understanding. For example, in 1 Kings 3:9 Solomon prays, *Give your servant an understanding mind to govern your people, able to discern between good and evil.* According to Paul, some have the specific gift of the *discernment of spirits* (1 Cor 12:10).

More generally, the biblical writers attest to God's love for and investment in human beings. The psalmist attests that God is present with us, is manifest in varied ways, and provides direction regarding the divine will. *I will instruct you and teach you the way you should go; I will counsel you with my eye upon you* (Ps 32:8).

Spiritual discernment enabled the prophets to speak. Spiritual discernment enabled Joseph to think about Mary in a new way (Matt 1:19-25). Spiritual discernment enabled Jesus to know God's will. When they faced a major turning point, the apostles and elders knew what to do. They communicated their decision, saying, in part, *it has seemed good to the Holy Spirit and to us . . .* (Acts 15:28).[2]

The Practice of Holy Discernment

Holy discernment assumes that God is self-disclosing, that God yearns for us to know God's will, and that God gifts us with the Holy Spirit. The Holy Spirit is God's active and ongoing guide in personal and corporate discernment.

Generally in the process leading up to making a major decision, there is a sense of leading and being led. In the Baptist and other free church traditions, listening to Scripture and to the Spirit are primary. Discerning a call is often couched in the question, "What would Jesus do?" In the tradition of the Religious Society of Friends, Quakers speak variously of being drawn to an action, feeling under the weight of a concern, or being called or led to act in a specific way.

If we are to discern God's call, several dispositions are necessary. These include a commitment to follow Jesus; a deep sensitivity to the ways of God; a willingness to detach ourselves from our natural desires for wealth, prestige, and security; an openness to the promptings of God's Spirit; a readiness to test our leanings; and being taught by the Spirit.[3]

Holy discernment can take place on an individual basis or in community. As individuals, we may seek a spiritual director, whose training and practice is to assist people to develop their relationship with God. While long-term, general spiritual direction can be a great benefit, there are a number of situations in which it is especially suitable to seek the help of a spiritual director, including decisions about relationships, vocations, and call. The qualities that one should look for in a "spiritual friend" are loyalty, right intention, discretion, and patience.[4]

Generally, holy discernment involves choices in which there is more than one possible outcome. In addition to individual discernment, we may want to explore options in community. Historically, Christians have used small group processes to assist individuals to discern God's purposes. In the Baptist and other free church traditions, there is a constant interplay between the personal and the corporate. The Religious Society of Friends uses a clearness committee when two members of a local meeting (congregation) ask to be married. A small group gathers with the couple several times to pray, to ask caring but probing questions, to explore issues the couple might not have considered on their own, to listen carefully to how the couple answers, and to let the couple listen anew to themselves. Many meetings have expanded this approach beyond marriage, using it to help individuals make a variety of crucial decisions.[5]

When a community seeks to discern God's will for the community, members agree to listen to one another, to respect the diversity of gifts represented, and to seek to avoid disunity. Generally, the process does not entail taking votes but enables the community to picture a different world and consider the steps it might take to get there.

Holy discernment is a desideratum. One reason is that, while religious freedom is a great strength of North American society, there are some perils.

Individuals can claim to hear the call of God. "God wants me to become a pastor." "God has given me a word of prophecy." Communities can claim to follow the leadings of God. "God has told us to move to the suburbs." "God is calling us to become more intentional in the area of racial reconciliation." How is the individual or the community to know that God is directing them in the direction that they say?

In the arena of new religions with their new gods, messiahs, scriptures, and rituals, many individuals masquerade as Christian. Some recruit members for potentially dangerous mind development groups and cults. In thinking about groups outside the religious mainstream, we do well to remember that the behavior and ideas of many of our own bodies once seemed misguided, eccentric, or evil. Some groups challenged religious institutions and authority of the day. Many disappeared, but some have flourished in North American society. Baptists, for example, were once among the most despised of all religious misfits. Unwelcome in Europe and then in England, Baptists breathed new life into dead ecclesiastical bodies. Courageously they pioneered constitutional protection of religious liberty and the separation of church and state.

Holy discerning encourages us to ask of individuals and groups, who is worshiped? Is the decision faithful to Jesus? What is the source of authority? Are the individuals or is the community faithful to Scripture and tradition? Does the decision bring inner peace and communal harmony? What are the fruits of the individual's or group's leading? *The fruit of the Spirit is love, joy, peace, patience, kindness, generosity, faithfulness, gentleness, and self-control* (Gal 5:22-23).

Holy discernment has extraordinary potential to enable us to see people with spiritual eyes and to look to something that lies beneath the surface. In the words of the little prince, "What is most important is invisible . . . ."[6]

Psychiatrist M. Scott Peck tells a story that makes this point.[7] The abbot of a dying monastic house visited the hermitage of a Jewish rabbi. They shared how the spirit had gone from their people. They wept, then read parts of Torah together and quietly spoke of deep things. When the time came for the abbot to leave, they embraced each other, and the abbot said, "It has been a wonderful thing that we should meet after all these years, but I have still failed in my purpose for coming here. Is there nothing you can tell me, no piece of advice you can give me that would help me save my dying order?"

The rabbi replied, "No, I am sorry. I have no advice to give. The only thing I can tell you is that the Messiah is one of you."

The abbot returned to the monastery. His discouraged community gathered around him. "What did the rabbi say?" they asked.

"He couldn't help. We just wept and read the Torah together. The only thing he did say . . . was that the Messiah is one of us. I don't know what he meant."

In the days and weeks and months that followed, the old monks pondered the rabbi's words. Wondering if the rabbi might have meant the abbot, one of the brothers who had long grumbled about matters came to recognize the gift of leadership that the abbot had exercised faithfully for so long. He began to see Brother Thomas as a man of holiness, Brother Elred as one who could give sound advice, Brother Philip as constant in support, himself as a real somebody. He began to treat the others with extraordinary respect. Gradually, an aura of extraordinary respect began to beam through the entire region.

So it happened that, without even being conscious of it, people came to sense something strangely attractive, even compelling, about those five old men. Hardly knowing why, they began to return to the monastery more frequently to picnic, to play, to pray. They began to bring their friends to show them this special place. Friends brought others. Some joined the order. Within a few years, the monastery began to thrive once again. Thanks to the rabbi's gift, it became a vibrant center of light and spirituality in the whole realm.

An application of corporate discernment involves the call, training, and ordination of individuals into ministerial orders. Most churches and denominations have a formal process by which an individual that has experienced the call of God on her or his life seeks the wisdom of the wider community and is guided for several years.

A danger to be avoided is to assume that the only vocation to which God calls people is in professional ministry. A Christian community does not consist solely of preachers and teachers of the word. Writing about life in a German community of resistance during the period of Hitler's rise to power, Dietrich Bonhoeffer observed that in a Christian community everything depends on whether each individual is seen as an indispensable link in a chain. "It will be well, therefore, if every member receives a definite task to perform for the community, that he may know in hours of doubt that he, too, is not useless and unusable. Every Christian community must realize that not only do the weak need the strong, but also that the strong cannot exist without the weak. The elimination of the weak is the death of fellowship."[8]

An example of a service of worship that grew out of a process of discernment took place in 1990. MacNeill Baptist Church in Hamilton, Ontario, was about to install Christopher Page as its pastor. Rather than focusing on him and on his call, we saw this as an occasion to recognize the call to ministry of every person in the community. During the service, every member who could brought to the altar a symbol of his or her service: the moderator brought a copy of the church constitution; a deacon brought a list of her watch-care group members; a member of the Ontario Human Rights Commission brought a copy of the Bill of Rights; a maintenance person brought a wrench, and so on. We then asked Chris if, in taking up his role as pastor of this community, he would nurture all of us in our respective calls.

We cannot separate the process of discernment and call from our vocational choices. All of us work. Some of us work in positions that generate income. The work we do can be a response to a call. Beyond that, individuals can bring spiritual values to our work. A discerning congregation needs to help individuals work in a balanced rhythm of worship, play, and rest and to support working people. (This is illustrated through a Labor Day liturgy included in an appendix.)

Discernment is a risky business. According to Elizabeth O'Connor, one of my mentors at the moment of decision, Jesus calls his disciples to take risks. In fact, those who appear to risk nothing risk more those who do so intentionally. To respond to a call necessitates setting out from a familiar and relatively secure place for a destination that can be only dimly perceived and that we cannot be certain of reaching. "One of the ways to test the authenticity of call is to determine whether it requires a journey. This journey is not necessarily geographical although, as in the case of Abraham and Moses, it is not at all unusual for it to involve leaving one's work and home . . . . We need to be delivered from all that binds and keeps the real self from breaking into music and becoming joy to the world." On the journey, God inevitably gives a new vision to reach toward. "Hope begins to grow and we are summoned to the work that will give us a feeling of wellness, and make possible that which we envision."[9]

Prayer

From his monastery in Trappist, Kentucky, Thomas Merton wrote a prayer that reflects our journey of discernment. I share it for companions seeking God's will in their lives.

> My Lord God, I have no idea where I am going. I do not see the road ahead of me. I cannot know for certain where it will end. Nor do I really know myself, and the fact that I think I am following your will does not mean that I am actually doing so. But I believe that the desire to please you does in fact please you . . . lead me by the right road . . . I will trust you always though I may seem to be lost and in the shadow of death. I will not fear, for you are ever with me, and you will never leave me to face my perils alone.[10]

---

[1] Frank Rogers Jr., "Discernment," in *Practicing our Faith: A Way of Life for a Searching People*, ed. Dorothy C. Bass (San Francisco: Jossey-Bass, 1998), 106.

[2] Danny Morris and Charles M. Olsen, *Discerning God's Will Together: A Spiritual Practice for the Church* (Nashville: Upper Room, 1997), 22-26. Morris and Olsen offer an invaluable guide for enabling religious groups to make decisions in spiritual ways such as coming to consensus (the sense of the meeting) and recognizing the leading of the Holy Spirit. Suzanne G. Farnham et al., *Listening Hearts: Discerning Call in Community* (rev. ed., Harrisburg: Morehouse, 1991) is also excellent. These books inform my use of *call* as a specific leading at a particular time.

[3] Paul A. Lacey, *Leading and Being Led*, Pendle Hill Pamphlet 264 (Wallingford: Pendle Hill Publications, 1985).

[4] Tilden H. Edwards, *Spiritual Friend: Reclaiming the Gift of Spiritual Direction* (Ramsey: Paulist, 1980), 46. Other excellent writings on spiritual direction include William A. Barry and William J. Connolly, *The Practice of Spiritual Direction* (San Francisco: Harper & Row, 1982); Katherine Marie Dyckman and L. Patrick Carroll, *Inviting the Mystic, Supporting the Prophet: An Introduction to Spiritual Direction* (Ramsey: Paulist, 1981); John J. English, *Spiritual Freedom* (Guelph: Loyola House, 1979); and Richard J. Foster, "Guidance," in *Celebration of Discipline: The Path to Spiritual Growth* (San Francisco: Harper & Row, 1988).

[5] Parker J. Palmer, "The Clearness Committee: A Way of Discernment," *Weavings* 3 (July–August 1988): 37-40.

[6] Antoine de Saint-Exupéry, *The Little Prince*, trans. Katherine Woods (San Diego: Harcourt, Brace and World, 1943), 76.

[7] M. Scott Peck, *The Different Drum: Community Making and Peace* (New York: Simon and Schuster, 1987), 13-15.

[8] Dietrich Bonhoeffer, *Life Together*, trans. John W. Doberstein (New York: Harper & Row, 1976, paperback), 94.

[9] Elizabeth O'Connor, *Cry Pain, Cry Hope: Thresholds to Purpose* (Waco: Word, 1987), 82, 85.

[10] Thomas Merton, *Thoughts in Solitude* (New York: Farrar, Straus, 1958), #83.

For Reflection and Conversation

- Why is holy discernment a practice of walking humbly with God?

- What are the most important ways of testing whether a decision is of God?

- Can you think of a time when you turned to God, family, or the faith community for direction in making a decision?

- How is your work a vocation from God?

- What is the relationship between discernment and evangelism?

Practices of Loving-kindness

Introduction

*What does the L*ORD *require of you but ... to love kindness?*
(Micah 6:8)

This book has a straightforward premise. As Christians, we proclaim the gospel of Jesus Christ by living faithfully in response to his gracious invitation to follow him. In the words of Paul, we become all things to all people that we might by *all means* save some (1 Cor 9:22).

All means leads to a broad evangelistic lifestyle. True evangelical faith cannot lie dormant. It feeds the hungry. It provides something to drink to those who are thirsty. It welcomes the stranger. It clothes the naked. It brings healing to those who are sick. It visits those in prison. It comforts the sorrowful. It serves those who harm it. It shelters the destitute. It binds up those who are wounded. In short, it becomes life-giving sustenance to everyone.[1]

We, the whole people of God, share the whole gospel for the whole person in the whole of society throughout the whole world. This definition is not unique to me and has gained wide acceptance over the last thirty years.[2] Five components of an evangelistic lifestyle follow.

Whole People of God: Every local manifestation of the church and all individual members of the church are responsible for God's mission. Evangelism is not an option, something we choose to do or *not* to do. Evangelism belongs to everyone. To evangelize alone is theologically misguided and a recipe for burnout.

Whole Gospel: We are gospel-bearers. Evangelism flows naturally from our baptism and incorporation into Christ's church. Through worship, programs, and other activities we evangelize intentionally. More generally, evangelism is walking in the light of God. In the words of a well-known chorus, "This little light of mine, I'm going to let it shine."

Whole Person: It is wrong to talk of saving "souls" as though we are disembodied. We share a gospel for the whole person that includes body, mind, and spirit.

Whole of Society: A biblical perspective on evangelism holds centripetal activity (the nations flowing to Jerusalem) in tension with centrifugal activity (going out to the nations). Aware of the contexts in which such practices arose, I appreciate the model of early ascetics who fled to the wilderness or of groups like the Amish who respond to the communitarian impulse suggested by passages such as Acts 2:37-42. While these may not be suitable models for most of us, it is clear that God calls us to bring the gospel to bear on all aspects of the social world in which we live.

Whole World: A biblical perspective on missions is hostile to narrowness of vision. Flung into God's world with a global consciousness, we are to think globally but act locally.

As Christ-bearers, we must resist three tendencies. The first is to be possessive. It is unacceptable to claim that the gospel of Jesus Christ is ours as though it is not something for others or is compatible only with our culture. The second is to live exclusively inward-directed or outward-directed lives. We must be as concerned with inner holiness and sanctification as we are with life in the world. The third is to accent one aspect of evangelism to the exclusion of others. We must be as concerned with personal witness as we are with justice.

Followers of Jesus Christ adopt a wide variety of practices. As we have seen in Part I, the interior practices such as prayer or Sabbath observance do in fact lead outward. In words of the eighteenth-century antislavery advocate John Woolman, "It is good for thee to dwell deep, that thou mayest feel and understand the spirits of people."[3]

Jesus and his friends, Mary and Martha, offer a model of evangelism that links prayer and action. They practiced the interior disciplines of personal holiness and journeyed as well into worldly service.

A third-century story recorded in *The Sayings of the Desert Fathers* illustrates how the inward-outward journey manifests itself. Abba Agathon, a third-century monk, was going to town to sell articles. On the roadside, he met a cripple with paralyzed legs who asked the monk where he was going. Abba Agathon replied, "To town, to sell some things." The cripple replied, "Do me the favor of carrying me there." So Agathon carried him to town. When they arrived, the cripple said, "Put me down where you sell your wares." He did so. After Agathon sold something, the man asked, "For how much did you sell it?" Agathon told him. The man said, "Buy me some food." Agathon did. When he had sold all his wares and was preparing to leave, the cripple asked, "Will you do me the favor of carrying me back to the place where you found me?" Agathon picked him up and carried him back to that place. Then the cripple said, "Agathon, you are filled with divine blessings, in heaven and on earth." Raising his eyes, Agathon saw only an angel of the Lord.[4]

This story in three movements leads to the heart of an evangelistic lifestyle. First, each of us, like Agathon, when we surrender to a call to follow Jesus, must simply let the Holy Spirit be our guide. Second, and again like Agathon, as we resolve to follow Jesus, we probably have no great plans. Generally we are not thinking about specific ministries. More likely, we are focused on holiness and salvation. Almost certainly, we are not thinking about the hungry, the helpless, the hopeless, and the hugless. These are, nonetheless, the ones Jesus beckons us to serve. We simply make ourselves available to those in need if we are Christ-bearers. Finally, and again like Agathon, when we follow all the directions that come from God, angels in heaven and on earth take note and fill our hearts to overflowing with God's love. This love is a divine gift. This love guides our ministry.

From Jesus I have learned that we are without power apart from that to which we are open. When we are open to a divine call, when we are ready to serve, and when we are humble before God, God fills us with love and lets love flow through us to minister to others.

This section explores four practices of loving-kindness: loving, listening, compassion, and testimony. Each arises out of Jesus' instruction that we observe all he has commanded (Matt 28:20). Many books about evangelism emphasize sharing the faith verbally. Adopting the practices discussed in this section does not preclude using words. Indeed, one of the practices discussed in this section, testimony, is a key means by which we share our life in Christ in word as well as by deed. But in this section, words are not a priority. People in North American society are already inundated by too many words. Rather, our main concern is with practices that help mend the world and restore the fabric of human community. Words may be only one part of carrying out these practices.

Evangelism is always specific, contextual, and incarnational. Specificity means sharing the gospel within a framework of a particular culture in the language of that culture. We do not do evangelism in general. We do evangelism in specific circumstances, in specific contexts, and with those whom

God specifically places in our lives daily. If we agree that Jesus is the answer for everyone's need, several questions follow. For what specific need is Jesus the answer? Are we to focus on the spiritual needs of an individual? Are the individual's immediate needs physical or mental? Does social injustice impinge upon the person? Are we to empower the individual or become an advocate? To practice an evangelistic lifestyle through localized expressions of the gospel, we must address the human condition as specifically as possible. Spiritual and physical needs are manifested concretely within each particular community.

Second, evangelism is contextual. One's needs are linked to one's life situation. While Christians do make an impact on large issues, most of us are not able to do a great deal about big issues such as environmental decay, hunger, inadequate housing, religious persecution, or poverty. We can act in an awareness of the need for Jesus in the lives of non-Christian family members, neighbors, and friends. We can respond to a need for food, clothing, or shelter on the part of marginalized people in our own cities and towns.

Third, evangelism is incarnational. Just as God became one of us in Jesus, we share Jesus by making him manifest in our lives. We incarnate Jesus' love and compassion as we bless, encourage, give testimony, heal, listen, love, strengthen, and watch. In these and other ways, we live out of the prophet Micah's call to love kindness.

---

[1] Inspired by Matt 25:31-45 and the Beatitudes as recorded in Matt 5:3-11 and Luke 6:20-22, these words arise out of the insistence of Protestant reformers that a Christian naturally gives outward expression of God's justifying grace in love and obedience to God. In 1520, the German Reformer Martin Luther (1483–1546) wrote, "A Christian is a perfectly free lord of all, subject to none. A Christian is a perfectly dutiful servant of all, subject to all. . . . Works themselves do not justify him before God, but he does the works out of spontaneous love in obedience to God and considers nothing except the approval of God, whom he would most scrupulously obey in all things" ("Freedom of a Christian" in *Martin Luther*, ed. John Dillenberger [New York: Anchor, 1961], 53, 68).

In 1539, the Dutch Anabaptist Menno Simons (c. 1496–1561) wrote, ". . . true evangelical faith . . . cannot lie dormant, but manifests itself in all righteousness and works of love; it . . . clothes the naked; it feeds the hungry; it comforts the sorrowful; it shelters the destitute; it aids and consoles the sad; it returns good for evil; it serves those that harm it; it prays for those that persecute it" (in *The Complete Writings of Menno Simons*, ed. J. C. Winger [Scottdale: Mennonite Publishing House, 1956], 307).

[2] A gathering in Lausanne, Switzerland, in July 1974 marked openness to holistic evangelism by so-called evangelical Protestants. For the Lausanne Covenant, see James A. Scherer and Stephen B. Bevans, eds., *New Directions in Mission and Evangelization*, vol. 1, *Basic Statements 1974–1991* (Maryknoll: Orbis, 1992). The All Africa Baptist Fellowship meeting

in Ibadan, Nigeria, on 22 October 1987 reflects grass-roots appropriation of a holistic approach. The declaration of theological principles includes, "We declare the task of evangelization to be the mission of the whole church, with the whole Gospel, for the whole person, in the whole of society, for the whole world."

[3] Richard J. Foster, *Celebration of Discipline: The Path to Spiritual Growth* (rev. ed., San Francisco: Harper and Row, 1988), 1.

[4] Benedicta Ward, trans., *The Sayings of the Desert Fathers: The Alphabetical Collection* (London: A. R. Mowbray, 1975), 21-22.

Practices of Love

Beloved, let us love one another, because love is from God. (1 John 4:7)

As we reflect on the practices of loving-kindness, we begin of course with love. This is where Jesus tells us to concentrate. Jesus calls us first and foremost to follow him and to love. Jesus does not call us primarily to journey a set path. Nor does he call us to serve institutional structures. He does not even call us to reshape the world around us. Rather, he calls us to let his sight and touch and sound and love be seen in us. He calls us to journey along a path he shares with us. Where his love and footsteps lead, we move and love and grow into Christ-likeness, his love being manifest in and through us.[1]

Someone asked Jesus to name the most important of the commandments. He answered, *The first is, "Hear, O Israel: the Lord our God, the Lord is one; you shall love the Lord your God with all your heart, and with all your soul, and with all your mind, and with all your strength."* Jesus continued, saying the second important commandment is to love your neighbor as yourself. *There is no other commandment greater than these* (Mark 12:28-31). When asked to clarify what he meant, Jesus indicated that when we love, we are not far from God's realm (Mark 12:34). In a parallel text, Jesus responded to a lawyer who asked the question in the first place, *do this, and you will live* (Luke 10:25-28).

Love God. Love neighbor. Love oneself. Do this and you shall live.

Loving is a practice. Loving is a requirement of holy living. Jesus summarized the love commandment and illustrated by concrete example how we are to love.

Who is my neighbor? the inquirer asked. Jesus replied, citing the case of a man who was going down from Jerusalem to Jericho and fell into the hands of robbers. They stripped him, beat him, and went away leaving him half-dead. Both a priest and a Levite passed him by, but a Samaritan was moved with pity and cared for him. Jesus then turned the question around, *Which of these three, do you think, was a neighbor to the man who fell into the hands of the robbers?* The answer came, *The one who showed him mercy.* Jesus said, *Go and do likewise* (Luke 10:25-37).

Similarly, when the time of his own death approached, Jesus had a final meal with his friends. He rose from the table, took off his outer robe, took a towel and water, and washed the feet of his disciples. He instructed them that if he as Lord and Teacher washed their feet, so should they wash one another's feet. He went on to give a new commandment: love one another. *Just as I have loved you, you also should love one another. By this everyone will know that you are my disciples, if you have love for one another* (John 13:34-35).

When Jesus met Peter and the other disciples after the resurrection, Jesus reiterated that he wants his disciples to love. Three times he asked Peter, *Do you love me?* He used one of three Greek words for love, *agape* (divine love). The first time Peter replied, *Yes, Lord, you know that I love you.* Peter used another Greek word for love, *phileo* (fraternal love). Jesus said to him, *Feed my lambs.* Jesus asked Peter a second time, *Simon, son of John, do you love me?* Again, Jesus used *agape*. Peter replied, *Yes, Lord, you know that I love you.* Again, Peter used *phileo*. Jesus said, *Tend my sheep.* Jesus asked a third time, *Simon, son of John, do you love me?* This time Jesus addressed Peter using *phileo*. Exasperated, miffed, and hurt, Peter affirmed, *Lord, you know everything: you know that I love you.* He used the word *phileo* for a third time. Jesus replied, *Feed my sheep.* Finally, Jesus said to Peter, *Follow me* (John 21:15-19).

Jesus did not ask, "How much are you going to accomplish?" He did not say to discouraged Peter, "Get a grip." No, Jesus said, "Feed my lambs, tend my sheep, feed my sheep, follow me." Jesus also cautioned Peter that his journey into loving in the world would not be easy.

In the Greek, Jesus changed the verb for love. Commentators have differed as to why Jesus shifted the verb from *agape* to *phileo*. A plausible explanation is that Jesus kept asking Peter a foundational question. Consistent with his teaching about love, Jesus used *agape* to connote a superior type of love. *Agape* love is deep-seated, purposeful, and self-sacrificing. It is a loving that one wills to be. It is a loving that is independent of emotional feelings one may have. This love is stronger than communicated by the Greek *phileo,* which connotes a spontaneous natural affection.

From a linguistic perspective then, it seems that Jesus came to accept that Peter simply did not understand what sort of love Jesus expected of his followers. Jesus was saying in effect, "Peter, you say that you love me. I wonder if you really do. Just as you denied me more than once, you really do not grasp that, by loving, I mean a costly kind of love. All right, then, Peter, I accept your human friendship for me. So let us begin here."[2]

Jesus related to the disciples on their terms. Peter denied Jesus three times. The other disciples did no better. It is unlikely any of them grasped the magnitude of what Jesus had taught before his death about love. Even after Jesus' resurrection, the disciples had a hard time grasping what Jesus was asking of them. So Jesus began with the basics. Love me in any way you can. Minister to my people however you are able. Let my love be grown in you and your love in them. In this way, Jesus simplified their task. Over time, Peter and the other early Christians learned to love with a deeper kind of love, *agape* love.

Do you love me? Jesus puts the same question to us many times and in terms we can understand. Yet, like Peter, it takes a long time for most of us to "get it."

Years ago, I watched a television interview of Mother Teresa of Calcutta (1910–1997) from Beirut, Lebanon. It was 1982 and a time of war. She stood amid the rubble of a bombed-out building, holding a child in her arms. A reporter asked her why she was there. He wanted to know what good she was doing. He pressed her to justify helping one child when a war was raging all about. The reporter asked her three times what good she was doing. Each time, she replied, "Jesus loves this child." *Feed my lambs. Tend my sheep. Feed my sheep.* Mother Teresa modeled what Jesus meant when he told Peter to follow him (Acts 21:19).

Some years ago, I participated in a Maundy Thursday Tenebrae service. The twelve of us participating extinguished twelve candles. This action symbolized what we do to Christ. We fail to let his light shine through us. As the twelve disciples deserted Jesus, we still desert him.

Throughout the service, the Christ candle remained lit and was still burning Sunday morning. At the end of the Easter worship, everyone in the congregation lit a candle from the Christ candle. One by one, we went out in the light and love of the resurrection carrying the light and love of Christ into the world. Our candles symbolized our going out to those in pain, to the lonely, the addicted, the children, the elderly, the prostitutes, and others. We went out to love.

Feed my lambs. Tend my sheep. Feed my sheep. Follow me.

What about the other dimensions of the love ethic? We are to love God. We do so through our praise, adoration, and love of God. We also love God by loving others. In words of the popular musical *Les Misérables*, to love another person is to see the face of God.[3]

Finally, we are to love ourselves. When we think about Jesus, we might not appreciate that Jesus expects us to love ourselves. The capacity to practice love of others arises from God's loving us. The evangelist John makes clear that God is love, that God has gifted us with love, and that we should be called God's beloved children. That is who we are (1 John 3:1).[4]

God loves me. Jesus loves me. How do I know? The Bible tells me so. This pretty much sums it all up.[5]

Overwhelmingly, biblical teaching makes it impossible to think of practicing love of God, neighbor, and self as a luxury. If love is a luxury, it is expendable. To be consistent with Jesus' teaching, we understand love as a necessity. To deny love is to perish. African American spiritual mentor Howard Thurman put it this way: "So simple is the reality, and so terrifying. Ultimately there is only one place of refuge on this planet for any man—that is in another man's heart. To love is to make of one's heart a swinging door."[6]

The practice of love arises from the teachings of Jesus, who reveals love as fundamentally the nature of God. We love because God loves, because Jesus loves, because it is in our nature to love. The following story offers one illustration of love as a natural overflow arising from our journey through life with Jesus. I am confident you can multiply such stories, for ordinary Christians have been practicing love a long while.

Thomas S. Klise's novel *The Last Western* concerns Willie, an Irish-Indian-Negro-Chinese boy who grows up in abject poverty, who is absolutely uneducable, but whose baseball skills are discovered in the slums and sandlots of Houston. In his first major league baseball game, Willie strikes out twenty-seven consecutive players and becomes a national sensation.

Quickly, Willie finds that the baseball executives exploit him. When riots strike his home area, he leaves the team and returns to Houston where his family and friends are dead. He finds his home razed. Overcome by horror, he runs. Somewhere outside the city, he collapses. People who call themselves the Silent Servants of the Used, Abused, and Utterly Screwed Up find him and nurse him back to health. Klise describes the community as follows:

> The Servants will always choose the way of serving the poor, the lonely, the despised, the outcast, the miserable and the misfit. The mission of the Servants is to prove to the unloved that they are not abandoned, nor finally left alone. Hence, the natural home of the Servants is strife, misfortune, crisis, the falling apart of things. The Society cherishes failure for it is in failure, in trouble, in the general breaking up of classes, stations, usual conditions, normal routines that human hearts are open to the light of God's mercy.[7]

Willie subsequently joins the Silent Servants of the Used, Abused, and Utterly Screwed Up. Klise's story makes compelling reading. It is a powerful description of the church of which I dream. Though very few of us are able fully to identify with Willie, there is a sense in which we are all Willies. We are all sinners. Until God touches us, we are utterly screwed up. Healed, we have the great calling to join with others of Christ's servants in the world. There, we encounter strife, misfortune, crisis, and the falling apart of things. Can Christians love as Jesus taught and commanded us to love?

Another practice of love is forgiveness. The command to forgive seventy times seven is among the hardest of Jesus' instructions. The letters by Paul, James, and other disciples were written to young churches suffering from grievances, complaints, lies, deceit, bad temper, anger, shouting, abuse, malice, bitterness—attitudes that reveal just how hard it was to live out the new life in Christ. We experience these attitudes in our own inner lives, not to mention our congregations. (We rarely discuss this reality.) We prefer to emphasize intrinsic worth of our worship, prayer, and outreach. Our mission statements emphasize that our congregations are places of welcome and community. All too glibly, we repeat phrases of Martin Luther King Jr.'s "I Have a Dream Speech" and uphold a mental picture of the Beloved Community. We easily ignore King's harder teaching that we must love as Jesus taught us to love. This includes love of enemy.

> How do we love our enemies? First, we must develop and maintain the capacity to forgive. He who is devoid of the power to forgive is devoid of the power to love . . . . Forgiveness does not mean ignoring what has been done or putting a false label on an evil act. It means, rather, that the evil act no longer remains as a barrier to the relationship. Forgiveness is a catalyst creating the atmosphere necessary for a fresh start and a new beginning . . . . Forgiveness means reconciliation, a coming together again. Without this, no man can love his enemies. The degree to which we are able to forgive determines the degree to which we are able to love our enemies . . . .

Love is the only force capable of transforming an enemy into a friend. We never get rid of an enemy by meeting hate with hate; we get rid of an enemy by getting rid of enmity. By its very nature, hate destroys and tears down; by its very nature, love creates and builds up. Love transforms with redemptive power.[8]

In 1984 five prisoners escaped from Fort Pillow State Prison near Jackson, Tennessee. One of them, Riley Arceneaux, found his way to the home of Nathan and Louise Degrafinried. Louise was aware of who Riley was. Nevertheless, she greeted him the way she received everybody, with love. She gave Riley clean clothes and prepared him breakfast. She had him put down his gun. Hers was a house of God, she told him, not of violence. Before they ate she offered grace. Her prayer disarmed Riley and, with a tear in his eye, he explained his grandmother prayed much like she did. Shortly after they ate, police arrived on the scene, and Riley surrendered peacefully.

Feed my lambs. Tend my sheep. Feed my sheep. Follow me.

To the Colossians, Paul wrote that Christ is the *icon* (the Greek word) of the invisible God (Col 1:15). That is, Christ is the image or representation of who God is and of what God is like. God is love. God is concerned for us. God wants us to be cared for. For Riley, Louise became a living icon of the loving God known through the loving Christ. I was not surprised to read that when Louise died a few months ago at age eighty-seven, Riley was among the pallbearers at her funeral. God bless Louise Degrafinried who risked all she had to love in faith and hope.

Most of us know people like Louise Degrafinried: a parent, grandparent, relative, or friend who practices love fully and becomes for us a model of what it means to follow Jesus. Perhaps this person leads us to faith. As we too practice love, so may we show others the way of love.[9]

In his book *Living Faith*, former President Jimmy Carter wrote of the most unforgettable funeral he had ever attended, with the possible exception of those of his own family members.[10] It was the service for Mrs. Martin Luther King Sr. Matriarch of the King family, she was shot while playing "The Lord's Prayer" on the church organ at Ebenezer Baptist Church. The Revered Otis Moss from Cleveland, Ohio, preached a brief but remarkable sermon about "the little dash in between." Carter remembers Moss's words in this way: "He said there would be a marker on Mrs. King's grave, with her name and a couple of dates—when she was born and when she died—and a little dash in between. He said he didn't want to talk about when she was born or when she died but about that little dash. He described Mrs. King's great life and then shifted his attention to the audience. He said that everybody has what might be considered just a tiny dash." With God, that dash is everything. God would have us reflect on the question, what do we do with that little dash in between? It represents our life on earth.

My prayer for each of you who read this book is that your little dash may be marked by love. When we love our brothers and sisters with the same love our Lord showed us, we experience God's love. When we so love our sisters and brothers, we enable them to experience this love. In this way, the practice of love becomes the foundation of an evangelistic lifestyle. Words by John Greenleaf Whittier, a nineteenth-century member of the Society of Friends, express this idea:

> Immortal Love, for ever full,
> For ever flowing free,
> For ever shared, for ever whole,
> A never-ebbing sea!
> Blow winds of God, awake and blow
> The mists of earth away:
> Shine out, O Light Divine, and show
> How wide and far we stray.
> We may not climb the heavenly steeps
> To bring the Lord Christ down;
> In vain we search the lowest deeps,
> For Him no depths can drown. . . .
> The healing of His seamless dress
> Is by our beds of pain;
> We touch Him in life's throng and press,
> And we are whole again.
> The letter fails, the systems fall,
> And every symbol wanes;
> The Spirit over-brooding all,
> Eternal Love remains.[11]

God has shown Eternal Love in Jesus. Over time, this love has changed the world. My prayer is that each reader will let him be known through us.

Prayer
We praise you, Triune God, to whom there is no alien race, no foreign shore, no child unsought, no person unnamed. Holy God, revealer of all that is good and true, in Whom all hearts find rest, help us to spread your love to

all; empower us to make your love known. May greed, hatred, and all else cease that disfigures the world into which you became incarnate in Jesus. Sanctify us that in some measure we may love. Help us to live into that time when every tongue might confess Jesus Christ as Lord. Amen.

---

[1] "The Summons," a hymn of the Iona Community, opens as follows (John Bell and Graham Maule, *Heaven Shall Not Wait* [Glasgow: Wild Goose Publications, 1987], 117):

Will you come and follow me
If I but call your name?
Will you go where you don't know
And never be the same?
Will you let my love be shown,
Will you let my name be known,
Will you let my life be grown
In you and you in me?

[2] Leon Morris, *The Gospel according to John* (Grand Rapids: Eerdmans, 1971), 872. My reading draws on the 1995 revised edition, pp. 768-70. Other commentators minimize the importance of the supposed difference in Jesus' use of different words for love (Herman N. Ridderbos, *The Gospel of John: A Theological Commentary*, trans. John Vriend [Grand Rapids: Eerdmans, 1997], 666).

[3] "To love another person is to see the face of God," finale, *Les Misérables*, a musical by Alain Boublil and Claude-Michel Schonberg (Los Angeles: Warner Brothers, 1986).

[4] Henri Nouwen, *Bread for the Journey* (San Francisco: Harper, 1997), 3 June, writes, "When we think about Jesus as that exceptional, unusual person who lived long ago and whose life and words continue to inspire us, we might avoid the realization that Jesus wants us to be like him. Jesus himself keeps saying in many ways that he, the Beloved Child of God, came to reveal to us that we too are God's beloved children, loved with the same unconditional divine love . . . . This is the great challenge of the spiritual life: to claim the identity of Jesus for ourselves and to say, *We are the living Christ today!*"

[5] "Jesus Loves Me, This I Know." Most readers will know these words of Anna Bartlett Warner with hymnody by William Betchelder Bradbury. Theologian Karl Barth cited the hymn to summarize his work.

[6] *Disciplines of the Spirit* (Richmond: Friends United Press, 1977), 127.

[7] Thomas S. Klise, *The Last Western* (Niles: Argus Communications, 1974), 150.

[8] Martin Luther King Jr., *Strength to Love* (Philadelphia: Fortress Press, 1963), 48-49, 52.

[9] Obituary, Louise Degrafinried, *Memphis Commercial Appeal*, 20 August 1998.

[10] Jimmy Carter, *Living Faith* (New York: Times Books, 1996), 236-37.

[11] John Greenleaf Whittier lived from 1807 to 1892. These words, not always included in hymnbooks, are in *The Hymnary* (Toronto: Ryerson Press, 1936), #123.

For Reflection and Conversation

- Do you have problems thinking of yourself as a child of God? Can you let go of this resistance?

- Can you think of others, even enemies, as God's beloved children?

- Identify *someone* who has shown you the love of God. Can you pray, "Thanks be to God"?

- Identify *a situation* in which someone has gone the extra mile to show the love of God. Can you pray, "Thanks be to God"?

- What is the relationship between loving and evangelism?

Practices of Listening

Let anyone with ears listen! (Matthew 11:15)

Listening as Following God

The quality most characteristic of a heart open to God is a listening heart. In the Bible, references to the ear express a comprehensive process of listening and hearing in a literal, physical sense and also of understanding and acting on the basis of what is heard. To listen is an active practice that entails recognition, discernment, obedience, and action.[1]

The most important religious expression of Jews begins *Hear, O Israel . . .* (Deut 6:4). The great commandment follows, namely to love God and teach children to honor God's ways. The prophets appealed to the people to listen and take heed. *Listen to me, O coastlands, pay attention, you peoples from far away!* (Isa 49:1). The psalmist used expressions such as *incline your ear to my cry* (Ps 88:2) to express the idea that the one who hears should pay attention and be ready to respond to what is heard.

When God's word is delivered, the human responses to God are hearing and doing what is communicated. One of the fruits of paying attention is understanding. That an individual hears God's word is a criterion of judging whether one is attuned to God. *Whoever is from God hears the words of God. The reason you do not hear them is that you are not from God* (John 8:47).

By contrast, it is possible that people have ears but do not listen, hear, comprehend, or act. In a despondent prayer, Job asks, *Who is there that will contend with me? For then I would be silent and die* (13:19). God judges people who fail to listen. *And now, because you have done all these things, says the* LORD, *and when I spoke to you persistently, you did not listen, and when I called you, you did not answer, therefore . . . I will cast you out of my sight . . .* (Jer 7:13-15).

Jesus couples the word *listen* with an expectation that his hearers will act upon what he is saying: *. . . listen, Love your enemies, do good to those who hate you* (Luke 6:27). Jesus expects that as his hearers listen they will take heed, understand, and act. *Then pay attention to how you listen; for to those who have, more will be given; and from those who do not have, even what they seem to have will be taken away* (Luke 8:18). In the parables, Jesus again employs the word *listen* as an imperative, a command. Thus, he concludes the parable of the sower with the words, *Let anyone with ears to hear listen!* (Luke 8:8).

Paul begins his letters with salutations and words of gratitude for the practices of Christian living that flow from hearing the gospel. *Just as it* [the gospel] *is bearing fruit and growing in the whole world, so it has been bearing fruit among yourselves from the day you heard it and truly comprehended the grace of God* (Col 1:6). John equates hearing with wakefulness, repentance, and obedience: *Remember then what you received and heard; obey it, and repent. If you do not wake up, I will come like a thief . . .* (Rev 3:3).

God communicates partly through the spoken and written word. Words may or may not be of God. The biblical world is replete with powers, principalities, and demonic forces that seek to obstruct our hearing and responding to God. For this reason, a discernment process is crucial, as discussed in chapter 4.

In Luke's account of Pentecost, the Holy Spirit overcame early believers with power. As the Spirit gave them power, they spoke many languages. In a sermon preached on that occasion, Peter attested that God did this that the nations might *both see and hear* (Acts 2:33).

In his first letter to the Corinthians, Paul suggested that the gift of tongues is spiritual and must be accompanied by interpretation. These are lesser endowments. *Do all speak in tongues? Do all interpret? But strive for the greater gifts. And I will show you a still more excellent way* (1 Cor 29:30-31). This is the way of love.

Twentieth-century spiritual writers acknowledged the importance of listening to God and to one another. In *Life Together*, German theologian Dietrich Bonhoeffer encouraged us to think of listening as a practice of the evangelistic life: "The first service that one owes to others in the fellowship [Christian community] consists in listening to them. Just as love to God begins with listening to His Word, so the beginning of love for the brethren is learning to listen to them. It is God's love for us that He not only gives us His Word but also lends us His ear."[2]

Douglas V. Steere of the Religious Society of Friends also stressed the ministry of listening with a listening heart. We are to listen "discerningly" to the other person. This requires maturity, "a certain self-transcendence, a certain expectation, a patience, and openness to the new. In order really to listen, there must be a capacity to hear through many wrappings, and only a mature listener, listening beyond the outer layer of the words that are spoken, is capable of this."[3]

We do not readily listen. In a confessional mode, I acknowledge that too often when I listen, I am listening in order to speak. My attention is then split between the other and myself. Worse, I commonly find that my anxiety about what to say means my focus is more on me than it is on the one to whom I should be paying attention. Or I am simply saying words that have no meaning. Unless I am willing for the other to tell me about the condition of his/her soul, I have no right to ask, "How are you?" or "How goes it in your spiritual life?"

Good listening takes energy. Good listening can consume time. Good listening may overwhelm or become emotionally draining for both the listener and the one sharing. At the same time, good listening can be an act of sacredness in which someone entrusts you with the essence of who they are, the utter completeness of what they feel. To let the other occupy the center of my stage is a precious gift. Genuine listening to another allows the other to become a channel through which God speaks to me. We must learn to respect that of God in the other. When I listen simply to listen or to be aware, I direct my concern wholly to the other: to God, to the journeyer, or to God through the journeyer.

Listening to God

We begin with listening to God. How do we listen to God? Waiting on God is a major path in the spirituality of listening. The Christian practice of prayer entails being still and opening heart and mind to God that we may hear God. *Be still, and know that I am God!* (Ps 46:10) literally means letting our hands fall that we embrace God, relying on God in everything.[4]

Set a guard over my mouth, O LORD, keep watch over the door of my lips! (Ps 141:3). How often, when I have prayed, have I not kept watch over the door of my lips! For years I did not. My pattern of prayer centered on talking. Gradually have I come to understand that growth in prayer necessarily involves talking to God less and listening more for the word God has for me.

This is not to suggest that I cease showering God with words of adoration, confession, petition, thanksgiving, and self-abandonment. It is crucial to praise God and express devotion to God. But God has helped me learn how important it is to wait upon God in silent expectation. God wants to speak to me. To hear God, I must quiet myself, become aware of God's presence, and attend to God's word. *The Lord is good to those who wait for him, to the soul that seeks him. It is good that one should wait quietly for the salvation of the Lord* (Lam 3:25-26).

In listening to God, we allow a crucial place for silence. What happens when God is silent? It is possible, of course, that God is not silent, but rather that we are not hearing what we want. It is also possible that God is silent. Divine silence can be positive. Thomas Merton writes of a "silence that ought to be sweet with the infinitely productive darkness of contemplation."[5] God's silence may elicit fear and terror. We cannot pray. We sense God abandoning us. We experience what the sixteenth century Spanish Catholic John of the Cross called "the dark night of the soul," a period of anguish and dread in the spiritual life.

In Christian history, a spiritual stream that includes John of the Cross and Merton accents God's darkness and unknowability. This stream takes the journeyer along the path of silence.

Jesus was silent before his accusers. Silence prompted Jesus to cry out from the cross, *"Eloi, Eloi, lema sabachthani?" which means, "My God, my God, why have you forsaken me?"* (Mark 15:34).

From the perspective of the cross, God appears silent. The empty tomb proves that God was not, but this became apparent only after the fact. In our context, a culture that insists on immediate response, it is hard to be patient. Yet God's word is not always transparent. As we listen for God, we sometimes must wait.

In her classic *Waiting on God,* French religious writer Simone Weil described prayer as paying attention.

> God rewards the soul which thinks of him with attention and love . . . . We have to abandon ourselves to the pressure, to run to the exact spot whither it impels us and not go one step further, even in the direction of what is good. At the same time we must go on thinking about God with ever increasing love and attentiveness . . . becoming the object of a pressure which possesses itself of an ever growing proportion of the whole soul.[6]

Waiting on God, God waits on us. When we wait on God and when we give voice to the innermost joys, concerns and longings of our hearts we inevitably find God is already listening to us. We read in Psalm 139:1-6, 23-24,

> O LORD, you have searched me and known me.
> You know when I sit down and when I rise up; you discern my thoughts from
>   far away.
> You search out my path and my lying down, and are acquainted with all my
>   ways.
> Even before a word is on my tongue, O LORD, you know it completely.
> You hem me in, behind and before, and lay your hand upon me.
> Such knowledge is too wonderful for me; it is so high that I cannot attain
>   it . . .
> Search me, O God, and know my heart; test me and know my thoughts.
> See if there is any wicked way in me, and lead me in the way everlasting.

One way to listen to God is to listen to Scripture. Ephrem the Syrian, an early theologian, says Scripture brings us to the gates of paradise, and the mind stands in wonder as it enters.[7] A slow, meditative reading of a particular text allows one to resonate with God's word. There are other ways to listen to Scripture. Some find it helpful to read the Scripture straight through. I have done so more than once, though I confess that I have found myself more engaged in completing the task than listening to the word.

It can also be helpful to follow devotional guides such as *Encounter with God* or *The Upper Room*. Both are readily available in religious bookstores for daily Bible study by individuals or groups. Over a period of time, these guides cover a great deal of the Bible and attend to all aspects of one's life. You may want to use a writing utensil or perhaps a journal as well as a Bible, preferably in more than one of the excellent contemporary translations that are available.

If you follow the guide alone, it is helpful to set aside a regular time each day. Begin by praying to God. Ask the Holy Spirit to help you to understand and receive God's word. Then read the passage carefully, perhaps more than once. Finally, meditate on what you have read and probe questions such as these: What is the main point of the reading? What is God revealing to you through the text? What are you learning about yourself? If you follow the guide with a group, set aside a regular time to gather, preferably weekly. A useful format is to begin with prayer, to read the text selected for study, and to reflect in silence before you discuss the passage. In addition, you may want to set aside time for singing, worship, refreshments, and sharing joys and concerns.

Another listening practice is to follow the lectionary. The lectionary follows the liturgical year and identifies Old Testament, Psalm, Epistle, and Gospel readings for each day of the year over a three-year period. Developed by representatives from many churches, the lectionary transcends divisions of denomination, nationality, or theology. To illustrate how truly unitive following the lectionary can be, I recall a summer when I studied Spanish in Bolivia at a Catholic institution shaped by liberation theology. Each Thursday in class, we read and discussed the lectionary passages for the following Sunday. At the end the course, I returned to Canada. That Sunday, in my evangelical Baptist congregation, I heard the same texts read and proclaimed.

Preachers may find it creative to follow the lectionary. The readings cover a great deal of Bible. Preaching the lectionary plunges one into the whole range of experience. It is a way to resist the temptation to go to the Bible seeking particular texts to substantiate personal beliefs; instead, you cover the Bible with Christians around the world. One can be flexible in the practice. Preaching the lectionary does not prevent accommodating to special circumstances.

Listening to Self

Listening to God is the first dimension of a listening heart. The second is listening to ourselves. Christians make a radical claim. God has come to us and saved us through Jesus Christ. God has chosen to be among us as one of us, as a human being. It is for this reason that true growth in the Christian life lies in listening to God within us.

I am a participant in the divine nature (2 Pet 1:4). I am God's beloved, loved with the same unconditional divine love of which John writes in 1 John 3:1: *See what love the Father has given us, that we should be called children of God; and that is what we are.* Created in the image of God, I am God's beloved. God calls me for the purpose of knowing and loving God and others, and of being loved in turn.

Intellectually, I know this! However, it has been difficult for me to let these radical claims reverberate in every corner of my being. My power to bless God and others comes from claiming who I am. For this reason, our most urgent need is to take time to listen and look inward to our own depths, to center ourselves on God, and to receive an infusion of God's love so that we can minister in God's name to those crying out to us. For there is more than enough of God's love to go around. *I took them up in my arms . . . I healed them . . . I led them with cords of human kindness, with bands of love . . . I bent down to them and fed them* (Hos 11:3-4). *How many of my father's hired hands have bread enough and to spare* (Luke 15:17). Poet Elizabeth Barrett Browning expresses her sense of God's presence in everything and everyone:

> Earth's crammed with heaven
> And every common bush alive with God.
> Only he who sees takes off his shoes;
> The rest sit around and pluck blackberries.[8]

Listening to Others

Listening to God and to ourselves, we must also listen to others. Too often, when we are in the company of others, we fail to listen. Preoccupied, we neither listen nor look nor pay attention. We think we must always contribute something to any conversation. This is especially true of pastors and teachers. Too often we think this is the one service we have to render. We forget that listening often can be of greater benefit than speaking.

As we listen to people share their joys, concerns, and needs, we take on the role of spiritual nurturers. Spiritual nurturers are companions along the path toward a deep relationship with God. Spiritual nurturers help the one journeying to God to discern how God is working in his or her life and how the journeyer may respond more fully to God. Spiritual nurturers tell the truth concerning the destructive dimension of personal and social sin in the lives of their companions. They bear witness to God's forgiveness of sin and the possibility of new life in Jesus Christ.

Spiritual nurturers must listen. One of the benefits of listening to others is that we may hear the voice of God through the other. Through the one to whom we are listening, God may be speaking to us. Too readily we listen for the dramatic voice of God—for example, when Moses heard God in a burning bush or Paul on the road to Damascus. We neglect the still small voice of God speaking to us through the people who enter our lives.

In *The Wounded Healer*, Henri Nouwen provides an illustration of what can happen when we fail to listen in this way.[9] People in a small village took in a young fugitive and gave him a place to stay. Eventually, enemy soldiers came and demanded the young man. When the people hesitated to tell of his whereabouts, the soldiers threatened to destroy the village and kill everyone. Frightened, the people turned to their pastor for guidance.

Torn between deserting his people and betraying the young man, the pastor went to his room and began reading his Bible in hope of finding an answer before dawn. He read all night. Finally, just before sunrise, he came to John 11:50: *it is better for you to have one man die for the people than to have the whole nation destroyed.* Trembling, the pastor walked outside and told the soldiers where to find the youth. As they took the fugitive away to be executed, the villagers celebrated, for their lives had been spared. However, the pastor did not celebrate with them. Instead, he went to his room smitten with a deep heaviness. In the evening, an angel appeared to him and asked, "What have you done?" The pastor replied, "I betrayed a fugitive." "But didn't you know," said the angel, "that the fugitive you betrayed is the Messiah? . . . If you had set down your Bible and gone to the fugitive and looked into his eyes you would have known."

Listening to Culture

A fourth dimension of a listening spirituality is listening to culture, by which I mean the specific angle of vision through which any of us perceive reality. We tend to take *our* culture for granted because it is transmitted as a given. We pass on these shared values through institutions such as family, church, school, and civic rituals. These forums tend to reflect what is important in a given setting and shape how one looks on other people.

The Christian faith is always imbedded in culture. We must listen to culture. When we do, we may hear God in the same way that, when we listen to others, we may hear God. How may listening to culture help our witness? As a practice in mission, listening to culture is an antidote to the barriers we encounter in evangelism. Culture is a barrier to the transmission of gospel for at least two reasons. First, people tend to be unaware of idiosyncrasies, limitations, or errors of their own culture and of the fact that they are part of one culture and not some other. Whoever has not traveled thinks his or her mother is the only cook!

Secondly, one's culture is always there. No matter how aware of and how sensitive to cultural differences people may be, they will almost always generalize from the perspective of their own culture. Even if one learns a language, a major aspect in communication in a culture, there is still the silent language of nonverbal communication. Efforts to learn these can be especially amusing. Someone trying to "go native" can really look quite foolish because their body language, gestures, facial expressions, clothes, and humor are not congruent with their identity.

Some years ago, the anthropologist Donald Larson studied a farming community in the northwest United States. He found that the farmers there divided the world into three different categories that Larson called Landscape, Machinery, and People. Trees and other scenery not manipulated by the farmers belonged to Landscape. Landscape was there as something to look at. Sometimes it could be enjoyed and other times only tolerated. Machinery had a higher value because it helped you to be productive. Machinery included livestock as well as tools. Machinery was an important and valuable means to an end. People were the third category: neighbors, family, friends, those with whom you grow up, share a meal, marry. But not all humans were People. The Mexicans who helped on the farms belonged to the Machinery category. They contributed to productivity and thus were regarded more highly than Indians. Indians belonged to Landscape. Like their art, Indians were something to look at, but they were not People. In the community Larson studied, only some humans were friends, potential family, and therefore People.

This study shows how listening to culture can reveal deeply felt patterns. Just as we must listen to God, ourselves, and others, we must listen to culture if we are to minister in any locale. For gospel-bearers to learn the oral language of the culture is not enough. One must also learn how that language functions in specific contexts. Listening to culture can help one avoid mistakes.

I can think of many situations when I have not listened adequately to culture and, as a result, have failed in my attempt to evangelize. Let me cite two examples. I moved to the South eight years ago. As a professor of evangelism, I am asked to preach revivals from time to time. In my first revival, I suggested closing the service each evening with "Here I Am, Lord." The host pastor gently suggested that "Just as I Am" would be more suitable. I held my ground, but no one in the congregation knew the contemporary song. What happened? I did not make this mistake the next time.

Another example comes from my life as an urban person. I am used to carrying business cards. Recently, I helped develop a place of retreat in rural Mississippi. I called on neighbors and presented them with a card. This gesture did not lead to building relationships. Friends suggested I should have taken them a pie! The kind of listening that takes culture seriously is not simply auditory; it requires the deepest attentiveness to people in their context.

Listening and Evangelism

All things being equal, effective evangelism is a result of listening. It is unlikely that we will hear God's voice unless we have contact with God, God's people, and the rich diversity of God's world. Moreover, it is unlikely we will share the gospel of Jesus Christ with others or do anything about the conditions that adversely shape their lives unless we have listened to them. People will pour themselves out to those who have loving hearts and ears to listen.

Listening is not one-directional. God listens to us. We listen to God and to others. As we listen we take heed, understand, and act; we open ourselves to ways in which God is speaking to us. And God is speaking to us through the Bible, through others, through our own wisdom, and through life around us! Listening is not simply to prepare to evangelize. Listening requires that we be willing to change. Surely, God intends that we grow throughout life. To live without listening is to atrophy or drift in one's own backwater.[10]

Prayer
With the Apostle Paul, Lord, I pray that we who evangelize will learn to grow in our love and in our capacity to listen. According to the riches of your glory, may each person be strengthened in his or her inner being with power through your Spirit. May Christ dwell in our hearts through faith as we are being rooted and grounded in love (Eph 3:16-17). Amen.

---

[1] R. C. Dentan, "Ear (Hearing)," *Interpreter's Dictionary of the Bible* (Nashville: Abingdon, 1962), 2:1.

[2] Dietrich Bonhoeffer, *Life Together*, trans. John W. Doberstein (New York: Harper and Row, 1976, paperback), 97.

[3] Douglas V. Steere, *On Listening to Another* (Garden City: Doubleday-Galilee, 1978), 207.

[4] Tryggve N. D. Mettinger, "Fighting the Powers of Chaos and Hell—Towards the Biblical Portrait of God," *Studia Theologica* 39 (1985): 28-29.

[5] Thomas Merton, *The Seven Storey Mountain* (New York: Harcourt, Brace & Co, 1948), 410.

[6] Simone Weil, *Waiting on God*, trans. Emma Craufurd (London: Fontana, 1959), 14-15.

[7] Quoted by Kathleen Norris, *The Cloister Walk* (New York: Riverhead, 1996), xv.

[8] Marcus Borg, *The God We Never Knew: Beyond Dogmatic Religion to a More Authentic Contemporary Faith* (San Francisco: Harper, 1998), 47.

[9] Henri J. M. Nouwen, *The Wounded Healer* (Garden City: Image, 1979), 25-26.

[10] Joan Chittister, *Wisdom Distilled from the Daily, Living the Rule of St. Benedict Today* (San Francisco: Harper, 1991), 21.

For Reflection and Conversation

- Why is listening a practice of loving-kindness?

- How do I know when I listen to God or God's word that it is indeed God who speaks?

- When I listen to another person, do I respect God in the other? Do I hear God speaking to me through the other?

- Why is listening to culture important in evangelism?

- What is the relationship between listening and evangelism?

Practices of Compassion

Be compassionate just as your Father is compassionate. (Luke 6:36, Jerusalem Bible)

Our Compassionate God

In the 1950s God called me to join the company of Jesus' followers. God provided caregivers to nurture me in my newfound faith and to equip me for the vocation to which I was called. Over the next few years, Paul Lindholm became one of my spiritual mentors. Then in 1965, when I was readying to go to Chad on a church-related work project and possibly to attend seminary, Paul said to me, "As you enter into the pain of the world, go with the compassion of Christ." He wanted me to understand that I could not practice a pie-in-the-sky spirituality and that along this journey into the pain of the world, the Holy One from Galilee would introduce me to some of his friends: the poor, the wounded, the marginalized, the handicapped, saints, sinners.

This has in fact been true for me. I have met many who experience life as overwhelming. I have met people who hunger for meaning in life, for comfort and consolation, for forgiveness and reconciliation, for healing and restoration. I have met the poor and the wounded, the marginalized and the handicapped, saints and sinners. I have heard God calling me to make my experience of new life in Christ evident through the practice of compassion toward them.

Hebrew Scripture refers to God as full of compassion and mercy.[1] Psalm 78:38 praises God who, being compassionate, forgives the iniquity of people and does not destroy them. Psalm 111:4 and other texts refer to God as gracious and merciful. As a people mindful of their covenant with a compassionate and merciful God, ancient Israel likewise was to show mercy and live with compassion.

As Christians we believe God's compassion became visible to us in Jesus. God became one with us in Jesus. Jesus consistently manifested God's compassion. In the feeding stories, for example, Jesus attracted crowds. The lame, the maimed, the blind, the mute, and others approached Jesus. Looking upon them, he said, *I have compassion for the crowd, because they have been with me now for three days and have nothing to eat; and I do not want to send them away hungry, for they might faint on the way* (Matt 15:32 and parallels). In this passage, translators render the Greek *splangchnizomai* as compassion. Literally the word means to have one's bowels yearn, to ache in the guts. The English derives from the Latin *pati* and *cum*, which together mean to suffer with. Distressed by conditions he saw, Jesus took pity on the people, responded with a visceral feeling, and was moved to act with compassion.

When Jesus saw people hungry, he had compassion. Jesus reacted to other situations with the same visceral response. Matthew records that Jesus moved about, teaching in the synagogues, healing, and proclaiming the good news of God's realm. Once he met two blind men. Jesus touched their eyes and healed them. When they had gone away, a mute demoniac was brought to him. Jesus cast the demon out, and the man who had been speechless spoke. Jesus met harassed and helpless people whom he likened to sheep without a shepherd. When he saw them, he had compassion on them and then commissioned his disciples to do likewise (Matt 9:27-38; Mark 6:34). Luke records Jesus' encounter with the widow of Nain. Jesus had compassion on her and comforted her (Luke 7:11-17). Matthew, Mark, and Luke record a story of Jesus healing an epileptic boy. According to Mark, someone asked Jesus to exercise compassion (Mark 9:22).

Jesus was known to act in a consistent way. He made God's compassion tangible and made clear to his followers that they, too, were to be compassionate. *Be compassionate just as your Father is compassionate* (Luke 6:36, *Jerusalem Bible*).

The Compassionate Life

The preaching, teaching, and healing practices of Jesus were like a magnet. Jesus attracted the blind, the hungry, the ignorant, the lepers, the widows, and others in need. Jesus responded with compassion and incorporated into his community those who would likewise practice compassion. He thus widened the circle of compassion. The compassion of Jesus flowed from

God's compassion. As followers of Jesus, his disciples were in turn to be transparent with the compassion of God.

What about us? How can we believe in a God of compassion when suffering abounds? How can we manifest the compassion of Jesus amid an uncompassionate world? Not only humankind, but animals, plants, and the entire created order are dying for lack of compassion. We have just marked the end of a century of unparalleled warfare, species elimination, and wholesale assault on features of the natural world on which we depend. The rain forests are being destroyed, the water and the air are polluted, and the ice caps are receding due to global warming. A few of us are overwhelmingly affluent at the expense of the vast majority who live in poverty. Unjust prejudice on the basis of ethnicity, gender, race, or religion contributes to discrimination and violence against others.

God does not expect us to speculate about such matters. Nor does God anticipate that we will eliminate these or other problems. God requires only a response. In Judaism one is expected to help somebody daily. This is called *Mitzvah,* a good deed. But there is a catch that, when you perform a *Mitzvah*, the truly holy person cannot tell.

An old story about a rabbi who was so addicted to golf that he even played on holy days illustrates this point. On Yom Kippur, the High Holy Day, the rabbi made a hole in one. As he danced about with exultation, thunder rumbled and lightening flashed. God's voice boomed down to him. "So who are you going to tell?"[2]

So who are you going to tell? This is a way of asking whether we have done something for someone today that we did not have to do according to the standards of society. But followers of Jesus must daily see those who need Jesus and respond to them as Jesus did: helping in caring ways, bold yet unassuming with loving-kindness and humility. Men, women, and children are waiting for compassionate people to reach out to them. By being compassionate as God is compassionate, we daily share good news in the way Jesus did.

It is possible *not* to do so. It is possible *not* to see what needs to be done. One can choose *not* to read a newspaper, watch televised news, or listen to public radio. By use of e-commerce, one can choose *not* to notice the underemployed in our stores and malls. One can choose to live behind protective barriers. Some would have this country erect fortifications to screen out the poor world. Three million US households live behind gated communities. New ones are under construction in the neighborhood where I live and write this. Building prisons is a growth industry in our economy. Violence and the fear of victimization are growing rampantly in our society. Recently, an advertisement arrived in the mail featuring handgun permit training, with free gun rental and ammunition. The price tag was $79.00.

What motivates people to receive such instruction, to move behind walls, or to buy security locks? Perhaps they feel insecure. Though we can never insulate ourselves entirely from the heedless ones among us, it is reasonable to protect ourselves from terrible things that can and do occur.

Why do some people maintain their own privilege rather than promote the common good? Perhaps one reason is that they have imbibed cultural norms that encourage the hoarding of wealth and economic power. From the perspective of loving-kindness, however, the analysis of James 4:1-3 is pertinent.

> *Those conflicts and disputes among you, where do they come from? Do they not come from your cravings that are at war within you? You want something and do not have it; so you commit murder. And you covet something and cannot obtain it; so you engage in disputes and conflicts. You do not have, because you do not ask. You ask and do not receive, because you ask wrongly, in order to spend what you get on your pleasures.*

From the standpoint of loving-kindness, we share what we have. *We know love by this, that he* [Jesus] *laid down his life for us—and we ought to lay down our lives for one another. How does God's love abide in anyone who has the world's goods and sees a brother or sister in need and yet refuses help?* (1 John 3:16-17). Greater equality in distributing the goods of this world will in the end mean better lives for all!

Another reason some people turn away is that they feel powerless. Besieged by requests for money or overwhelmed by the need, some people may hear the cry of others but fail to act. As crisis after crisis enveloped planet earth some years ago, commentators observed a phenomenon called compassion fatigue. Spiritual writer Henri Nouwen explained, "Exposure to human misery on a mass scale can lead not only to psychic numbness but to hostility."[3] Prime Minister Lee Kuan Yew of Singapore manifested this as he turned back Vietnamese Boat People. He insisted that one has to develop calluses on the heart or else bleed to death.

I can identify with this response. In 1965, I went to Chad with Crossroads Africa, a non-government organization founded by the Reverend James Herman Robinson.[4] Our journey took us through Nigeria. On the brink of civil war, the country could not meet the dietary needs of children whose bloated stomachs revealed they had kwashiorkor, a disease that results from malnutrition. Subsequently I visited camps of Biafran refugees in western Cameroon. The abyss between the scenes I saw and God's immense, inexhaustible, and unfathomable tenderness was palpable. I felt powerlessness.

In 1999, Hurricane Floyd followed Hurricane Mitch. News of random violence in Littleton, Colorado, gave way to coverage of a mass murder of children in Fort Worth, Texas. Kosovo, East Timor, and other hot spots screamed for attention. I wanted to shut all this out. I wanted to scream, "It's a tough world! Won't somebody do something?"

One does not have to travel afar to enter the pain of the world. An urban sprawl of nearly a million people at the confluence of three southern states—Arkansas, Mississippi, and Tennessee in the Mississippi River Delta—Memphis is one of the poorest cities in the United States. When it claims to be "Home of the Blues," Memphis claims a parentage of music steeped in Delta blood, sweat, and tears. The music rocks, writhes, and tells of hard times that "hurt so good."

One-third of Memphians live below the poverty line. Homeless poor go through the green garbage bins before city sanitation workers do their collection runs. Single mothers work double shifts. Health care is not available for countless thousands. How can such neglect of God's children during a period of unprecedented prosperity be?

Half a world away, refugee camps teem with the refuse of wars. Half a world away, castaway children are sold for body parts. The poor poke around city dumps for food and material with which to build shanty homes. How are Christians to respond?

The Reverend Simea Meldrum of Olinda offers a model of what Christians in northeast Brazil do. Simea serves those in Brazil who inhabit cardboard shacks and rummage for food in garbage dumps. This is the poorest and least developed region of the country. In the fall of 1998, as part of an ongoing parish partnership between her Living Water Mission in Brazil and St. Mary's Episcopal Cathedral in Memphis, several members of St. Mary's visited Olinda. A year later Simea and her husband, the Reverend Ian Meldrum, came to Memphis accompanied by two lay colleagues, Josenaide Maria Lopes Pereira and Magaly Melo de Mendonca Ramos. It was apt that they joined in activities recalling Memphis martyrs Constance and her companions who died of yellow fever in 1878 while caring for those affected by the epidemic.

In the course of her visit, Simea preached. During her sermon, she told of growing up in a "simple" family. They were so poor that they had only pumpkins to eat. As a girl, she once shared a pumpkin with a neighbor who was equally poor. The neighbor returned with a special dish. It was a wonderful lesson that God does provide manna in the form of pumpkins in the morning, at noon, and in the evening.

Simea explained that Jesus led her into the pain of the world. "We can't leave the work to full-time clergy." One of the street children she rescued is now leading her parish's struggle against the empire that is the International Monetary Fund and World Bank. She cited Dom Helder Camara, who died recently and was formerly Archbishop of Olinda and Recife. At his funeral, someone read one of his prayers: have pity on those who have no home to live in, and even greater pity on those who live in mansions.

Simea closed by inviting us to eat pumpkins in the morning, at noon, and in the evening. It will be enough. Like love, when you give it away, who knows what will come back? Truly blessed are Simea and the poor with whom she serves.

We all can think of people like Simea who practice compassion. They are basically good, gentle, and understanding. They are vessels through whom God's compassion flows. Through them, the world is learning about God's compassion.[5]

Four Principles for Nurturing Compassion

Compassion is not abstract. It is a concrete, specific practice by which we reach out to others in the name of Jesus. Amid all the need, how are we to know what to do? Where are we to begin? Let me identify four principles by which we may nurture compassion.

Principle One: Grow Where You Are Planted

A primary model by which Christians respond to need is to undertake development or relief projects in international contexts. Examples include medical teams that provide inoculations and other basic medical procedures in a region without an adequate health infrastructure and a youth group that helps with a building project.

Often, this approach entails organizing a group to visit an area of identified need and to provide short-term relief or development assistance. For those served, the intervention can achieve some good. For those who make the journey, the experience can be life-changing. But there are three major problems with this approach to compassion. First, language and other barriers make it impossible for participants to develop relationships in unfamiliar cultural contexts. Second, time, expense, and distance limit opportunities for education, ministry, or follow-up. Third, such travel contributes to today's global tourism industry.[6]

As an alternative, I encourage Christians to begin where they are planted. Think of the one who needs a compassionate response as something other than an abstraction. Put a human face on large issues of homelessness, hunger, and poverty. Tackle these larger-than-life issues as determinative realities for those around us. In workshops and evangelism classes, I encourage participants to connect with their communities in a four-stage process:

• *Preparing.* Human need often is invisible. One reason is that members of congregations are strangers to the community around the church facilities. The first step to engagement is to become aware of need and of the destructive dimensions of personal and social sin in one's immediate vicinity. To prepare for engagement, walk through your community. If you live in a rural area, drive through it. What do you see? Get basic demographic information about the community. Generally, one can access census data or other crucial information readily.

• *Listening/sharing.* Build relationships in the neighborhood through participation in community events, home visitation, shared meals, and other experiences. Invite a social worker to lunch. Ride a police beat. Create space for members of different cultural groups to be heard during forums, discussions, and other events.

• *Assessing.* Seek to understand by assessing and evaluating the data gathered. Formulate possible courses of action. Be sensitive to how any activity will impact the people most affected.

• *Acting.* Participants inevitably respond to contextual learning by wanting to make a difference in the lives of those in need. Myriad students and workshop registrants have thereby grown where God has established them in ministry. Let me cite a few examples.

In one evangelism class, student projects resulted in four new ministries. The Reverend Sarah Salazar served the growing Latino population in

Memphis. She developed a variety of specific ministries such as language training and job skills that gave them power to improve their lives. The Reverend Janjia Liu established a Mandarin-language congregation for Chinese newcomers without a spiritual home. The Reverend Rosalyn Regina Nichols sensitized African Americans to the needs of South East Asian refugees. The Reverend Mike Wilkinson reached shut-ins through a rural Tennessee Cumberland Presbyterian congregation.

In another class, a United Methodist Church parish nurse program has started in and around Norfork, Arkansas. Lives have been saved! Co-pastors Bob and Kay Burton envision three hundred congregations adapting their model throughout the tri-state Delta area. The Church Health Center in Memphis, Tennessee, has joined in this effort to offer hope and healing to the working poor in both rural and urban areas.[7]

In Ottawa, Ontario, Canadian Baptists created a place of hospitality for children left alone on city schoolyards through an innovative preschool breakfast program. In an overwhelmingly poor area of Hamilton, Ontario, the Reverend Alan R. Matthews started diverse programs for the needy, including a ministry to prisoners. For Baptist and Mennonite Central Committee volunteers, Welcome Inn has been a school of compassion.[8]

Failure to know one's community can produce catastrophe! I think of a Hamilton, Ontario, congregation that spent millions for refurbished offices and worship space but ignored the three largest categories of people around the church: the homeless, the poor, and the elderly. The congregation did not elicit from people what they thought they needed or address these needs. The congregation might have provided facilities such as washrooms, kitchens, and beds for street people. They might have undertaken an AIDS ministry for those vulnerable to drug trafficking. They might have provided wheelchair access for the elderly. They did none of these. They did not grow where they were planted.

Principle Two: Respond to a Call

A second strategic principle is to encourage response to a specific call. It does little good to harangue people from the pulpit regarding what they should or should not do. A person will not respond to human need unless she or he hears God's call and understands that God equips each of us with gifts appropriate to that call. An authentic call is hard to discern. If one hears a call and tests its authenticity, it is a powerful impetus to enter the pain of the world.[9]

In my life there have been periods of vocational struggle including my call to Memphis. In 1993, I attended a conference in Birmingham, Alabama, during which I shared in manual labor at a Catholic Worker house run by James and Shelley Douglass. I inquired why they had moved there from the Pacific Northwest. Jim stated that in the United States, Christians concerned about compassion and justice must locate themselves in cities such as Birmingham and Memphis. Naming Memphis, Jim sounded a call analogous to the calls of Moses, Isaiah, and Jeremiah. At the time, my résumé was only theoretically open. I was not looking for new employment. Yet a voice stirred within me to address poverty and racism in the city where Martin Luther King Jr. struggled for economic justice on behalf of sanitation workers and died.

I felt the force of T. S. Eliot's words:[10] "Human kind cannot bear very much reality." I feared the blessing of God, the loneliness of the night of God, the surrender required, and the deprivation inflicted. Did I fear the injustice of men and women less than the justice of God?

"The loneliness of the night of God" is a striking image. From my late teen years I have felt the call of God to enter into the pain of the earth. Yet here I was wrestling with a particular call. I experienced something like a vision of a fire singing away all resistance. Words came: *You are not alone in this. Fear not. Take courage. I have conquered the world* (John 16:33). And that is how I came to be in Memphis.

Phoenix Place in Hamilton, Ontario, a ministry to battered women and children, provides another example of Christians responding to a call. The origins of Phoenix Place can be traced to the professional and volunteer involvement of members of MacNeill Baptist Church. Personal experience and training led some of them to engagement at a shelter for battered women and children. A few women responded to an invitation to attend MacNeill. A small group developed. Members of the group began to ask what they could do. A period of study and discernment followed. Group members discovered that a major lacuna existed in Hamilton for women who flee to shelters. Generally, they could remain only a short period of time. A need for second-stage housing existed. Women needed a safe place to live beyond the shelter. As the call developed and the challenges of developing a second-stage home seemed too great for a small group, they recruited additional members from other churches. Fund-raising followed. Phoenix Place came to be. It grew out of five years of meetings and work.

At the start of the process, those involved in Phoenix Place responded to a call. Initially, they did not believe they could undertake a project on the scale of providing housing and other forms of assistance for battered women. Yet God blessed their faithful response. As Margaret Mead has observed, "Never doubt that a small group of thoughtful committed citizens can change the world. Indeed it's the only thing that ever has."

Principle Three: Empower Those Served

A third principle is to empower those served. A truism that builds on this idea goes as follows: give a hungry person a fish, and the individual eats that day. Teach a hungry person to fish, and the individual eats for a lifetime. An old Chinese saying underscores this:

> Go to the people
> Live among them
> Learn from them
> Love them
> Start with what you know
> Build on what they have:
> But of the best leaders
> When their task is done
> The people will remark
> "We have done it ourselves."[11]

Contemporary events are full of great catastrophes. When tragedy strikes, it is important to respond to immediate needs. But we risk perpetuating misery if we do not enable those helped to reduce their vulnerability to disaster or to extricate themselves from sources of problems embedded in the structures of society. In any calamity, the short-term goal of humanitarian intervention must give way to rehabilitation, reconstruction, and sustainable development.

Principle Four: Strike a Balance between the Local and Global

This final principle acknowledges human limits. Compassion does not focus on statistical results. What matters is that, to the best of one's ability, one lives with compassion with those given to love. It is important, therefore, to strike a balance between seeking to change the world and making a small difference in somebody's life. This means holding in tension the long-term goal of structural change with the call to make tangible God's great compassion. We do so when we act as individuals. Each person can make a difference. It matters that we act. As we work through organizations, we multiply our efforts and intensify the possibility that our efforts will impact more widely. Amnesty International members advocate on behalf of prisoners of conscience. Habitat for Humanity volunteers build houses. Heifer Project International sends what is needed to provide eggs, honey, meat, and draft animals to aid agricultural production. These three, of hundreds of voluntary bodies, manifest the truth that God's compassion is wide. Individuals benefit. Over time, political discourse and structures change. Such compassionate responses to human need illustrate another axiom: we can aspire to something *big*. If we accomplish what we dream, we really have not dreamed *big*.

There is a great difference between the Jesus one typically meets in Sunday school and the Jesus one meets along the journey of compassion. Each of us is growing into Christ-likeness. Each of us has a special concern that the God of compassion brings to our attention. We can direct our gifts and respond to the call of God to practice compassion. Pray that God will kindle within us true evangelical faith. We cannot let faith lie dormant. May it clothe the naked, feed the hungry, comfort the sorrowful, shelter the destitute, serve those that would do harm, bind up that which is wounded, and heal the broken-hearted. Heaven rejoices as we live compassionately.

Prayer
Be with me, Jesus.
Open my eyes that I may see those to whom to offer your compassion.
Open my ears that I may hear those you would comfort.
Open my hands that I may offer your healing touch.
Open my heart that I may radiate your deep caring to all creation. Amen.

[1] Translators of the Hebrew word *rachum* use "compassionate" and "merciful" interchangeably.

[2] Northumbria Community, *Celtic Daily Prayerbook*, cited 4 November 2000, *Tablet* 1509.

[3] Henri Nouwen, "Coping with the Seven O'clock News," *Sojourners* 6 (September 1977): 15; Henri J. M. Nouwen, Donald P. McNeill, and Douglas A. Morrison, *Compassion: A Reflection on the Christian Life* (New York: Doubleday, 1983), 15-16.

[4] *Road without Turning: The Story of Reverend James H. Robinson* (New York: Farrar, Straus, 1950). Founded in the 1950s, Crossroads Africa became the seed of the Peace Corps.

[5] Frank Laubach, *The World Is Learning Compassion* (Westwood: Fleming H. Revell, 1958).

[6] Jo Ann van Engen, "The Cost of Short-term Missions," *Other Side* 36 (January–February 2000), 20-23; Susan B. Thistlethwaite and George F. Cairns, eds., *Beyond Theological Tourism: Mentoring as a Grassroots Approach to Theological Education* (Maryknoll: Orbis, 1994).

[7] G. Scott Morris, ed., *Hope and Healing: Words from the Clergy of a Southern City* (Memphis: Guild Bindery Press, 1995).

[8] Alan R. Matthews, *Together We Can* (Hamilton: Fowler-Matthew, 1984; rev. ed., 1988). See *Welcome Inn Community Centre and Church 1966–1986* (Hamilton: Welcome Inn, 1986) for the congregation's ministries. For Memphis ministries, see Jericho Road at <http://www.jericho.org>.

[9] Elizabeth O'Connor, *Cry Pain, Cry Hope: Thresholds to Purpose* (Waco: Word, 1987); David Hilfiker, *Not All of Us Are Saints: A Doctor's Journey with the Poor* (New York: Ballantine, 1994).

[10] T. S. Eliot, "Murder in the Cathedral," *The Complete Poems and Plays 1909–1950* (New York: Harcourt, Brace & World, 1962), 209, 221.

[11] John M. Perkins, *Beyond Charity: The Call to Christian Community Development* (Grand Rapids: Baker, 1993), 86.

For Reflection and Conversation

- Why is compassion a practice of loving-kindness?

- Have you ever experienced compassion fatigue? How did you deal with this feeling?

- Describe a situation in which you or someone else has experienced outrage over injustice. By what steps can one begin to ameliorate conditions that produce such injustice?

- Can you think big? How big?

- What is the relationship between compassion and evangelism?

Practices of Testimony

I give thanks to my God always for you because of the grace of God that has been given you in Christ Jesus, for in every way you have been enriched in him, in speech and knowledge of every kind—just as the testimony of Christ has been strengthened among you—so that you are not lacking in any spiritual gift as you wait for the revealing of our Lord Jesus Christ. (1 Corinthians 1:4-7)

Aspects of Testimony: Evidence, Relationship, Community

Testimony is evidence. Discussing the practice of testimony, New Testament scholar and Christian Methodist Episcopal Church Bishop Thomas Hoyt Jr. underscores three aspects of testimony: truth telling, bearing witness to what is good, and community. Bishop Hoyt writes, "[Testimony] is a deeply shared practice—one that is possible only in a community that recognizes that falsehood is strong, but that yearns nonetheless to know what is true and good."[1]

In this passage, Bishop Hoyt borrows from the world of courtrooms and trials to make clear that testimony has to do with telling the truth. Testimony as truth telling begins early in life when parents ask children questions such as "How was school today?" or "Who ate the cookie that I put in the cookie jar for Grandma?" The child tells the truth, the whole truth, and nothing but the truth. If not, the child learns that lying leads one astray and to punishment.

Testimony as truth telling continues throughout life. As a legal term, testimony occurs in a courtroom where witnesses are summoned to give testimony in courts of law or before government hearings. When we die, credible people witness our last will and testament.

As a human practice that happens in our most ordinary relationships, testimony occurs all the time. When we tell family members or friends about a good movie or a bargain sale, we do so with the expectation that they will be interested in the film or product and that their positive response will do them good. If we respond to a marketing survey about a product, we speak the truth as we have seen, heard, and experienced it. In a court, witnesses testify, and others receive and evaluate the facts. Indeed, whenever we testify, we do so for good.

Testimony is personal and a part of an individual's story. Testimony grows out of relationships and community. In dedicating this book to people who have shaped my journey, I have shared some of my own story. My birth family nurtured me in faith. As I grew up, family and friends communicated a powerful witness to a God who really is and really cares for me and all God's children. My decision at a Billy Graham crusade intentionally to follow Jesus arose out of friendship with Alan Smith. We were school chums. We did Cub and Boy Scouts together. We camped together. In time, he shared his personal testimony with me. One evening, he invited me to accompany him to the Cow Palace in San Francisco. Initially, I was unmoved by the music, sermon, and ambiance. As a newcomer to this style of worship, I was uneasy. Resistance rose up within me as though a voice was saying, "What are you doing here? Wouldn't you rather be across the way at Candlestick Park where the San Francisco Giants are playing? Isn't the hand-clapping and hand-waving pure emotion?"

At some point, we left. That did not stop the service or prevent the Holy Spirit from convicting me of the need to return and go forward. Later as we drove home, we sang "How Great Thou Art" and other hymns. Though distance has made it difficult to sustain the intimacy of our school years, we remain friends. I have never ceased to give thanks for Alan's testimony!

As Alan communicated God's love for me directly and naturally, lifestyle evangelism in general and testimony in particular entail sharing in direct and natural ways. Christians share the good news of God's love to others by deed or word out of the bounty of God's love. We do so that others may know the truth and goodness of new life in Christ and respond. Generally, we make our testimony accessible to people through relationships and through the faith community.

Testimony and Evangelism

Testimony has contributed to my ability to navigate crucial passages at several significant times during my life pilgrimage. The story of my personal decision to follow Jesus is typical. For most converts, family members and friends nurture passages to faith. Countless books and surveys conducted over recent years reveal that an overwhelming majority of converts identify someone's personal interest in them as key to their turning to Christ.

One such survey of 511 adult men and women who had recently made public professions of faith reported that conversion was the result of a long process. Only 4 percent of those surveyed said they had been brought to Christ through big evangelistic rallies. A few reported that events such as the birth of a child or death of a loved one were important occasions of conversion. But in most cases, new converts reported that the door of entry to faith was personal testimony by family and friends who lived out their faith in daily life. The report concluded that rallies and other methods traditionally associated with evangelism, such as special programs, door-to-door home visitation, and street evangelism, are no substitute for personal and incarnational evangelism in everyday living. Gavin Read, Bishop of Maidstone in the British Anglican community, observed, "As Christians we are all a lazy bunch." Referring to a national Billy Graham crusade he directed in the 1980s, he continued, "The onset of one of these missions sometimes gives us the heave to get out and do what we should have been doing all the time."[2]

Testimony occurs as people reach others within natural social networks. In a negative way, failure to practice testimony may mean a failure to respond to someone in need. Often, we practice testimony as much by what we do not do or do not say as by what we do or say.

What barriers exist to the practice of testimony? Perhaps the single greatest obstacle is lack of self-esteem on the part of believers and of small-membership congregations. In the case of individuals, many have heard so many negative voices that they have come to believe them. For the past five years, I have facilitated a small group that meets Sunday morning to pray and explore discipleship together. To further this goal, we read books by contemporary authors. Generally, we alternate biblical or theological studies with books that present images of faith through art or literature. Irrespective of the genre, the books have elicited early memories of religion that have emphasized our dark side. "I am no good." "I deserve God's punishment."

Within the group, friendship has nurtured trust. We have begun to hear other voices within and without. Some whisper softly, "You are God's Beloved." Others declare loudly, "God wills your well-being, life, and health. Live into the grace of God." As friendship and trust have grown, we have talked about evangelism. At the outset, several participants expressed typical worries such as What do I say? How do I say it? What if I offend? What if they reject me? These concerns have dissipated as we have become comfortable with one another.

One Sunday, a newcomer arrived in the middle of our time of prayer. We welcomed her and invited her to settle in. We were quiet for some minutes. Listening prayer let us clear away the rubble of our busy lives. We became present one to another and to Christ. The newcomer gained confidence that she was in a safe place. Without a word being spoken, she learned it was okay to be wherever she was in her spiritual life. As our time ended, it was as though we had always known each other. Our new friend needed the Lord to speak peace to her. It happened. Our words were not necessary. We needed to give God space, as well as our heart-felt thanks and praise.[3]

In the case of congregations, a significant factor behind a weak corporate self-image is the tendency of members to recall the size they were back in the 1950s or 1960s or to compare themselves unfavorably with mega-churches. Many members of numerically small congregations see their churches as unattractive, powerless, and lacking resources for growth. Many members feel that they lack communication skills by which they might practice testimony. These negative perceptions create a self-fulfilling cycle that produces policies and decisions inhibiting growth, however defined. The congregation's planning priorities are for institutional survival, not loving-kindness and growth. The congregation fails to understand that small can be beautiful.

Excellent resources exist to assist individuals and congregations struggling to recover a sense of self-esteem. In many books, renewal advocate Lyle E. Schaller and others have insisted that personal testimony in sermon, song, ritual, special events, and storytelling are crucial. When we give an account that Christ is alive and that his Spirit is active in our lives, we open channels by which God's Holy Spirit may effect transformation in our lives and the lives of others.[4]

Other obstacles to evangelism include over-clericalized congregations, discouraged clergy, change, doubt, and despair. There are ways pastors can encourage laypeople to overcome these difficulties. Pastors can create a sense of openness. They can incorporate testimony as a regular part of services of worship. They can build community through small groups in which people can share their wounds as they move toward health and wholeness. They can respect, affirm, and encourage members. They can emphasize grace. They can nurture the practices of love, gratitude, listening, hope, and compassion in members.

I have visited many centers of Christian renewal: the Church of the Saviour in Washington, DC; Corrymeela in Northern Ireland; Iona in Scotland; Koinonia Farm in Georgia; L'Arche in the Holy Land; Madonna House in Ontario; Taizé in France; Wildfire in Birmingham, England; the Community of Hospitality in Atlanta; and the Toronto (Ontario) Vineyard Church. Some are well known. Other are less so. Some are theologically more conservative. Others are less so. Generally, however, Christians in these contexts bear witness to the new creation in Christ in four radical ways.

First, they reclaim a sense of unity through personal allegiance to Jesus Christ. The simple confession, "Jesus Christ is Lord," cuts through theological differences. Effective Christian communities manifest little interest in the fine points of doctrine or denominational label.[5]

Second, they adopt inward spiritual disciplines such as extensive devotional use of Scripture, prayer, and meditation. Christians practice these disciplines both individually and corporately. Through them, they discern God's call, both individually and corporately, to be present for those needing compassionate care, for one another and for those beyond the community.

Third, they commit themselves to serving the poorest, weakest, most abused members of the human community. They develop practices by which they participate in the struggles of the marginalized for recognition and wholeness.

Finally, they embrace more spontaneous and varied worship. Some try house church styles of worship together, and others experiment in the arts. No one mode of worship will meet the needs of every individual. Perhaps because I was raised in a tradition of more formal worship, I appreciate liturgical forms; others prefer informal styles of worship. What is crucial is to multiply opportunities by which people may share their testimony.

Testimony involves beginning where people are. When I hear someone say, "Christ is the answer," I ask, "What is the question?" The Christ-bearer must create a bridge to the person's desire and culture. As a sharing between humans, testimony inevitably entails a person telling his or her truth to another in specific contexts. Donald Soper, a British Methodist evangelist and peacemaker, stresses the importance of beginning where people are rather than where we would like them to be: ". . . we have to begin with the challenge of our years, however inchoate, imprecise, unordered and invalid its ideas may be. It is there that we can expect to find a point of contact, and it is there that we must begin today."[6]

Testimony in Practice

A friend serves as a hospice chaplain. Recently, she was called in the middle of the night to the home and bedside of a dying person. Other Christians had come before. According to the family, two itinerant evangelists had been by earlier in the day and invited the individual to visit their church. A member of a congregation where the patient occasionally worshiped also had been by and in effect criticized the individual for irregular attendance. By contrast, my friend sat with the person, listened to him, read Scripture, and prayed with him. She gave her testimony. In turn, the individual shared his love of the Lord and desire to be baptized. My friend offered the individual an opportunity to partake of the sacraments of baptism and Holy Communion. By these means, she offered nonverbal testimony of the love of God. The patient gladly responded. By the presence of this angel of compassion and love, God transformed the remaining hours of this individual's life from a deathwatch to a time of anticipation of glory.

Autobiographies present a written genre of testimony. In the early 1960s and 1970s, *Christian Century* featured a column titled "The Books that Shaped Lives." Two generations of intellectual giants frequently mentioned autobiographies including Augustine's *Confessions*, Pascal's *Pensées*, Schweitzer's *Out of My Life and Thought*, and Woolman's *Journal*.[7]

Testimony was a crucial practice of the Puritans, radical seventeenth-century reformers of the English church. Initially a party within the established church, the Puritans sought restitution of true religion by the outward church and inward purity on the part of believers. Leaders of the movement did not initially intend to form new ecclesial bodies. Nonetheless, several resulted: the Baptist, Congregational, and Presbyterian denominations and the Religious Society of Friends. Calvinist in theology, the Puritans struggled to know how they were saved and how they might know and act in truth. Self-styled "publishers of truth," they responded to such questioning through a literary outpouring of testimony. These remarkable testimonies were unique in Christian history and have continued to inform contemporary practice in such areas as family nurture and the Friends' peace testimony.[8]

One of the better-known converts to the Puritan cause was a tinker or handyman, John Bunyan (1628–1688). In his youth, Bunyan experienced a period of horrendous spiritual doubt. Weathering the turmoil, Bunyan studied Scripture and spiritual writers such as Augustine and Luther. Once he became convinced of his salvation, Bunyan became zealous to live in the light of the gospel. He suffered periods of imprisonment for reasons of religious conscience. He shared his testimony in sixty books, including two that have profoundly influenced readers ever since. In *Grace Abounding to the Chief of Sinners* (1660), Bunyan recorded his own journey of faith. In *Pilgrim's Progress,* published in two parts (1678 and 1684), Bunyan drew on traditional symbols to create an image of great mythic power, the figure of the lonely pilgrim on a purposeful journey. His testimony enabled others to experience God's grace.

A third example of specificity in testimony emerges from the experience of marginality. Conversion testimonies of Africans enslaved in the United States represent an early genre of autobiography. African American spiritual writers traced their freedom back to the acquisition of some sort of saving knowledge and to an awakening of the awareness of God's love. The recognition of one's true identity, unfettered by either the slavery of sin or the sin of slavery, set in motion a process by which early African Americans attained spiritual and secular freedom. The tradition of Sojourner Truth, Mary Ann Shadd Cary, Ida B. Wells, and W. E. B. Du Bois inspired twentieth-century prophets such as Howard Thurman and Martin Luther King Jr. to claim their "somebodiness." Dr. King wrote,

> Once plagued with a tragic sense of inferiority, resulting from the crippling effects of slavery and segregation, the Negro has now been driven to reevaluate himself. He has come to feel that he is somebody. With this new sense of "somebodiness" and self-respect, a new Negro has emerged with a new determination to achieve freedom and human dignity whatever the cost may be.[9]

Testimony entails plainly speaking the truth in love. Many are trying to find a vision of a life worth living. God's dream is that we are called to live, love, and build a more just and peaceful society. I want for myself, for each reader, and for children—the next generation of witnesses—to know God's dream that our lives be filled with joy and peace. Without the baggage of proselytism and triumphalism, we are called to the practice of testimony.

Prayer
God, whose love is limitless, I thank you that you have redeemed me through Jesus Christ. May I ever look upon my Savior with gratitude. Sustained by the presence of your Holy Spirit, I look to the future in trust. Enlarge my vision to the wideness of your grace. Let me know that no saving

word, no healing touch, and no act of mercy offered in Christ's name is too humble. Amen.

---

[1] Thomas Hoyt Jr., "Testimony," in *Practicing Our Faith: A Way of Life for a Searching People*, ed. Dorothy C. Bass (San Francisco: Jossey-Bass, 1998), 92.

[2] "Personal Evangelism Works Best," *Christianity Today* (9 November 1992): 72.

[3] Roberta C. Bondi, *In Ordinary Time: Healing the Wounds of the Heart* (Nashville: Abingdon Press, 1996), explores the work of introspection and memory that is sometimes necessary for the healing of painful injuries inflicted by the church. See also Frank Martin, *War in the Pews: A Foxhole Guide to Surviving Church Conflict* (Downers Grove: InterVarsity, 1995); G. Lloyd Rediger, *Clergy Killers: Guidance for Pastors and Congregations under Attack* (Louisville: Westminster, John Knox Press, 1997); Walter Wink, "The Angels of the Churches," in *Unmasking the Powers: The Invisible Forces that Determine Human Existence* (Philadelphia: Fortress, 1986).

[4] Lyle Schaller, *Growing Plans* (Nashville: Abingdon, 1983), 20. See also Ron Crandall, *Turn Around Strategies for the Small Church* (Nashville: Abingdon, 1995); Nancy T. Foltz, *Caring for the Small Church: Insights from Women in Ministry* (Valley Forge: Judson, 1994); H. Eddie Fox and George E. Morris, *Faith Sharing: Dynamic Christian Witnessing by Invitation* (Nashville: Discipleship Resources, 1996); Anthony Pappas and Scott Planting, *Mission: The Small Church Reaches Out* (Valley Forge: Judson, 1993); Kevin E. Ruffcorn, *Rural Evangelism: Catching the Vision* (Minneapolis: Augsburg, 1994).

[5] Donald C. Posterski and Irwin Barker, *Where's a Good Church?* (Winfield: Wood Lake Books, 1993); Reginald W. Bibby, *Fragmented Gods: The Poverty and Potential of Religion in Canada* (Toronto: Irwin Publishing, 1987). A sociologist, Bibby has replicated his findings from Canadian data in the United States. See his *Future Trends: Results of a Comprehensive Survey of Cumberland Presbyterians* (Memphis: General Assembly Council, 1997).

[6] Donald Soper, *The Advocacy of the Gospel* (New York: Abingdon Press, 1961), 45.

[7] Results of this survey are found in "Spiritual Resources for Ministry," *Theological Bulletin* 5/2 (May/June 1979): 17-29. In a course titled "Religions of Abraham," I introduce University of Memphis students to spiritual autobiographies of adherents of each of the three traditions.

[8] Elise Boulding, *Friends Testimonies in the Home* (Philadelphia: Friends General Conference, 1964); Wilmer A. Cooper, *The Testimony of Integrity in the Religious Society of Friends*, Pendle Hill Pamphlet 296 (Wallingford: Pendle Hill, 1991). On Bunyan, see Richard L. Greaves, *John Bunyan* (Grand Rapids: Eerdmans, 1969). James Blanton Wharey prepared the standard scholarly edition of *Pilgrim's Progress* (rev. ed., Roger Sharrock; Oxford: Clarendon Press, 1960).

[9] "The Case against 'Tokenism,'" *New York Times Magazine*, 5 August 1962, in *A Testament of Hope: The Essential Writings of Martin Luther King, Jr.*, ed. James M. Washington (San Francisco: Harper and Row, 1986), 108. Both Bishop Hoyt in his essay on testimony (n. 1) and Cheryl J. Sanders in *Empowerment Ethics for a Liberated People* (Minneapolis: Fortress Press, 1995) stress the role of slave testimonies.

For Reflection and Conversation

- Why is testimony a practice of loving-kindness?

- What are the most important aspects of testimony? What testimony is important to you?

- Describe an individual, a community, or a book that has offered testimony crucial to your life.

- What atmosphere fosters testimony?

- What is the relationship between testimony and evangelism?

Practices of Just Living

Introduction

What does the L<small>ORD</small> *require of you but to do justice?* (Micah 6:8)

In the Bible, justice or righteousness is the fulfillment of the demands of relationships between humans and God and between people. Biblical scholar Walter Brueggemann states this succinctly. Biblical justice is sorting out what belongs to whom and returning it to them. Such an understanding implies three things. There are basic entitlements for everyone. There is a right distribution of goods. There is a work of justice to be done. This justice work entails the work of giving things back so that people may know God's liberation, redemption, and salvation.[1]

In this section we explore four practices that ground lifestyle evangelism in doing justice. They are reconciliation, jubilee, dialogue, and servant leadership. For some readers, it may be a stretch to call these practices evangelism. Does not Jesus tell us to go throughout the world making disciples and baptizing them in the name of the Triune God? Is not evangelism ministering cross-culturally, going throughout the world and beckoning people to convert?

This rendering truncates the Great Commission (Matt 28:16-20; Mark 16:15). A story told by George MacLeod illustrates the point. During the apartheid period in South Africa's history, MacLeod was in Durban to preach. An Ulsterman approached him and said, "I hope you're going to give them the gospel red hot."

"Yes," MacLeod replied. "I am speaking of its social implications here in Durban."

The man said suspiciously, "Social implications? What is wanted is the gospel red hot."

"But is it not of the gospel," MacLeod asked, "that by right of Christ all men have an equal dignity?"

"Yes," he replied, "that is of the gospel."

MacLeod then asked what the hot gospellers were doing about the tens of thousands of black Africans and Indians without shelter that cold night. "Them?" replied the man. "I wish the whole damn lot were sunk in the harbor!"[2]

Jesus did not have in mind hot gospelling when he urged us to teach people to obey everything that he commanded of his followers (Matt 28:20). Graciously, Jesus invited people to follow him, to love, and to forgive. Jesus called people to obey everything he had taught.

Herb Miller, onetime executive director of the National Evangelistic Association of the Christian Church and consultant for Yokefellow Institute, stressed this point. In *Actions Speak Louder than Verbs*, Miller explored ten verbs Jesus commonly used. The key verbs are repent, follow, pray, believe, love, forgive, go, baptize, teach, and serve. Miller expanded this primary list by exploring related verbs. Under loving, Miller identified these additional verbs that Jesus used:

> Do not judge (Matthew 7:1; Luke 6:37, 41-42). Give (Matthew 19:21; Mark 4:24, 10:21; Luke 6:30, 38; Acts 20:35). Honor (Matthew 19:19; Mark 10:19; Luke 18:20). If your brother sins, go tell him (Matthew 18:15-17). Whoever divorces (Matthew 19:9, 18; Mark 10:11-12, 19; Luke 16:18; 18:20). Do not kill (Matthew 19:18; Mark 10:19, Luke 18:20). Do not steal (Matthew 19:18; Mark 10:19; Luke 18:20). Do not tell untruths (Mark 10:19). Be merciful (Luke 6:27-36). Humble yourself (Luke 18:14).[3]

To do justice is a verb. Doing justice, we move closer to the One behind the verb. This inevitably moves us toward the Jesus way. Doing justice, we proclaim the Jesus gospel. With Paul, I say *woe to me if I do not proclaim the gospel!* (1 Cor 9:16). We are to proclaim the gospel by doing justice. If necessary, we do so using words.[4]

According to Paul, our speaking and our doing are *a demonstration of the Spirit and of power, so that your faith might rest not on human wisdom but on the power of God* (1 Cor 2:4). Speaking and doing justice require a lifelong commitment. It is not good enough to want a better world. Now and always, we must speak, and we must act. Not to do so violates Jesus' announcement of God's inbreaking and contributes to injustice.

God is waiting on us. Jesus needs our response. An aphorism says that for evil to triumph it is not necessary that the good become bad, only that the good do nothing. In a collection of reminiscences, Jewish writer Elie Wiesel makes this clear. He retells a Passover story about Job. Job was in Egypt at the same time as Moses. Wiesel continues:

> What's more, he held the important position of advisor in the Pharaoh's court, the same rank as Jethro & Bileam. When the Pharaoh asked how he might resolve the Jewish question, Jethro spoke in favor of Moses' request—to let his people go. Bileam, however, took the opposite stand. When Job was consulted, he refused to take sides; he wished to remain neutral, so he kept silent, neither for nor against. This neutrality, the Midrash says, earned him his future sufferings. At critical times, at moments of peril, no one has the right to abstain, to be prudent. When the life or death—or simply the well being of a community is at stake, neutrality is criminal, for it aids and abets the oppressor and not his victim.[5]

Around the world, Christians as well as non-Christians long ardently to see a radically different world come into being. God created everything and pronounced creation good. Abuse of children and women, exploitation of workers, pollution, poverty, racism, war, and other evils were not part of God's good earth. They were products of human action. So God dreamed a better world and gave humans the capacity to live into that dream. Living the dream, we make visible a new world of justice.

---

[1] Walter Brueggemann, "Voices of the Night-Against Justice," in *To Act Justly, Love Tenderly, Walk Humbly* (Mahway: Paulist, 1986), 5. See also E. R. Achtemeier, "Righteousness in the Old Testament," and P. J. Achtemeier, "Righteousness in the New Testament," *The Interpreter's Dictionary of the Bible*, (Nashville: Abingdon, 1962) 4:80-85 and 91-99; and G. Klein, "Righteousness in the New Testament," *The Interpreter's Dictionary of the Bible,* supplementary vol., 750-52.

[2] George MacLeod, *Only One Way Left: Church Prospect* (Glasgow: Iona Community, 1956), 54. Founder of the Iona community in Scotland, MacLeod lived from 1895–1991.

[3] Herb Miller, *Actions Speak Louder than Verbs* (Nashville: Abingdon Press, 1989), 68.

⁴ Francis (c. 1182–1226), the "Little Poor Man of Assisi," is quoted as having said, "Preach the Gospel everywhere you go. Use words only if necessary." I have not found his exact words. The idea is consistent with the life of Francis as Celeno and Bonaventure recorded in early hagiographies. The *Little Flowers of St. Francis* records his time with the "Sultan of Babylonia." Impressed by the piety and deeds of Francis, the Sultan declined to convert to the faith of Christ for fear of the life of Francis and his own. Later, he received instruction in the faith and holy baptism (*Writings and Early Biographies: English Omnibus of the Sources for the Life of St. Francis*, ed. Marion A. Habig [Chicago: Franciscan Herald Press, 1983], 1355-56).

⁵ Elie Wiesel, *From the Kingdom of Memory: Reminiscences* (New York: Schocken, 1990), 151; Wiesel does not give a reference for the midrash.

Practices of Reconciliation

From now on, therefore, we regard no one from a human point of view; even though we once knew Christ from a human point of view, we know him no longer in that way. So if anyone is in Christ, there is a new creation: everything old has passed away; see, everything has become new! All this is from God, who reconciled us to himself through Christ, and has given us the ministry of reconciliation; that is, in Christ God was reconciling the world to himself, not counting their trespasses against them, and entrusting the message of reconciliation to us. (2 Corinthians 5:16-19)

The Biblical Concept of Reconciliation

Reconciliation is the word that best describes God's intentions for humankind. We are to live in harmony with God, within ourselves, with one another, and with all of life. Reconciliation has nuances nonspecific to Jewish or Christian usage. Reconciliation is about healing wounds and bringing people into relationship after a period of estrangement. Reconciliation is about people settling differences and achieving harmony. Reconciliation is about grassroot processes aimed at uprooting prejudice, discord, and disunity. Reconciliation is about people solving problems together.

In the ancient world, the vocabulary of reconciliation had rich meaning. Reconciliation referred to changing shape, color, and appearance or to bartering as in modern financial matters, for example, when we reconcile our bank accounts. Generally, in Hebrew Scriptures reconciliation was a catchword, an omnibus word embracing myriad concepts such as liberation, peace, and salvation.[1]

In the Septuagint Old Testament, the Greek word *katallasso* and several cognates expressed ideas close to New Testament usage. In 1 Samuel 29:4, the Philistine leaders expressed concern lest David and Saul be reconciled. David thereby regained Saul's favor. Second Maccabees 1:5, 5:20, 7:33, and 8:29 anticipated Paul's understanding of God's initiative to affect reconciliation.

There is scant linguistic basis to know the origins of Jesus' notion of changing enmity into friendship or of Paul's understanding of God acting to bring about reconciliation with humankind. As I understand words used in

Scripture to describe sacrifice (atonement, mediator, forgiveness of sin, penitence, ransom, redemption, restitution), God is affirmed as loving humankind despite our alienation from God. Humans sin. Humans fail to fulfill their covenant duties. The people pray. God reconciles. Our ultimate hope is that God hears our prayers and reconciles us to God's self.[2]

By the first century AD, God came to be understood as redeeming humans from physical misery *and* sin *and* death.[3] Jesus spoke of reconciliation as changing enmity to friendship: *when you are offering your gift at the altar, if you remember that your brother or sister has something against you . . . go; first be reconciled* (Matt 5:23-24).

The main source for the developing idea of God acting to make us pleasing to God was Paul or writers influenced by Paul. Paul was clear that God reconciles us to God's self. In the passage at the start of this chapter, 2 Corinthians 5:16-19, Paul used the language of new beginnings. *So if anyone is in Christ, there is a new creation . . . see, everything has become new!*

God sees us only in the light of Christ. In Clarence Jordan's vivid paraphrase, God has bridged the gap between God and humanity through Christ. Paul also makes clear that, *entrusting the message of reconciliation to us,* God has given us the job of bridging all that still divides. God has hugged the world. God no longer keeps track of our sins. God is helping us to get it all together. In this way, we know what God's goodness really is. God has looked out for us and at the right time given us a helping hand. The time is now. This is freedom time![4]

God has given us the job of bridging the gap. This image of reconciliation is vibrant and contemporary. In the period leading up to recent United States elections, two national organizations, the Call to Renewal and the Conference of Catholic bishops, invited faithful citizens to bridge myriad gaps. The Catholic bishops indicated that service to the poor and the vulnerable motivated them to enter the public forum:

> . . . this is not an easy time for faithful citizenship. By this we mean more than people who consistently participate in public life, but disciples who view these responsibilities through the eyes of faith and bring their moral convictions to their civic tasks and choices. Sometimes it seems few candidates and no party fully reflect our values. But now is not a time for retreat. The new millennium should be an opportunity for renewed participation. We must challenge all parties and every candidate to defend human life and dignity, to pursue greater justice and peace, to uphold family life, and to advance the common good . . . . How will we protect the weakest in our

midst—innocent, unborn children? How will we overcome the scandal of a quarter of our preschoolers living in poverty in the richest nation on earth? How will we address the tragedy of 35,000 children dying every day of the consequences of hunger, debt and lack of development around the world? . . . How will our society best combat continuing prejudice, bias and discrimination, overcome hostility toward immigrants and refugees, and heal the wounds of racism, religious bigotry and other forms of discrimination?[5]

We too can generate a long list of gaps to overcome. Gaps exist between those who are free and those who are not, between those who seek to be stewards of earth's resources and those who plunder earth's resources without pause for thought and so on. In Ephesians 2:11-22, the focus is on the gap between Jews and non-Jews. Christ establishes one new humanity and offers to Jews and Gentiles alike a new status as citizens with the saints. We are members of God's household built upon the foundation of the apostles and prophets with Christ Jesus himself as the cornerstone.

Theologically, Paul is describing what God has already done. Through his death and resurrection, Jesus the Reconciler effects a new reality between God and humans, as also between Jews and Gentiles and all parties otherwise antagonistic one to another. In Ephesians, according to E. C. Blackman, "it is not really Christ who is slain on the cross, but the hostility which separates men from one another and from God . . . . This is evidence of divine operation, since the gulf between Gentile and Jew was regarded in the ancient Roman Empire as more unbridgeable than the modern disparity between East and West, Communist and non-Communist."[6]

It is not always easy to see the good effects of God's divine operation. The history of enmity between Jews and Gentile Christians is doleful. Yet, we do live in more hopeful times. Offered a fresh start, we may live into a literal, actual period of Jewish-Christian reconciliation.[7] Let me mention two examples.

Many Palestinian Christians live in Israel as citizens of a state hostile to their existence. Many have lost family members and their homes. Yet many love Jews and seek to reconcile the two warring peoples. An Israeli Palestinian priest, Elias Chacour, struggles to become Christ-like, to care for the victim and victimizer alike. He feels deeply the torment of those who suffer. He calls prophetically to the oppressor to be liberated from fear, anger, and lust for power. He envisions the land of Israel as a place of safety and well-being for all.[8]

In 1970 a Dominican priest, Father Bruno Hussar, founded *Neve Shalom/Wahat al Salat* (Oasis of Peace) near the Latrun Monastery just off the main Tel Aviv-Jerusalem road. The settlement straddles the Green Line that marks the boundary separating Israel and Palestine. Jewish and Palestinian Christian and Muslim families live together and make decisions on the basis of equality. In addition to worshiping in accord with their separate traditions, they share a common worship. Among projects the members of Oasis of Peace undertake is *Partnership*, a weeklong school of peace that brings together over 5,000 Jewish and Arab children each year. The governing principle is simple: make so-called enemies friends (Matt 5:44).[9]

Elias Chacour and Oasis of Peace are harbingers of that day when all things hold together in Christ (Col 1:17). The point is crucial. In a world driven by division, we can see walls coming down! Thanks be to God for the fall of the Berlin Wall on 9 November 1989. Thanks be to God for Nelson Mandela's walk to freedom on 11 February 1990.

We may rejoice in these contemporary events, each the climax of long struggles marked largely by nonviolent resistance. Walls do come down. West and East Berlin are now united. President Mandela has led a post-apartheid government. But the writer to the Ephesians is not talking of political arrangements. These can be sources of violence among people. Ephesians claims something else. God has achieved a new humanity of non-strangers, a new people of God.

In Colossians 1:15-23, Paul says God makes peace by the blood of the cross. Christ is the head of the church. There is a new dimension as well. In Christ all things hold together. Beginning with the cross, God realizes the full dimensions of reconciliation with the resurrection. Again in Clarence Jordan's down-home prose, God puts all the eggs in one basket, showing friendliness toward everybody. By the blood shed at Jesus' lynching we have peace on the earth and in heaven.

In Romans 5:8-11, Paul depicts reconciliation as a result of God's reconciling work in Jesus:

> God proves his love for us in that while we still were sinners Christ died for us. Much more surely then, now that we have been justified by his blood, will we be saved through him from the wrath of God. For if while we were enemies, we were reconciled to God through the death of his Son, much more surely, having been reconciled, will we be saved by his life. But more than that, we even boast in God through our Lord Jesus Christ, through whom we have now received reconciliation.

Here Paul is saying we were God's enemies. By sin we were estranged from God. Through Christ we have gained reconciliation with God. Reconciliation, then, arises from our understanding of God whose basic nature is love, peace, and reconciliation. Jesus of Nazareth reveals a God who is source of life. Despite our sin, God freely and tenderly reaches out to us and invites intimacy. God wants to be our friend. God wants friendship with all people. God loves us. God restores us to our Edenic grandeur of the divine image and likeness. Reconciled with God, we too are reconcilers.

In the face of these high-minded affirmations, doubts may arise. Like lemmings rushing to the sea, we humans ignore warnings of potential consequences of our actions. In real life, many people feel estranged from God. In the real world, people experience discord within themselves, with the created order, and with others. In our daily lives, division is pervasive. Everywhere humans seem to erect walls of partition. Sources of polarization abound. Many oppose the ordination of women. Straights rail at gays. White people maintain privilege to the detriment of people of color. Ethnic groups strive against each other. Especially in rich countries, we consume resources at a pace that imperils future generations and, indeed, human existence.[10]

God needs us to fulfill the biblical vision of a reconciled world. God needs people to carry Christ's cross and show people the way to God. This hard, painful work is a work that God counts on us to do. How do we practice reconciliation in the Jesus way? In the words of Henri Nouwen,

> The God who loves us is a God who becomes vulnerable, dependent in the manger and dependent on the cross, a God who basically is saying, "Are you there for me?"
>
> God, you could say, is waiting for our answer. In a very mysterious way, God is dependent on us. God is saying, "I want to be vulnerable, I need your love. I have a desire for your affirmation of my love." God is a jealous God in the sense of wanting our love and wanting us to say yes. That's why in the end of the Gospel of John, Jesus asks Peter three time, "Do you love me?" God is waiting for us to respond. Life gives us endless opportunities for that response.[11]

Shalom Community, Beloved Community

The main biblical vision of history is of a reconciled creation with every creature living in harmony with God and all creation. According to this vision, the joy, security, and well-being of each individual is linked with the joy, security, and well-being of everyone else. The triumph of one person enhances the common good. When one person suffers, all suffer. If we destroy Earth's life support systems—the sea, the forests, and the protective ozone cover—we threaten ourselves. The vision of a reconciled creation is staggering and invites us to examine our individual self-interests in the context of the whole human family and cosmos. The reconciliation of people and in particular the reconciliation of Jew and Gentile, slave and free, and male and female are stages in a grander divine plan, a reconciled world (Gal 3:28).

As God's intended reconciliation of the whole cosmos unfolds, all people are being woven into a single family. Reconciliation thus requires that we see ourselves through the divine lens. We are God's beloved children. Biblical scholar Walter Brueggemann images the reconciled creation as a *shalom community*. Brueggemann writes that *shalom* is the Hebrew word that best defines the controlling vision. "*Shalom* is the substance of the biblical vision of one community embracing all creation . . . . The origin and destiny of God's people is to be on the road of *shalom,* which is to live out of joyous memories and toward greater anticipations."[12]

Howard Thurman and Martin Luther King Jr. developed a second image: *beloved community.* They probably owed the phrase to two mentors, Walter Rauschenbusch and Josiah Royce. Thurman and King valorized the image as the outcome of reconciliation.[13] Like the *shalom community* image, *beloved community* expresses two tenets of biblical anthropology. The first picks up the idea that we are God's beloved. According to King and Thurman, everybody is a somebody. No matter what one's circumstances may be, everyone is precious to God. We are God's beloved because of who we are. *See what love* [God] *has given us, that we should be called children of God; and that is what we are* (1 John 3:1).

Thurman and King enabled all God's children to claim who and whose they are. They affirmed as well that to be human is to live in community. God's intent for humankind is that we dwell in a reconciled community of justice and harmony; a community of love, understanding, goodwill, and nonviolence; a world without slavery, segregation, inferior schools, slums, or second-class citizenship; a world without war and violence.

Thurman and King described the march toward full community in terms of breaking down barriers. The *beloved community* cannot feed on itself for long; it flourishes where boundaries give way to the coming from beyond of others, formerly unknown or undiscovered sisters and brothers. Thurman wrote, "For this is why we were born: [people] all belong to each other, and he who shuts himself away diminishes himself, and he who shuts another away from him destroys himself."[14]

Practically, what do these images look like? *Shalom community* and *beloved community* are images of the new creation, reconciled cosmos, restored community, and new heaven and new earth. Are these utopian images? Is reconciliation a realistic goal? What blocks realization of God's dream of a reconciled world? From whence do all the conflicts and disputes come?

To this latter question, James 4:1 posited one solution. Cease the cravings that are at war within us. African American comedian Bill Cosby offered another. Speaking in Memphis at an event organized by an interfaith organization that serves the poor, Cosby responded to a youth who asked what should be done about drug use and gun violence among young people. After reflection, Cosby replied, "Change the object of desire."

Practices of Reconciliation

What are the practices by which we serve as emissaries of reconciliation? Three dimensions of life together in Christ are at the heart of the reconciliation: the personal, communal, and social. The personal dimension relates to our changed relationship to God. In part, the earthly mission of the church is to witness to God who unconditionally offers forgiveness to all who will believe. Liturgically, Protestants acknowledge forgiveness of sins during the ordinances of baptism and Eucharist while Roman Catholic and Orthodox Christians observe the sacrament of penance as a rite of reconciliation.

With Christians through the centuries and around the world, I affirm my faith in words of ancient creeds, including "I believe in the forgiveness of sins." Forgiveness is an important lens for viewing the rich meaning system associated with the practice of reconciliation. The letter to the Hebrews concentrates on forgiveness and reconciliation, identifying the work of Jesus as that of a blameless sacrifice, an innocent victim. Jesus is *the Lamb of God who takes away the sin of the world!* (John 1:29). According to Luke 23:34, the first words Jesus uttered from the cross were, *Father, forgive them; for they do not know what they are doing.*[15] These words provide the focal point in Luke's telling good news. Jesus' cry from the cross recalls his announcement of God's forgiveness and exemplifies the cost of forgiveness to God who is both victim, the one offended by human sin, and reconciler. In Acts, the second part of Luke's narrative, the Spirit of the Crucified and Risen One descends upon early Christians. Forgiveness of sins becomes manifest in the community through liberation from oppression, healing of pain, critique of self-righteous power, pacification of demonic forces, and restoration of destroyed relations.

What of the communal dimension of the church, the community of Jesus the Reconciler? Foot-washing is one ritual that highlights our restored friendship with one another in the body of Christ. The Mennonites and Brethren maintain foot-washing as an ordinance of the church. A time of confession, forgiveness, restitution, and expressed resolve to amend one's life precede the rite. Congregants wash one another's feet as a demonstration of reconciliation, not only a response to Jesus' command in John 13 to do so. Congregants embody a community who truly love and serve one another, as we do when we exchange the peace before celebrating the Lord's Supper.

Another ritual that connects the forgiving and the healing are litanies of remembering. Congregants come face to face with the burden of the past and seek to piece together that which was once whole. An example of this reuniting of that which has been severed, of again making complete what was broken, is a practice among some Christian congregations of *shoah* (Holocaust) remembrance. Congregants recall the painful history of anti-Semitism, which led in part to the Holocaust, and symbolically break the chains that have locked Christians in the dark.

Another example, from Australia, is the apology of Victorian Baptists to Aborigines of the Stolen Generation. During a service of worship, congregants remember; then they seek and offer forgiveness and resolve to go forward together in wholeness.[16] Such steps signify long-term commitment to journey toward reconciliation. Only by confession, forgiveness, and amendment of life do people model Christian love one for another (John 13:34).

A third dimension of reconciliation is social. To be in Christ is to take on a new identity. We are not Jew or Greek, Euro-American or African American, Serb or Croatian, but something new. Yet our worship often reflects our divisions. Martin Luther King Jr. decried a situation in which the 11:00 hour on Sunday mornings reflected alienation among the races. So too, denominational and other differences make it seemingly impossible for Christians to share communion. We desperately need social reconciliation within our ecclesial institutions.

The social dimension poses great challenges for Christians. Brokenness is concrete. Some people do horrible things to other people. A woman raped as a child by her father or mother's boyfriend comes to terms with these memories. Survivors of the Oklahoma City bombing on 19 April 1995 struggle to make sense of this tragedy. Survivors of the 28 April 1996 massacre in Port Arthur, Tasmania, where thirty-five tourists were shot and killed, confront a national debate about the death penalty or gun control regulations. White and black South Africans address the truth and reconciliation commission. Native Americans in Canada and the United States reveal the abuses they endured in the residential schools.

The list is virtually endless. How are Palestinian Christians to view those of the Christian right, largely a North American phenomenon that gives unconditional support to Israelis who oppose reconciliation with Palestinians? How are Catholic Croats to relate to Serbian Orthodox and both to Bosnian Muslims, when few of those who participated in genocide have been brought to accountability? It seems that so much of primordial emotions and tribal identities shape our behavior and make it difficult to transcend gender, race, and class. We have to begin to find ways to build a common society, especially through truth and reconciliation commissions and apologies.

To practice reconciliation in the social arena, we must acknowledge that conflict is part of life within ourselves, our families, churches, the nation, and the world. Conflict is not necessarily bad or evil; it arises from the clash between differing needs, wants, ideals, and power-interests. To practice reconciliation is not to trivialize conflict, to ignore memories of past wrongs, or to forgive and forget. Reconcilers enter the long-term journey of transforming conflict, restoring justice to those whose rights have been violated, repairing broken lives and seeking healing. To practice reconciliation is to be faithful to what Christ has done. The Christian is bold to affirm, in a world that seems unredeemed, that its redemption has already been accomplished.[17]

Contemporary theologians insist reconciliation must top the agenda of Christian evangelization. Robert Schreiter says we stand between the times. At the end of the twentieth century, we waited the birth of a new reality. In the twenty-first century, we find God's reconciliation welling up in the souls of people. Similarly, Charles van Engen states, "our primary role is to be involved in the transformation of our world by working for reconciliation."[18]

In our work for reconciliation, we must be sensitive to misconceptions associated with the concept. Often, talk of reconciliation connotes maintaining the status quo. The privileged can appear to offer to forgive and forget without any offer of justice. Reconciliation can be a false form of appeasement rather than of building a common society. True reconciliation can never postpone movement toward liberation. It can never be a hasty, brokered peace. It must lead to justice, healing, and creation of mutually satisfying relations.[19]

To summarize, we are created in the image and likeness of God. The root cause of our alienation from God is our pursuit of other objects of desire. As a result, in the depths of our being we are marred, out of sync, out of balance. God offers a solution. By the death and resurrection of Jesus, we are reconciled to God and to one another. We are to share with the great company of witnesses who from the time of Abraham and Sarah have responded to God's Spirit and participated in this new creation. Reconciliation is so central and powerful an ideal, yet its absence seems to define human experience. For Paul it is a cosmic reality, a way of seeing the world and an ethical imperative. Practices of reconciliation are at the heart of a lifestyle of evangelism.

Prayer
Loving God who is all-compassion, all-peace, comforter, Spirit of truth, everywhere present, filling all things, treasury of all goodness, and giver of life: enable us to respond to the gracious invitation of Jesus to journey toward a reconciled world. May we walk his way of healing, nonviolence, and love. May all your children experience the new humanity of your beloved son Jesus Christ. Amen.

---

[1] Stanley E. Porter, *Katallasso in Ancient Greek Literature, with Reference to the Pauline Writings*, Estudios de Filologia Neotestamentaria 5 (Cordoba: Ediciones El Almendro, 1994); E. C. Blackman, "Reconciliation, Reconcile," *Interpreter's Dictionary of the Bible* (Nasvhille: Abingdon, 1962), 4:16-17; J. Reumann, "Reconciliation," *Interpreter's Dictionary of the Bible*, supplemental vol., (Nashville: Abingdon, 1970), 728-29; Friedrich Buchsel in Gerhard Kittel, *Theological Dictionary of the New Testament* (Grand Rapids: Eerdmans, 1964), 1:251-59.

[2] Porter, *Katallasso*, 13; Cilliers Breytenbach, "On Reconciliation: An Exegetical Response," *Journal of Theology for Southern Africa* 70 (March 1990): 64-68.

[3] Augustine Stock, "The Development of the Concept of Redemption," in *Sin, Salvation and the Spirit*, ed. Daniel Durken (Collegeville: Liturgical Press, 1979).

[4] Clarence Jordan, *Cotton Patch Version of Paul's Epistles* (New York: Association, 1968), 81-82. In 1942 Jordan (1912–1969), a New Testament scholar, left the academy to found, with his wife Florence (1912–1987) and others, an interracial community at Koinonia, Georgia.

[5] United States Catholic Conference, "Faithful Citizenship: Civil Responsibility for a New Millennium," in *Origins* 29/20 (28 October 1999): 311.

[6] Blackman, "Reconciliation, Reconcile" 17.

[7] John Driver, *Understanding the Atonement for the Mission of the Church* (Scottdale: Herald Press, 1986), 177. (Catholic) Commission for Religious Relations with the Jews, "We Remember: A Reflection on the 'Shoah,'" *Origins* 27/40 (26 March 1998).

[8] Elias Chacour, *Blood Brothers* (Grand Rapids: Zondervan, 1984); and *We Belong to the Land* (San Francisco: Harper, 1990).

[9] Bruno Hussar, *When the Cloud Lifted*, trans. Alison Megroz (London: Veritas Books, 1989).

[10] D. H. Meadows et al., *Limits to Growth* (New York: New American Library, 1972) marks the beginning of serious discussion of sustainable economics. See also World Commission on Environment and Development, *Our Common Future* (New York: Oxford University Press, 1987).

[11] Henri Nouwen, *The Road to Peace: Writings on Peace and Justice*, ed. John Dear (Maryknoll: Orbis, 1998), 220.

[12] Walter Brueggemann, *Living toward a Vision: Biblical Reflections on Shalom* (Philadelphia: United Church Press, 1976), 16.

[13] Howard Thurman, *Disciplines of the Spirit* (Richmond: Friends United Press), 25; Martin Luther King Jr., *Stride Toward Freedom: The Montgomery Story* (San Francisco: Harper and Row, 1958), 105-106, 224. Coretta Scott King, "Foreword," in Martin Luther King Jr., *Strength to Love* (Philadelphia: Fortress, 1963). Kenneth L. Smith and Ira G. Zepp Jr., *Search for the Beloved Community: The Thinking of Martin Luther King, Jr.* (Lanham: University Press of America, 1988).

[14] Howard Thurman, *The Search for Common Ground: An Inquiry Into the Basis of Man's Experience of Community* (New York: Harper and Row, 1971), 104.

[15] For a brief discussion of exegetical issues related to the Luke text, see L. Gregory Jones, *Embodying Forgiveness: A Theological Analysis* (Grand Rapids: William B. Eerdmans, 1995), 101. This is the best book on forgiveness in English. See also Geiko Muller-Fahrenholz, *The Art of Forgiveness: Theological Reflections on Healing and Forgiveness* (Geneva: WCC Publications, 1997); Robert J. Kennedy, ed., *Reconciliation: The Continuing Agenda* (Collegeville: Liturgical Press, 1987).

[16] Paul R. Dekar, "Australian Baptists apologize to Aboriginal peoples," *Baptist Peacemaker* 18 (spring 1998): 14. For a century, Australia's state governments supported the forced removal of Aboriginal children from their homes and their placement in residential schools. The policy ended in 1968. *Bringing Them Home* (Sydney: Human Rights and Equal Opportunity Commission, 1997) is a summary of findings of a national inquiry into the "stolen generation." In Canada and the United States, the churches ran similar schools for Native American children.

[17] Biblical authors encourage bold witness. Paul and Barnabas *spoke boldly for the Lord who testified to the word of his grace by granting signs and wonders to be done through them* (Acts 14:3). Jesus enables us to *approach the throne of grace with boldness, so that we may receive mercy and find grace to help in time of need* (Heb 4:16). A twentieth-century Jew, Martin Buber, highlights the boldness of Christianity in *Israel and the World* (New York: Schocken, 1948), 40.

[18] Robert J. Schreiter, *Reconciliation: Mission and Ministry in a Changing Social Order* (Maryknoll: Orbis, 1992), 81. Charles van Engen, *International Review of Mission* 86 (October 1997): 452.

[19] Carter Heyward, *Touching Our Strength: The Erotic as Power and the Love of God* (San Francisco: Harper and Row, 1989) for an evocative treatment of "right relations."

For Reflection and Conversation

- Why is reconciliation a practice of justice?

- What are the most important aspects of reconciliation?

- What image do you have of a reconciled world?

- Describe an individual or a community that demonstrates the processes of reconciliation.

- What should be done about drug use and gun violence among young people?

- What is the relationship between reconciliation and evangelism?

Practices of Jubilee

You shall not cheat one another, but you shall fear your God; . . . the land is mine. (Leviticus 25:17, 23)

A few years ago, I was doing research in the British Library and came across a speech by Victor Hugo before an International Peace Congress on 21 August 1849. Hugo stated that universal peace is a religious ideal emanating from God. God's law is peace, not war; justice, not oppression; universal prosperity, not an ever-growing gap between rich and poor. Deploring the immense sums that nations were squandering on armaments, Hugo urged nations to direct these funds to the arts, research, agriculture, and science. He pleaded that nations cease to traffic in arms. He called for international mechanisms for cooperation and conflict reduction.

In 1862, Hugo incorporated his vision of a better world into *Les Misérables*, a novel about love, justice, and revolution. Hugo was practical dreamer and his ideas bore fruit. Within fifty years, a peace gathering created the Permanent Court of Arbitration, the International Court of Justice, the Hague Academy of International Law, and a peace library. Within a hundred years, creation of the United Nations and adoption of the Universal Declaration of Human Rights institutionalized other aspects of Hugo's vision in purposeful ways. A modern production of *Les Misérables* inspires people:

> Do you hear the people sing
> Lost in the valley of the night?
> It is the music of a people
> Who are climbing to the light.
> For the wretched of the earth,
> There is a flame that never dies.
> Even the darkest night will end

> And the sun will rise.
> They will live again in freedom
> In the garden of the Lord.[1]

Dreamers, awake! Envision a different and better world. Now, as in Hugo's times, headlines scream out: War! Ethnic cleansing! Drug trafficking! Gun violence! Voices cry out from Kosovo, East Timor, Columbia, Sierra Leone, Littleton, Memphis, and elsewhere.

The Bible invites us to view this world in which we live in the light of what Verna J. Dozier calls "the dream of God."[2] God, whose loving initiative brought a good earth into being, created humankind in the divine image. God wills restoration of humankind to this status of original peace. This is why God became incarnate in Jesus and sustains us to live into the dream of God. *His divine power has given us everything needed for life and godliness, through the knowledge of him who called us by his own glory and goodness. Thus he has given us, through these things, his precious and very great promises, so that through them you may escape from the corruption that is in the world because of lust, and may become participants of the divine nature* (2 Pet 1:3-4).

Genesis 2 details conditions that existed before the expulsion of Adam and Eve from the Garden of Eden. In the garden, humankind did not struggle for existence. In the garden, gold and precious stones were not present. These symbols of material values were found outside the garden in the land of Havilah (Gen 2:10-12). In the garden, God had given humans everything they needed. Outside the garden, land and labor and wealth were objects of human desire and hence of sin.

Changing the object of desire was at the heart of the biblical plan to restore God's original peace. The plan was called Jubilee. Leviticus 25 spelled out the details. Though it is possible ancient Israel never implemented Jubilee legislation, it represented more than a utopian ideal. The Jubilee ideal sought to ensure the right of everyone to live honorably with a guaranteed minimum of economic means and thereby actualize divine justice in society.[3]

To do justice, the Jubilee practices mapped the right path. In Ezekiel 46, Isaiah 61, and other texts, the prophets drew attention to Jubilee. Jesus knew the Jubilee theme. In Luke 4:18-19, he said the time of Jubilee was at hand. Jesus did more than announce that God's commonwealth of justice was breaking in. He called for action. He told a rich young man to give what he had to the poor (Mark 10:17-22). He blessed Zacchaeus when the tax collector offered restitution to those he had defrauded (Luke 19:1-10). In this latter story, Jesus dispelled three myths about what it meant to be a righteous person. First, when Jesus went to the home of a sinner he demonstrated that holiness is this-worldly as well as otherworldly. Second, he affirmed that charity is inadequate. Zacchaeus did not simply give a handout. He repaid his debts and more. Zacchaeus knew he could not follow Jesus while continuing to enjoy the economic benefits of systemic evil. He had to repent, publicly giving reparations, and live in a new way. Third, Jesus proved again that God's love is not a scarce commodity. He came to seek and save *all* that are lost.

Few Christians today know about Jubilee practices. It is not hard to guess why. Jubilee envisions a periodic and fundamental restructuring of economic relations for all creation! Ancestral lands would be returned to the original inhabitants. Financial debts would be cancelled. Freedom from slavery would be granted. The land would lie fallow. Farm animals would have a year off. Imagine the reactions of politicians or bankers if Christians pressed home the implications of queries such as these: Who owns the land? Who profits from its resources? Yet this is happening. Christians are major actors in a modern Jubilee movement.

As Jubilee charted a way for ancient Israel to overcome the curse of banishment from the Garden of Eden, Jubilee now challenges us to do justice through restoring the land to God's intent; restoring liberty to those who suffer oppression; restoring economic hope; and restoring community.

Restoring the Land to God's Purpose

God provided ancient Israel a place to live on the basis of a new relationship with the land, animals, and crops. The land of Israel is God's; humans are *aliens and tenants* (Lev 25:23). Leviticus 25:4 offers one strategy to restore the land to God's purpose: a Sabbath of complete rest for the land.

Inherently, the idea that the earth is God's, and therefore a gift, is at odds with the actions of some Jews and some Christians. In Jewish tradition, the role of the land of Israel is to concretize and implement the covenant given to Israel at Sinai. Yet, ancient Israel does more than receive the land. It takes the land and keeps the land in the hands of Israel.

Martin Buber and David Hartman are two modern Israeli writers who wrestle with this tension between gift and grasp. For both, Zionism offers Jews the opportunity of fully realizing the universal thrust of Judaism without abandoning its intense particularism. According to Buber, "God does not give any one portion of the earth away, so that the owner may say as God says in the Bible: 'For all the earth is Mine' (Exod. 19:5). The conquered land is, in my opinion, only lent even to the conqueror who has settled on it—and God waits to see what he will make of it." Hartman seeks new ways of balancing various tendencies in the tradition: "The perennial risk facing Jews is that instead of regarding Israel as an 'echo of eternity,' they will idolize the people and the land and will sever the historical link of the people of Israel with the Torah of Israel."[4]

Five principles follow from their challenge. The first is that creation has intrinsic worth. The entire cosmos has value in and of itself, independent of human norms. No scientist can synthesize, no economist price, and no technology replace the created order.

The second principle is that all things are connected. The earth is a community of living things interconnected and mutually dependent on each other for life and survival. Whatever we humans do to the web of life, including God and the whole of creation, we do to ourselves.

The third principle has to do with custodianship. Each generation has responsibility for future generations through the care of land and other resources. We are stewards on behalf of future generations. The best interests of children and youth should govern our behavior.

The fourth principle is the indivisibility of justice. We cannot separate ecological justice from defending the rights of the occupants of the land in question or respecting the rights of children and youth. Exploitation of resources must address the needs and experiences of the people directly affected by resource extraction: the people who may be removed to clear the way for so-called development, or future generations.

The final principle is resistance. The earth and its components suffer due to the unjust activities of people. People must resist those forces that damage the integrity of creation. We must cultivate concern for humanity and earth through advocacy, education, prayer, and openness to join in nonviolent direct action.[5]

Restoring Liberty to Sufferers of Oppression

Leviticus 25:10 calls for hallowing the fiftieth year and proclaiming liberty throughout the land. Other passages indicate that no Israelite is to be enslaved. Aliens are to be welcomed. One thing not permitted is oppression of others. In the words of Spanish poet Antonio Machado, "Look for your other half / Who walks always next to you / And tends to be who you aren't."[6]

Under the umbrella of the ancient Jubilee theme, a grassroots movement made a global priority of eliminating the debts of poor countries to donor nations by the year 2000.[7] Built up over many decades, these debts passed more than two trillion US dollars by 1997. This broke down to a debt of $400 for every person in the poor world. Most of the increased debt by so-called developing countries was to pay interest on the loans.

In the poorest countries where the average income is less than a dollar a day, financing the debt burden condemns hundreds of millions of people to live in poverty and undermines human dignity. International debt diverts resources from addressing the basic needs of people including education, nutrition, health, clean water, and sanitation. International debt creates political, social, and economic instability. International debt contributes to destruction of the environment.

For some time, individuals and groups worked on the issue of debt relief in relative obscurity. In the 1990s, an international movement gained momentum. By 1999, over seventeen million people worldwide signed a Jubilee petition, a figure that has since doubled. In June 1999, forty thousand people from around the world gathered in Cologne, Germany, calling for the rich nations to erase the debts of poor countries. On behalf of the Jubilee 2000 campaign, Archbishop Oscar Rodriguez Maradiaga of Tegucigalpa, Honduras, presented the petition to German Chancellor Gerhard Schroder. Host of meetings of heads of state of the world's seven wealthiest countries, Schroder pledged, "I take you all with me . . . . With one heart and one hand you will all be there."[8]

During their meetings, the world leaders took note of the Jubilee movement and moved to relieve some of the debt. In addition to corporate action through organizations such as the World Bank and International Monetary Fund, individual countries had to act. In the United States, President William Jefferson Clinton proposed to remove $27 billion from the debt of the world's poorest countries (many of them in Africa). He said, "Unsustainable debt is helping to keep too many poor countries and poor people in poverty." A year later on 6 November 2000, he signed a bill that provides $435 million in debt relief.[9]

The Jubilee movement resembles the civil rights struggle in the United States in the 1960s and the move against apartheid in South Africa in the 1980s. People of faith have not lost the ability to dream God's dream. This healthy religious vocation is consonant with a concept that assigns to humankind co-creation or co-partnership with God in the work of redeeming history.

Seventeenth-century Jewish mystic Isaac Luria said that the Creator of the universe, deciding to make a world, contracted or drew in the divine breath in order to make room for the creation coming into being. In this enlarged space, the Creator then set vessels and poured the brilliance of divine light into them. This shattered the containers. Ever since, humans have been responsible to refashion the dispersed shards of creation, a work known as mending or fixing the world, *tikkun olam*.[10] The concept has inspired me and others to assume partnership with God in realizing the dream of God.

Restoring Economic Hope

Many details of Leviticus 25 have to do with the right economic ordering of society. For example, there should be no usurious interest. Fallow land should be distributed. Such passages have fueled the contemporary theological current known as the theology of liberation. Writing especially from the poor world, liberation theologians have focused attention on the need to give priority to and to work unreservedly for the liberation of the poor and oppressed.

We need a similar theology of liberation for the rich. Speaking for myself, I live in chains. They are not the prison doors behind which women and men are incarcerated. They are not barbed wire fences that confine refugees to camps or keep illegal aliens out of the United States. They are the more invisible chains of affluence. They shackle me and prevent me from discerning their evil effects on me. They prevent me from seeing my complicity in the suffering of others. They lead me to worship false gods. As the epistle of James states, they are a major cause of war.

What practices by the privileged will restore economic hope to the poor? Aldo Leopold made a suggestion fifty years ago. Commenting on the greed of the rich, symbolized by the "need" for more bathtubs, Leopold warned that earth has lost the capacity to sustain our obsessions. We have lost the capacity to remain healthy. "Nothing could be more salutary . . . than a little healthy contempt for a plethora of material blessing."[11]

Among other voices, Brazilian educator Paulo Freire (1921–1997) and Bishop Oscar Romero of El Salvador (1917–1980) called for humanization of the rich. Freire wrote, "As the oppressors dehumanize others and violate their rights, they themselves also become dehumanized. As the oppressed, fighting to be human, take away the oppressors' power to dominate and suppress, they restore to the oppressors the humanity they had lost in the exercise of oppression." In a letter to the churches of North America, Romero said that the idolatry of wealth and private property inclines people toward *having* more and lessens their interest in *being* more. This absolutism supports structural violence and oppression.

> The god of money forces us
> to turn our backs
> on the God of Christianity.
> Because people want a god
> who turns his back on them,
> instead of the true God—
> therefore many criticize the church.
> They kill every movement
> that tries to destroy false idols
> and give us the true God.[12]

The Jubilee campaign addresses more than the issue of international debt. It also encourages local initiatives in the arena of economic justice. In Memphis, a coalition of over a thousand religious bodies have supported several initiatives including these: (a) Participating congregations will contribute $1.00 per member for early intervention on behalf of infants at risk. One program seeks to engender learning skills on the part of preschool children and to offer their beleaguered mothers and fathers parenting skills. (b) The coalition enters into solidarity with the poor by working for elimination of the Tennessee sales tax on food. (c) The campaign supports local groups monitoring toxic wastes. (d) The campaign does education in the arena of racial and ethnic reconciliation and social justice.

Restoring the Community of God's Children

A major component of the Jubilee agenda is restriction of slavery (Lev 25:39-55). The enslavement of peoples did not stop with the demise of the Atlantic Slave Trade. Black Africans continue to be bought and sold, notably in two North African countries: Mauritania and Sudan. Moreover, millions of children around the world work in conditions of bondage. Many are given away or sold by their families and then abandoned. Children and youth work because of poverty. Many are vulnerable, especially the girl child, the disabled child, minority children, migrants, and refugees.

In 1999, two Guinean boys, Yaguine Koita (age fourteen) and Fodé Tourakana (age fifteen), were found dead in the cargo hold of an airplane in Brussels, Belgium. In a letter discovered on their dead bodies, they reveal the extent to which many are denied the basic freedoms promised all God's children. The letter read in part,

> We beseech you on behalf of your love for your continent, your people, your families, and above all your children, whom you cherish more than life itself. And for the love of God, who has granted you all the experience, wealth, and power to ably construct and organize your continent. We call upon your graciousness and solidarity to help us in Africa. Our problems are many: war, sickness, hunger, lack of education, and children's rights.
> . . . we suffer too much in Africa. We need your help in our struggle against poverty and war.
> Be mindful of us in Africa. There is no one else for us to turn to.[13]

God's people are to establish human society on the basis of right relationships both within and without the covenant community. God's people are to keep God's commandments and observe them faithfully. Then God will acknowledge them as God's people. *I will walk among you . . . and you shall be my people. I am the* LORD *your God who brought you out of the land of Egypt, to be their slaves no more; I have broken the bars of your yoke and made you walk erect* (Lev 26:12-13).

In this new millennium, to acknowledge Jubilee practices as part of God's plan to restore the original order of creation might seem unduly sanguine. Viewed from a panorama of the evils of the twentieth century, the emergence of a Jubilee movement is an extraordinary act of faith. Yet at the beginning of a new century, more people are working for justice, peace, and reconciliation than ever before.

Not only that, their work is bearing fruit. Over the past three decades, human rights organizations have made the *Universal Declaration of Human Rights* a yardstick by which we measure human progress. A campaign to promote the well-being of children contributed to adoption by the United Nations General Assembly of a Convention on the Rights of Children. A campaign to ban antipersonnel land mines led to an international treaty banning them. A similar push led to creation in 1998 of an International Criminal Court in Rome.

Massive resistance to tyranny in Eastern Europe, South Africa, Latin America, Indonesia, and the Philippines foreshadowed an international crescendo of nonviolent social change. Thousands of delegates met in May 1999 at The Hague, Holland. Living recipients of the Nobel Peace Prize launched an Appeal for Peace for the children of the world. They called upon the United Nations to declare the first decade of the new millennium, the years 2000–2010, a decade for a culture of nonviolence, and to declare the start of the decade, the year 2001, a year of education for nonviolence. The Nobel laureates stressed that nonviolence must be realized in daily life through reduction of violence and suffering.

God knew that human greed, which caused our expulsion from paradise, would lead to imbalance. Some would accumulate more than others would. Disparities would grow and threaten to overwhelm humans. So every fifty years, a grand leveling would take place. Jubilee entails release from every form of bondage and imprisonment. Jubilee practices challenge empires, patriarchal institutions, churches, nation-states, and corporations at war with God's word. Jubilee means that the meek really will inherit the earth, that the wolf and lamb one day really will lie together in peace, that one day the hungry really will have plenty to eat, and that the rich will be turned away.

Confession, forgiveness, and thanksgiving are key practices of Jubilee. Jesus admonished sinners to repent and amend their lives (John 8:11). He called upon the wealthy to set their affairs right (Mark 10:17-31 and parallels). He denounced injustice (Mark 11:15-19 and parallels). In sum, he called upon his followers to take on a new way of living. Through the practices of Jubilee, we journey the way Jesus intended and extend Jesus' *shalom* to all.

Another practice of Jubilee is worship. In Memphis from time to time, I attend a Taizé service. Canons such as *Jubilate servite, raise a song of gladness, peoples of the earth* and *Laudate omnes gentes, sing praises, all you peoples, sing praises to the Lord* pick up the Jubilee theme.[14] Jim and Jean Strathdee's collection titled *Jubilee* opens with these words:

> JUBILEE! Let the slave and the captive go free
> JUBILEE! Save the land and return it to me
> JUBILEE! Let people stand in their dignity
> In the year of God's Jubilee.[15]

The ancient prophets call us to dream dreams and nurture Jubilee practice. *The LORD . . . does not faint or grow weary . . . those who wait for the LORD shall renew their strength, they shall mount up with wings like eagles, they shall run and not be weary, they shall walk and not faint* (Isa 40:28-31). *The LORD has anointed me . . . to proclaim liberty to the captives, and release to the prisoners; to proclaim the year of the LORD's favor* (Isa 61:1-2). Isaiah and other prophets dreamed that God's redemptive work of Jubilee would unfold. Jesus proclaimed it was indeed unfolding.

Sometimes it is difficult to see God's salvation breaking in. Sometimes it is difficult to see God's reign of justice and peace unfolding, but believe this: the Lord is with us, watching over us, challenging us to bear fruit worthy of repentance. And because the Lord is with us, we may pray with confidence that one day, God's day of Jubilee will be a reality. God will see to that. Let the effect of our praying, ultimately, be righteousness, peace, and trust forever (Isa 32:16-17).

A new heaven and a new earth are on the way. One day every tear will be dried and God's purposes in creation will be fulfilled. Even death itself will be no more. The fate of the earth is bound up with the whole Jubilee agenda that sees humans and nonhumans alike as part of the drama of redemption. The fate of the earth is at stake. God is counting on us.

Prayer
God, send peace upon the earth, a deeper and more lasting peace than the world has ever known. Grant us a vision of your coming realm of justice, mercy, and peace. As you have planted a seed of virtue in every person, grant that we may water it and harvest the fruits of your peace. May truth and freedom flourish. May your name be hallowed throughout the universe. Amen.

---

[1] *Finale, Les Misérables*, a musical by Alain Boublil and Claude-Michel Schonberg.

[2] Verna J. Dozier, *The Dream of God* (Cambridge: Cowley, 1991). John Milbank writes of "the ontological priority of peace" and "infinite peace" in *Theology and Social Theory: Beyond Secular Reason* (Malden: Blackwell, 1993), 363, 432. See also David Burrell and Elena Malits, *Original Peace: Restoring God's Creation* (Mahway: Paulist, 1997).

[3] Yairah Amit, "The Jubilee Law—An Attempt at Instituting Social Justice," in *Justice and Righteousness: Biblical Themes and Their Influence*, ed. Henning Graf Reventlow and Yair Hoffman, JSOT Supplement Series 137 (Shefield: JSOT Press, 1992), 59.

[4] Martin Buber, "The Land and Its Possessors," *Israel and the World: Essays in a Time of Crisis* (New York: Schocken Books, 1948), 232. David Hartman, *Joy and Responsibility: Israel,*

Modernity and the Renewal of Judaism (Jerusalem: Ben-Zvi-Posner, 1978), 285. I am grateful to my colleague, Dr. Steve Parrish, for his comments on the Jubilee idea.

[5] Alice Walker, "The Universe Responds: Or, How I Learned We Can Have Peace On Earth," in *Mother Earth through the Eyes of Women Photographers and Writers*, ed. Judith Boice (San Francisco: Sierra Club, 1992). Sallie McFague, *Super, Natural Christians: How We Should Love Nature* (Minneapolis: Fortress, 1997).

[6] Antonio Machado, "Moral Proverbs and Folk Songs," *Times Alone*, trans. Robert Bly (Middletown: Wesleyan University Press, 1983), quoted by Maria Harris, *Proclaim* Jubilee*! A Spirituality for the Twenty-first Century* (Louisville: Westminster John Knox, 1996), 7.

[7] *New Internationalist* 312 (May 1999) provides a good overview.

[8] M. Hebblethwaite, "Chain-gang in Cologne," *Tablet* (26 June 1999); S. Lu, "Peace Power to the People," *ABCNews* (1 June), <http://abcnews.go.com>.

[9] *Memphis Commercial Appeal*, 30 September 1999 and 7 November 2000. In the United States, Pat Robertson of Christian right and relief organizations such as Bread for the World represent the wide political and religious spectrum that supports the Jubilee campaign.

[10] Harris, *Proclaim* Jubilee*!*, 15; Emil L. Fackenheim, *To Mend the World: Foundations of Future Jewish Thought* (New York: Schocken Books, 1982).

[11] Aldo Leopold wrote these words in 1948 (*A Sand County Almanac* [New York: Ballantine, 1970], xix).

[12] Paulo Freire, *Pedagogy of the Oppressed* (New York: Seabury, 1970), 42. Oscar Romero, *Voice of the Voiceless: The Four Pastoral Letters and Other Statements*, trans. Michael J. Walsh (Maryknoll: Orbis, 1985), 173; Romero cited in Daniel Berrigan, *Steadfastness of the Saints: A Journal of Peace and War in Central and North America* (Maryknoll: Orbis, 1985), 66.

[13] "A Prayer for Africa," *Harper's Magazine* (November 1999), 22.

[14] Jacques Berthier, *Songs and Prayers from Taizé* (Chicago: GIA Publications, 1991), 18, 48.

[15] Harris, *Proclaim* Jubilee*!*, 94, quotes words for *Jubilee*.

For Reflection and Conversation

- Why is Jubilee a practice of justice?

- What are the most important aspects of the biblical idea of Jubilee?

- Describe individuals or a community putting Jubilee themes into practice.

- What atmosphere fosters Jubilee?

- What is the relationship between Jubilee and evangelism?

Practices of Dialogue

The earth is the LORD's *and all that is in it, the world, and those who live in it* . . . . (Psalm 24:1)

Defining Dialogue

As I am using the word, *dialogue* means conversation coupled with embrace. If one understands dialogue as speaking words or discussing amiably in an open or pleasant manner, one misses the significance of dialogue as something fundamental to an evangelistic lifestyle. The practices of dialogue arch over virtually all the practices discussed in this book, including prayer and discernment, loving and listening, being compassionate and forgiving.

"Dialogue is a fundamental relationship with the world to which we are called."[1] The word in English comes from the Greek *dialogos* and *dialegesthai*, through the word. Broadly, dialogue is an embrace of the world, in part through words. Dialogue wells up from our being in such a way that the practitioner holds all life very close.

"All actual life is encounter."[2] By these few words, Jewish thinker Martin Buber (1878–1965) encapsulated a viewpoint that holds dialogue to be a categorical imperative. Buber's views predate contemporary interest in interfaith dialogue. From his perspective, dialogue is something *a priori*. Dialogue is a path to God leading to self-actualization. As described in autobiographical passages in his writings, Buber derives this stance from his own experience. Let me mention two incidents that led Buber to formulate his dialogical theology.[3]

When Buber was eleven years of age, he spent the summer at his grandparents' estate. As often as he could, he went unobserved to the stables where he gently stroked the neck of a broad dapple-gray horse. Ears flicking, the horse would gently raise his massive head and snort quietly. Even if young

Buber had not begun to pour oats for him, the horse always responded to Buber with an element of vitality. This routine was always a matter of delight and deeply stirring. Whenever he stroked the horse's mane, Buber felt the life beneath his hand. It was as though the two beings merged into one.

One day, it struck Buber what fun this activity was. Buber did not recall precisely what came over him, but he became conscious somehow of his hand. The next day, when Buber stroked and fed his friend, the horse did not raise his head. The horse and Buber's hand were objectified. What had been an *I-Thou* experience, a relationship between two subjects, became an *I-It* experience, an encounter between two objects.

The second crucial incident occurred in autumn 1914 after the outbreak of the First World War. Buber spent a morning of "religious enthusiasm." Without describing that experience, Buber said he received a visitor that afternoon. He did so in a friendly manner but without being there in spirit. The lingering glow of his ecstatic experience prevented Buber from being present to the essential content of the visit. Buber answered questions as though he were an *I* speaking to an *It*. A short while later, Buber learned that his visitor had sought him out "not for a chat but for a decision." The young man died. Buber was overwhelmed with remorse for having neglected the anguish and need that had led the young man to his door.

Buber called the moment "a conversion." Up to that time, he considered religion as the experience of otherness. Religion had nothing to do with everyday life. From then on, he regarded every encounter as having the potential for communion. "We expect a theophany of which we know nothing but the place, and the place is called community."[4]

Dialogue, then, is not one practice among others. It is foundational to others. It is to see the world charged with God's grandeur (this is the title of a poem by Gerard Manley Hopkins, 1844–1889) and to move toward wholeness and the well-being of *all* creation.

Interfaith Dialogue as a Long-term Christian Commitment

A specific practice of dialogue arises from the fact that we live in a religiously plural world. We cannot share a word with others in mutuality and embrace without considering the faith by which people live. Kenneth Cragg (b. 1913) often makes this point. Former Anglican Bishop of Jerusalem, Cragg has lived throughout the Middle East and writes, "Christianity cannot address men and ignore their gods: it may not act in the present and disown the past or wisely hold forth salvation and withhold salutation. In seeking men for Christ's sake, it is committed to the significance of all they are in their birth and their tradition, both for good or ill."[5]

The interest of Christians in other religions is not new. Early Christians seriously grappled with issues raised by their encounters with adherents of the religions and philosophies of late antiquity. Now, dialogue has tended to be seen as a profession with denominational or academic career tracks, formal times, and criteria to guide discussion and worship. So to constrict dialogue is unfortunate. It has the effect of limiting Christian witness amid people of other faiths to academics or church bureaucrats who earn a living from the dialogue process.

Religion is both individual and communal. This latter, communal dimension arises because religion is an aspect of culture. Religion and culture are not the same. However sensitive you may be to culture, however well you learn the language and mores of a people, however sensitive your presentation of the universal gospel may be to a specific context, interreligious dialogue takes the practitioner to the depths of his or her being. Bishop Cragg asks, "Are we not faced with an otherness which cannot be reduced, abated, merged, or interchanged?"[6]

A few solitary explorers have taken up this challenge. Buber's seminal ideas about dialogue led him to study and embrace adherents of other religions. His encounters with Christianity enriched his life as a Jew and the lives of Christians as well. His practice of dialogue revealed a striking feature of the great spiritual adventurers of this century. Buber plumbed the depths of religions other than his own yet remained true to his tradition.[7]

Christian practitioners of dialogue include Mother Teresa (1910–1997) of Calcutta. She loved Indians of all religions. When she died in 1997, they expressed their love for her. Another person I think of in terms of dialogue as a genuine meeting of peoples is Charlotte Digges (Lottie) Moon (1840–1912). A Baptist from the southern United States, she spent forty years in China and developed strong friendships with adherents of traditional Chinese religion. Similarly, the Catholic monk Thomas Merton (1915–1968) befriended the Zen Buddhist scholar D. T. Suzuki (1870–1966) and Vietnamese Buddhist monk Thich Nhat Hanh (b. 1926). French Catholic scholar of Islam Louis Massignon (1883–1962) was described, when he died, by a Muslim authority, "He was a true Christian and a true Muslim."[8]

In India, Charles Freer Andrews (1871–1940), Eli Stanley Jones (1884–1973), and Henri Le Saux (1910–1973) each became part of an ashram where they undertook instruction in Hindu traditions guided by Hindu sages. Each believed that such study must precede the emergence of an Indian church. Under the name of Swami Abhishiktananda, Le Saux incorporated his studies of the Upanishads and other classic Hindu texts in his writing. His successor Bede Griffiths (1906–1993), a Benedictine monk, wrote a commentary on the *Bhagavad Gita*, another classic Hindu text.

These exemplars of mutuality and openness in interfaith dialogue make some truths foundational to Christianity very clear. God has become one with us (John 1). God receives us as we are (Luke 15:11-32). We are to become all things to all people (1 Cor 9:22).

It is important to notice the relational aspect of Jesus' practice and the practice of his early followers. First, Jesus and his friends entered into dialogue with all sorts of different people, including people of different faiths. Second, Jesus and his disciples met all people with acceptance, freedom, and love. Third, Jesus and his friends met people on their own terms. In short, Jesus and his followers met people at the level of relationship rather than of dogma. Jesus practiced a dialogue of love that led toward deeper levels of encounter and embrace.

The Practice of Encountering "The Other"

Another important practice of dialogue is to encounter difference in a positive light. Many Christians in North America do not often meet people of other faiths or engage in interfaith dialogue. Yet daily they may encounter a great deal of diversity.

There has been a good deal of contemporary discussion about the meaning of difference. Edward Said, Edith Wyschogrod, and other scholars explore how people craft "the Other" in different images. For example, Europeans once tended to project the image of nobility upon people of color. This idea of the noble savage gave way, subsequently, to the image of "the primitive," an idea foundational to the racist contamination of Christianity in the West.[9] To paraphrase words of the musical *South Pacific*, we have to be taught very carefully to hate.

When we practice dialogue, the Other is freed to represent himself or herself. A possible outcome is desire for justice on behalf of the Other. This requires that we meet people on their own terms. When we recognize and appreciate the Other, we allow the Holy Spirit to work. Religion becomes *a* if not *the* source of embrace. *When the Spirit of truth comes, he will guide you into all the truth; for he will not speak on his own, but will speak whatever he hears, and he will declare to you the things that are to come* (John 16:13).

The converse is that, when we do not recognize and appreciate the Other, religion becomes *a* if not *the* source of friction. A daughter of a missionary in a contemporary novel, Adah Price, writes, "Illusions mistaken for truth are the pavement under our feet. They are what we call civilization."[10] Woe to us if, after proclaiming to others the things that are to come, we should ourselves be disqualified from God's embrace (1 Cor 9:27).

Religion is a factor in destructive conflicts in former Yugoslavia, Northern Ireland, the Holy Land, Lebanon, Sri Lanka, and elsewhere. In these and other cases, religion is not the sole or even primary cause of strife. Historically, however, misuse of religion in the manufacture of the Other has fueled intractable violence toward the Other.

Commenting on the pathos of religion, Jewish scholar Jacob Neusner suggests a possible explanation. He observes that religions have proved incapable of forming a useful theory of the Other. By erecting powerful barriers that differentiate groups of believers, or believers from nonbelievers, religious teachers encourage adepts to confront otherness through excess. One result is "that believers not only love one another, they hate everybody else."[11]

French-born literary critic René Girard (b. 1923) discloses the violent mechanisms of human culture in the manufacture of otherness. Since ancient times, the central problem in all societies has been violence. All evil hinges on this one evil. Religion must deal with it. The sacred must remove the veil of violence through sacrifice. Girard writes, "The function of sacrifice is to quell violence in the community and to prevent conflicts from erupting."[12]

The role of religion, according to Girard, is to save communities from the destructive effects of violence by deflecting the violence onto a surrogate or scapegoat, which is sacrificed ritually. Thus, sacrifice and scapegoating are religiously justified, romanticized, sacralized, and imitated means to sublimate internal strife and prevent violence from erupting in such forms as a blood feud.

Sacrifice may have served this function in Lebanon or former Yugoslavia before violence erupted in the recent, tragic histories of these countries. In these and other cases, Christians (not Christians alone) became enmeshed in the violence. Mechanisms intended as antidote to fear and hate ultimately failed.

Always and inevitably, we humans fail. God alone sets in motion the only mechanism that can end our imprisonment to violence. The cross alone breaks the escalating spiral of violence. God suffers violence rather than sponsors it. God forgives rather than blames those who perpetuate evil.

Girard's theory cannot be validated or falsified and is too complex to discuss further here. His reconstruction fits with many stories. In Genesis 4–5, for example, Cain kills his brother. God intervenes to protect Cain's life. At stake is a threatening cycle of vengeance. The story reaches a dead end when Lamech, Cain's distant ancestor, kills a man and boasts that he will be avenged seventy-sevenfold. Lamech claims he acted justifiably. He killed a man who had wounded him. Developing an ethic of forgiveness is needed to halt the engine driving a cycle of violent revenge.

Genesis 22 records another ancient story, the binding of Isaac. In Jewish practice, it is read and discussed on the second day of *Rosh Hashanah*, the New Year. Typically, commentaries stress the faith of Abraham. An exception is the Danish theologian Soren Kierkegaard (1813–1855), who was clearly nauseated by the idea of faith in a story about a father who would kill his son. In his praise or panegyric to Abraham, a section of *Fear and Trembling*, Kierkegaard questions Abraham's ethics. Is there such a thing as an absolute duty toward God? Do we really believe that no sacrifice, even human sacrifice, is too great a duty if God demands it? Who is this God who lusts for blood? Kierkegaard says that the real question is how we should live. The real ethical duty is to love.[13]

This is the crucial point. Through the ages, Christians have failed to live out the love ethic manifest in God's sacrificial act in Christ. We have failed for many reasons. These are reasons of history, cultural blindness, nationalism, ideology, and our common humanity. Christians must change gears. Christians must shift from confrontation and violence to dialogue and embrace. If and only when we meet the Other will we do justice. "We have marched around alien Jerichos the requisite number of times. We have sounded the trumpets. And the walls have not collapsed."[14]

How do we embrace the Other? What constitutes "otherness" is not always self-evident. Usually, religion entails belief in God or ultimate reality, though some Buddhists, Taoists, and secularists are essentially atheistic. Usually, religion entails certain prescribed behavior (ethics, worship, and institutional membership). Here again, there are differences and exceptions. Judaism and Hinduism blur the distinction between religion, ethnicity, and nationality. Generally, a mosque functions differently for the Muslim than does the church building for Christians in the West.

Powerful conceptions of reality and pervasive patterns of thinking, being, and doing shape a person's *religious identity* as *religious*. Knowing a person as a fervent Shiite Muslim tells you more about that person than knowing his or her Arab or Iranian or Indonesian background. Meeting a religiously observant Jew is substantially a different and more intense experience than encountering a Jew in the broad sense of ethnicity or an Israeli or a member of a local Jewish benevolence organization.

The practice of dialogue becomes, therefore, a most challenging and vexing desideratum. Dialogue requires an engagement with others in openness and mutual concern. To live by dialogue creates an environment in which mutual transformation can occur.

Through this book, we have considered evangelism in the light of God's choosing us as beloved children. Christ has restored our belovedness. The Holy Spirit invites people to become what they already are, children of God, loved with the same unconditional divine love as God loved Jesus. Evangelization is inviting another person to respond to God's acceptance in and through the Beloved. How does this happen when the other is a member of another religion?

It happens quite simply when we present Jesus in our lives. This is what Paul concluded as he wrestled with the issue in relationship to Judaism. Disappointed that Jews did not accept Jesus as the Christ, Paul concluded, *I ask, then, has God rejected his people? By no means! I myself am an Israelite, a descendant of Abraham, a member of the tribe of Benjamin. God has not rejected his people . . .* (Rom 11:1-2).

We may present Jesus in our lives with integrity. Among contemporary writers on dialogue, I have found Lesslie Newbigin (1909–1998) to be an especially creative guide. Ordained in 1936 by the Church of Scotland for missionary work in India, he served as a village evangelist and was an architect and bishop of the Church of South India. In Britain during retirement, Newbigin promoted active engagement of Christians with the traditions and worldviews of modern society. Without question, he affirmed that salvation comes through Jesus Christ. In humility, he acknowledged that God's salvific work is not complete. With risk, he walked the road of dialogue as a way to find common ground with all people. With boldness, he glorified God.

Newbigin suggests seven essential steps if we are to practice dialogue. These steps are a roadmap to the widest experience of dialogue. First, we must be prepared for a journey. A pilgrim must be ready to take risks and determined not to be put off by discouragement. Jesus walks with us. We may trust him to guide us. Second, we must acknowledge the freedom of every individual to search and be embraced by the truth. Third, dialogue requires a genuine engagement by all Christians with culture. Fourth, if we are self-critical and open in dialogue, we are granted the freedom to critique other cultures and religions. Fifth, we must acknowledge horrors done in the name of Jesus Christ. At the same time, we may point others to Christ by our grace-filled living, by our doing justice, and by our becoming stewards of earth's resources. We may help people see Jesus in the saints who mirror Christ. Sixth, we must have the courage to hold to what we believe to be true, though it cannot be proved. *We have become partners of Christ, if only we hold our first confidence firm to the end* (Heb 3:14). Finally, we must make our churches places of joy, praise, surprise, and laughter. In Christ, we experience a foretaste of the endless surprises of heaven.[15]

Despite the massive efforts of Christians to share Christ with peoples of other faiths, two-thirds of humanity is not Christian. A fruit of modern Christian missions is that, in most parts of the world, Christians daily witness to the love of God in their lives. Young Christians in the two-thirds world manifest the enduring validity of dialogue.

In the 1970s, a Baptist denomination appointed my wife and me as missionaries to what was then called Zaire. We did not serve at the time for various reasons. Notably, this was a period in which churches in the two-thirds world called for a moratorium on sending new appointments and for "authenticity" in native practice. North American and European boards withdrew missionaries from foreign fields.

Fortunately, we live in a new day of mutuality and partnership. Internationally, the sending and receiving of missionaries is a two-way phenomenon. As a result of a renewed commitment to live dialogically, Christianity grows numerically in many parts of the world. Moreover, a generation of younger missiologists, including Lamin Sanneh of Gambia, Kwame Bediako of Ghana, and Marcel Oyono of Cameroon acknowledge an enormous debt of gratitude to missionaries as pioneers, cultural bridges, and translators.

Interfaith dialogue as well as mutually satisfying encounters of trust and embrace are needed if humanity is to survive. According to Art and Jocele Meyer—farmers, teachers, and former Mennonite Central Committee volunteers in Grenada—people of faith must cooperate if we are to deal with ten issues crucial to our survival. The global agenda requires cooperation in areas such as environmental degradation; the arms race; threat of nuclear proliferation; blind adherence to political-economic systems incompatible with biblical justice; the scandal of hunger in a world that has the capacity to feed everyone adequately; the need for everyone to have meaningful employment; the growing gap between the rich and the poor; food and agricultural policies that contribute to the collapse of rural societies; population growth; and the legacy of neocolonial policies manifest in the global debt issue.[16]

We can expand the list. Christians must reach out to people who are different. In an interdependent world, Christians following Jesus must fight all that destroys life in community with others. By our living, we make known the great reality that God, creator and sustainer of all, exists. God sent Jesus to give us life. The Spirit sustains us in our living. Knowing the reality of the triune God, we experience an ocean of infinite love overflowing to all creation, to all human beings.

Regarding "True Religion," William Penn (1644–1718) wrote, "The humble, meek, merciful, just, pious and devout souls are everywhere of one religion; and when death has taken off the mask, they will know one another, though the divers liveries they were here makes them strangers." I believe Jesus is eagerly welcoming the signs of faith among men and women outside the Christian house. One day, all will see Jesus, hands outstretched on the cross, lovingly welcoming those whom others cast out.

Prayer
Eternal God, we praise you for love, wisdom, and light present since the beginning of the universe. Help all to grow toward the fullness of life and love seen in Jesus. May all be free from evil. May you be recognized by all people, by the few I know and by the many of every place on earth I do not know, that they may come to know the happiness of loving you who first loved us and taught us to love through Jesus Christ. Amen.

---

[1] David Lochhead, *The Dialogical Imperative: A Christian Reflection on Interfaith Encounter* (Maryknoll: Orbis, 1988), 85.

[2] Martin Buber, *I and Thou*, trans. Walter Kaufmann (New York: Charles Scribner's Sons, 1970), 62. Published in 1923 in German. *I and Thou* first appeared in English translation in 1937. In the prologue to his translation, Kaufmann describes the work as a masterpiece that deals centrally with relationships and with the development of a new sense of community among humans (38).

³ Martin Buber, "Autobiographical Fragments," trans. Maurice Friedman in *The Philosophy of Martin Buber*, ed. Paul Arthur Schilpp and Maurice Friedman (La Salle: Open Court, 1967), 10, 25-26; *Between Man and Man*, trans. Ronald Gregor Smith (New York: Macmillan, 1947), 13-14, 22-23.

⁴ Buber, *Between Man and Man*, 7.

⁵ Kenneth Cragg, *Christianity in World Perspective* (London: Lutterworth Press, 1968), cited by John V. Taylor, *The Go-Between God: The Holy Spirit and the Christian Mission* (London: SCM, 1972), 181.

⁶ *Alive to God: Muslim and Christian Prayer* (Oxford: Oxford University Press, 1970), 4.

⁷ Martin Buber, *Two Types of Faith*, trans. Norman P. Goldhawk (New York: Macmillan, 1951). In his essay "Apologies to an Unbeliever," Thomas Merton described himself as a "solitary explorer who, instead of jumping on all the latest bandwagons at once, is bound to search the existential depths of faith . . . ." (*Faith and Violence: Christian Teaching and Christian Practice* [Notre Dame: University of Notre Dame, 1968], 213).

⁸ Donald Nicholl, *The Beatitude of Truth: Reflections of a Lifetime* (London: Darton, Longman and Todd, 1997), 150. See Gerald H. Anderson, ed., *Biographical Dictionary of Christian Missions* (New York: Macmillan Reference USA, 1998) for entries on several figures mentioned in the text. For Griffith's commentary, see *Bhagavad Gita, River of Compassion* (Warwick: Amity House, 1987).

⁹ Edward W. Said, *Orientalism* (New York: Vintage, 1979); Edith Wyschogrod, *Saints and Postmodernism: Revisioning Moral Philosophy* (Chicago: University of Chicago, 1990); Ashley Montague, ed., *The Concept of the Primitive* (New York: Free Press, 1968); Alan Davies, *Infected Christianity: A Study of Modern Racism* (Kingston: Mc-Gill, Queen's University Press, 1988).

¹⁰ Barbara Kingsolver, *The Poisonwood Bible* (New York: HarperCollins, 1999), 532.

¹¹ Jacob Neusner, "Thinking about 'the Other' in Religion: It Is Necessary, but Is It Possible?" *Modern Theology* 6/3 (April 1990): 273; reprinted in *Ministry and Theology in Global Perspective: Contemporary Challenges for the Church*, ed. Don A. Pittman, Ruben L. F. Habito, and Terry C. Muck (Grand Rapids: Eerdmans, 1996), 466.

¹² René Girard, *Violence and the Sacred*, trans. Patrick Gregory (Baltimore: Johns Hopkins University Press, 1979), 14. For a significant engagement with Girard's ideas, see Gil Bailie, *Violence Unveiled: Humanity at the Crossroads* (New York: Crossroad, 1995).

¹³ Soren Kierkegaard, *Fear and Trembling*, trans. Walter Lowrie (New York: Doubleday, 1954); Walter Kaufmann, introduction, in Soren Kierkegaard, *The Present Age*, trans. Alexander Dru (New York: Harper, 1962).

¹⁴ Max Warren, cited by Wilfred Cantwell Smith, *The Faith of Other Men* (New York: New American Library, 1963), 120. See also Miroslav Volf, *Exclusion and Embrace: A Theological Exploration of Identity, Otherness, and Reconciliation* (Nashville: Abingdon, 1996); Charles Taylor, "The Politics of Recognition," in *Multiculturalism and "The Politics of Recognition"* (Princeton: Princeton University Press, 1992).

¹⁵ Lesslie Newbigin, *Foolishness to the Greeks: The Gospel and Western Culture* (Grand Rapids: Eerdmans, 1986); *The Gospel in a Pluralist Society* (Grand Rapids: Eerdmans, 1989); *Unfinished Agenda: An Autobiography* (Grand Rapids: Eerdmans, 1985).

¹⁶ Art and Jocele Meyer, "Ten Global Issues for Christian Reflection," in *Earthkeepers: Environmental Perspectives on Hunger, Poverty, and Injustice* (Scottdale: Herald Press, 1991), 36-39.

For Reflection and Conversation

- Why is dialogue a practice of justice?

- What are the most important features of dialogue?

- What are the most important impediments to dialogue?

- What has been your experience with people of religious traditions, worldviews, and philosophies other than your own? What atmosphere fosters dialogue with these friends?

- What is the relationship between dialogue and evangelism?

Practices of Servant Leadership

For I have set you an example, that you also should do as I have done to you. Very truly, I tell you, servants are not greater than their master, nor are messengers greater than the one who sent them. (John 13:15-16)

"Servanthood" Is a Good Word

Commonly in ancient Israel, a servant referred to a slave, in Greek *doulos*—a person of either sex serving a master. When the prophets applied the concept of servant to a leader such as Moses or a king, they generally understood the role of servant in relationship to a sacred calling.

The prophets judged servant leaders by what they did or did not do to fulfill Israel's responsibility to the covenants. Isaiah gave the title *servant* to a figure whose call, mission, sufferings, death, and glorification would bring liberation, healing, and justice to all. The servant referred to as being *my servant* (Isa 42:1; 49:3, 6; 52:13; 53:11) is sometimes called the servant of God (Isa 49:5) or the *suffering servant* (based on Isa 52:13–53:12). The religious significance of the servant lay in this: "he not only encountered and accepted suffering in the course of his work; in the final phase suffering became the means whereby he accomplished his work, and was effective in the salvation of others."[1]

> Here is my servant, whom I uphold, my chosen, in whom my soul delights;
> I have put my spirit upon him; he will bring forth justice to the nations.
> He will not cry or lift up his voice, or make it heard in the street;
> a bruised reed he will not break, and a dimly burning wick he will not
>   quench;
> he will faithfully bring forth justice . . . .
> I am the LORD, I have called you in righteousness,
> I have taken you by the hand and kept you;

*I have given you as a covenant to the people, a light to the nations,
to open the eyes that are blind, to bring out the prisoners from the dungeon,
from the prison those who sit in darkness* (Isa 42: 1-3, 6-7)

Generally, Christians associate the servant figure with Jesus. Jesus inverts the relationship between servant and master. Jesus is the Servant King who enters Jerusalem on a donkey. Jesus is the Servant Messiah who hangs on the cross. Jesus is the Servant Prophet who models servant leadership to followers. *Servants are not greater than their master, nor are messengers greater than the one who sent them* (John 13:16).

When Jesus began his active ministry, he was blessed by God as the Beloved (Mark 1:11 and parallels). He gathered disciples to be with him. He formed them and sent them out to widen the circle of his friends, sent by Jesus into the world. Jesus established a new way to think of leadership. To be a servant leader meant *voluntary* subordination and radical obedience in *service* (*diakonia*) to his call and sending out, not the *involuntary* work of a slave on behalf of a master.

Throughout the history of Christianity, servant leadership has been risky. Sometimes it has culminated in death. In 1665, someone sent a box of clothes from London to Eyam, a village in Derbyshire, England. Unwittingly, this transmitted the plague. To stop it from spreading farther, the villagers of Eyam isolated themselves voluntarily. Within a year, some 259 of the 350 villagers died.

Each year on the last Sunday of August in Eyam, a service of worship commemorates their voluntary sacrifice. In Memphis, Tennessee, we recall the sacrifice of Constance and her companions who died in 1878 while nursing others during a yellow fever epidemic. The annals of Christian history highlight the voluntary sacrifice of Damien of Molokai (Joseph Damien De Veuster, 1840–1889), the Flemish missionary who died of leprosy contracted from those he served. These are but a few of countless servant leaders who model their lives on Jesus' life.

Servant leadership *can* correct the pride and power implicit in hierarchy and patriarchy. Some traditions dramatize the example Jesus set through the practice of foot-washing on Maundy Thursday. In Catholicism, the Pope washes the feet of some of the faithful who gather in Rome. In the Anglican tradition, bishops wash the feet of some of the clergy and laity of various dioceses. In traditions that do not practice foot-washing, other ritual acts reverse roles to express Jesus' model of servant leadership. Baptist congregations, for example, are egalitarian at least in principle. Pastors, deacons, or other leaders distribute bread and juice to congregants and one another during the ordinance of the Lord's Supper.

However, we often ignore the deep significance of Jesus' actions. Gertrude Lebans, a priest of the Anglican Church of Canada, states, "For women, the image of servanthood has created a trap of millennial proportions."[2] Using the biblical image of servant as a weapon, men tell women that women are to submit graciously to the authority of men and to the authority of patriarchal institutions. Citing "household" texts like *Wives, be subject to your husbands as you are to the Lord* (Eph 5:22; see also Col 3:18), men tell wives to submit to their husbands, even when husbands fail to honor the ironclad law of love.

In modern North America, many women, especially women of color, shoulder economic duties as a form of virtual slavery. In Memphis each morning, along a busy thoroughfare, a stream of cars—not any cars but commonly a torrent of Lexus, Mercedes, and sports utility vehicles—transport "haves" to center city from gated communities and suburban homes. Along the same route in the opposite direction, a trickle of less ostentatious vehicles carry "have-nots" to their destinations. Low-paid workers, generally African American women, dismount from the city buses and go to the houses and nursing homes of the "haves."

There are other problems with the servant image of leadership. I am leery of people who want to serve others. Often, they are motivated to serve for the wrong reasons. Some think that they are earning merit. Some respond to the inner voice of parents: "You have to be good."[3] Some take jobs away from people or deprive grassroots organizations of the capacity to solve problems. Some violate a rule of empowerment, that one should never do for others what they can do for themselves. Servant leaders allow those served to feel that they have the power to do this or that themselves.[4]

Acknowledging that servanthood is a problematic concept, I use it primarily because Jesus offers a model of a genuinely egalitarian social order. Servant leaders must resist those powers and principalities that seek to undermine his model. Jesus cannot be used to justify the violation of human rights. Jesus cannot be used to create domination systems of oppression.

Becoming Friends of Jesus

In *The Blue Mountains of China* (1970), Canadian Mennonite Rudy Wiebe presents a modern story of servant leadership. Symbolically through the saga of the central character, John Reimer, Wiebe guides readers through a wilderness of crisis, despair, materialism, and the general falling apart of things. Reimer is on pilgrimage in search of the Beloved Community of peace and justice. The settings range from Russia to Paraguay to China. In the last chapter, "On the Way," Reimer lands at Toronto's Pearson International Airport and begins a trans-Canada trek. He picks up a cross and calls people to follow Jesus. Reimer describes what friends of Jesus do.

> The church Jesus began is *us living, everywhere, a new society* that sets all the old ideas of people living with others on its head, that looks so strange it is either the most stupid, foolish thing on earth, or it is so beyond our usual thinking that it could only come as a revelation right from God. Jesus says in his society there is a new way for us to live:
> you show wisdom, by trusting people;
> you handle leadership, by serving;
> you handle offenders, by forgiving;
> you handle money, by sharing;
> you handle enemies, by loving;
> and you handle violence, by suffering.
>
> In fact you have a new attitude toward everything, toward everybody. Toward nature, toward the state in which you happen to live, toward women, toward slaves, toward all and every single thing. Because this is a Jesus society and you repent, not by feeling bad, but by *thinking different.* Different. This is the new society of "church" and Jesus is its Lord. The kingdom of God is within your grasp, repent and believe the good news![5]

Throughout this book, I have written about claiming our identity as God's beloved children and following Jesus. I have introduced practices that allow us to deepen our walk with Jesus. I have cautioned that the practices are not new. At some level, we are familiar with each of them. Probably, I have written little that is new to most readers. Most of us know about praying. After all, we pray. Most of us know about loving. After all, we are loving people. Most of us know about forgiving. After all, we do forgive others. Well, usually. I am trying to emphasize that at a deep level, we are not to take these practices lightly. Each takes a lifetime to learn. Each takes a lifetime to risk.

Following Jesus is not ordinary. Writing in North America, I would say that following Jesus is utterly foreign to our culture. Participating in the culture at large, we can identify aspects of our common experience that make it difficult to befriend Jesus. Challenging features of our society include the lure of instant wealth, information without knowledge, manipulation of the body, sensory overload, sex without love, and vicarious adventure through celebrities.

Friends of Jesus listen to different music. We have already touched on several key practices by which we resist the allure of the dominant culture and maintain friendship with Jesus. These are the practices of holiness discussed in part I, including prayer, Sabbath observance, and godly play. Other disciplines such as study of Scripture and fasting are also crucial. We have looked at how we can discern Jesus' call on our lives. This can lead to meaningful action in Christ's name.

Another ingredient is the formation of community. There is no such thing as a solitary Christian. Nevertheless, many Christians do not find community in the churches and congregations of which they are a part. Many Christians do not experience the mutuality the Apostle Paul had in mind when he wrote, *We who are strong ought to put up with the failings of the weak, and not to please ourselves. Each of us must please our neighbor* (Rom 15:1-6).

New Testament scholar Paul S. Minear surveys several crucial images of the church: the people of God, the new creation, the body of Christ, and a servant- or slave-church. Minear emphasizes the mutual dependence of the community on Christ in the following list:

> to die with him — to live with him
> to suffer with — to be glorified with
> to be crucified with — to be raised with
> to be baptized with — to be made alive with
> to be buried with — to sit with
> to be planted with — to rule with
> to be conformed to — to come with.[6]

Every once in a while I glimpse the Beloved Community early Christians formed. One of these moments was in summer 1992. At the close of the second International Baptist Peace Conference in Nicaragua, women pastors from around the world led communion. Children from the countryside wove their way among us. I heard what sounded to me like the heartbeat from all over the world: eastern and western Germany, eastern and western Europe, North America, Indonesia, the Philippines, India, Cuba, El Salvador, South Africa, Nicaragua, and elsewhere. They represented a marketplace of grassroots communities: Amnesty International, peace movements, Greenham's Common, the Women's International League for

Peace and Freedom, Greenpeace, and others. Through liturgy and song, we were for that moment anyway a rainbow of hope, a sign pointing to a future, reconciled world. Mountains moved. People danced. Worshiping God, we represented the community of faithful witnesses to the length God has gone to restore broken community.

In a flash, we saw coming the time when swords will be hammered into ploughshares and nations shall not even study war; when the proud shall be scattered, the mighty pulled down, the lowly ones exalted, and the hungry filled with good things; when God will wipe every tear from our eyes. Death will be no more; mourning and crying and pain will be no more. And the holy one of God will give water as a gift from the spring of the water of life, sparkling like crystal, flowing from the throne of God and of the Lamb down the city streets. On either side of the river will be the tree of life. Its leaves shall be for the healing of the nations.

I was not alone in understanding this time as similar to that John experienced when he heard loud voices in heaven saying, *The kingdom of the world has become a kingdom of our Lord and of his Messiah, and he will reign forever and ever* (Rev 11:15). This transitory, ecstatic time did not fade but motivated participants to reclaim their responsibility as earthkeepers, stewards of *the world, and those who live in it* (Ps 24:1).

Community is needed as one begins to address another ingredient in servant leadership—just stewardship of money. Because our culture conditions us well in economic matters, it is hard to move from attitudes toward money characteristic in North America to a perspective shaped by New Testament teachings about economic justice. A society that does not provide for the health and well-being of all is toxic. The sickness affects the whole of society, including myself. I am not pleased by the extent that I am encumbered and become uneasy when I read the instructions of Jesus to the twelve disciples (Matt 10) and to seventy others (Luke 10) to take very little and rely on the good will of others. I am even more uncomfortable when I read the accounts of Jesus meeting a rich young man. Jesus told him to give everything to the poor and have his treasure in heaven (Matt 19:16-30 and parallels). It is no wonder that the early Protestant reformer Martin Luther observed, "There are three conversions necessary: the conversion of the heart, the mind, and the purse."[7]

As we move toward a just stewardship of money, a caring community of faith can help hold us accountable. We can implement basic practices including giving generously, practicing hospitality, and simplifying our lives.

We can run our businesses, institutions, and organizations justly. We can study basic principles of a nonviolent economy, including trusteeship, cooperation, social development, and equal access of all to basic resources, productive opportunities, and needed goods.

In November 1996, the United States Roman Catholic bishops approved a ten-point "Ethical Framework for Economic Life." It is a thoughtful and concise document useful for study in local congregations and groups of all types. The ten points follow.

1. The economy exists for the person, not the person for the economy.
2. All economic life should be shaped by moral principles. Economic choices and institutions must be judged by how they protect or undermine the life and dignity of the human person, support the family, and serve the common good.
3. A fundamental moral measure of any economy is how the poor and vulnerable are faring.
4. All people have a right to life and to secure the basic necessities of life.
5. All people have the right to economic initiative, to productive work, to just wages and benefits, and to decent working conditions, as well as to organize and join unions and other associations.
6. All people, to the extent they are able, have a corresponding duty to work, a responsibility to provide for the needs of their families, and an obligation to contribute to the broader society.
7. In economic life, free markets have both clear advantages and limits; government has essential responsibilities and limitations; voluntary groups have irreplaceable roles, but cannot substitute for the proper working of the market and the just policies of the state.
8. Society has a moral obligation, including governmental action where necessary, to assure opportunity, meet basic human needs, and pursue justice in economic life.
9. Workers, owners, managers, stockholders, and consumers are moral agents in economic life. By our choices, initiative, creativity, and investment, we enhance or diminish economic opportunity, community life, and social justice.
10. The global economy has moral dimensions and human consequences. Decisions on investment, trade, aid, and development should protect human life and promote human rights, especially for those most in need wherever they might live on this globe.[8]

A final ingredient in servant leadership is serving in the gaps. A servant church is a church at the margins. In biblical terms, the margins are on the periphery of the mainstream of society. The margins are places of vulnerability, holiness, and power. Structures are turned upside down. The weak are lifted up. By entering into the pain of the world, we are led to the margins. This is a good place to be. We come to know who we are, our limits, our sinfulness, our inability to fix things, whose we are, and those we are called to serve. Among the marginalized we discover the mission of God. In the desert places we enter into solidarity with the marginalized.

School of Servant Leadership

The Church of the Saviour in Washington, DC, offers a model of servant leadership. Begun in the late 1940s by Gordon Cosby and a few others, the church exists now as a network of servant leadership ministries around North America including Seattle, Washington; Toronto, Ontario; and Memphis, Tennessee.

Essential to the Church of the Saviour model is participation in small groups. Generally, each group has no more than a dozen members. Each develops a set of practices common to members of the group. Size of the group is deemed less important than faithfulness to both dimensions of the Christian journey. Members hold in creative tension the inward journey and outward journey. Unless one is involved in both, discipleship is shallow and not Christ-like.

The Memphis School of Servant Leadership has adopted the following statement:

> being transformed toward the image of Christ through spiritual discipline compassionate and well-versed in the art of loving;
> well-grounded in committed community;
> committed to building relationships with persons who are poor, outcast and lost;
> committed to the transformation of the world through courageous and sacrificial living.
>
> Our vision is to sponsor servant leaders who renew the church as servant in the world and, in so doing, recall us to our vocation as "the repairers of the breach and restorers of the streets to live in."[9]

Becoming a Servant Community

As a body of believers, Christians find their reason for being, their *raison d'être*, as the church becomes a loving community of disciples of the crucified and risen Jesus, confessing that Jesus is Savior. As witnesses to his forgiveness and reconciliation, we become a covenant community of solidarity and hope. We must be patient with people if they are slow to join in the process. Each generation has to find its own way, language, and symbols.

The church of my dreams is one place where all men, women, and children realize their humanity. The church is not same as the realm of God, but it is an anticipatory sign that points the way to God and to God's commonwealth of justice and peace.

We need to dream new images of the church in terms of servant leadership. One image is the church in the round. Theologian Letty Russell uses this image to evoke what kitchens are like.[10] Kitchens tend to be a bit messy. Kitchen tables often are round. A lot of community activity takes place at kitchen tables: passing food, table talk, trying out new dishes and new ideas and so on. We are describing a place of connection and freedom. For many the church in the round is a powerful symbol of servant leadership. The metaphor evokes creativity, diversity, equality, hospitality, humility, partnership, passion, service, and vulnerability. We are describing a church becoming a place where people respond to the despair, hopelessness, and pressures of life more effectively.

Another image may come to mind. What is crucial is to discover structures that will better enable us to live out our corporate call through which the redeeming work of Christ will be seen throughout the world.

Prayer
Jesus, you are God calling, God caring, God drawing, God loving, God saving, God serving. Thanks be to God for you! Thanks be to you for showing us God. Amen.

---

[1] C. R. North, "Servant of the Lord," *Interpreter's Dictionary of the Bible* (Nashville: Abingdon, 1962) 4:294. The "servant songs" are Isa 42:1-4; 49:1-6; 50:4-9; and 52:13–53:12. For a discussion of servant leadership, see John Howard Yoder, *The Politics of Jesus: Vicit Agnus Noster* (Grand Rapids: Eerdmans, 1972), ch. 9.

[2] Gertrude Lebans, "Liberating Our Images of Ministry," in *Gathered by the River: Reflections and Essays of Women Doing Ministry*, ed. Gertrude Lebans (Toronto: Artemis, 1994), 96.

[3] "Wild Geese," a poem by Mary Oliver, opens with these words: "You do not have to be good. You do not have to walk on your knees for a hundred miles through the desert, repenting" (*Dream Work* [New York: Atlantic Monthly, 1986], 14). See also John McKnight, "Why 'Servanthood' Is Bad," *The Other Side* (January/February 1989), 38-40.

[4] Saul D. Alinsky, *Rules for Radicals: A Practical Primer for Realistic Radicals* (New York: Vintage, 1972), 194.

[5] Rudy Wiebe, *The Blue Mountains of China* (Toronto: McClelland and Stewart, 1970), 215-16.

[6] Paul S. Minear, *Images of the Church in the New Testament* (Philadelphia: Westminster, 1960), 163.

[7] Cited by Richard J. Foster, *The Challenge of the Disciplined Life: Christian Reflections on Money, Sex and Power* (San Francisco: Harper, 1985), 19. See also his *Freedom of Simplicity* (San Francisco: Harper and Row, 1981). A useful exercise is to keep a money autobiography. For a brochure to guide readers, see Maryle Ashley, *Keeping a Money Journal*, available through Ministry of Money, 2 Professional Drive Suite 220, Gaithersburg MD 20979.

[8] *Baptist Peacemaker* 17/2 (summer 1997): 15. Severyn T. Bruyn develops similar criteria in *Quaker Testimonies and Economic Alternatives*, Pendle Hill Pamphlet 231 (Wallingford: Pendle Hill, 1980), 30.

[9] "Our Vision," *The Memphis School of Servant Leadership Newsletter* (winter 2001). For the Church of the Saviour model, see Dorothy Devers and N. Gordon Cosby, Handbook for Churches and Mission Groups (pamphlet); Elizabeth O'Connor, *Servant Leaders, Servant Structures* (Washington, DC: Servant Leadership School, 1991). These and other resources are available through The Potter's House Book Service, 1658 Columbia Road NW, Washington, DC 20009. Also, see Robert K. Greenleaf, *Servant Leadership* (New York: Paulist, 1977) and *The Power of Servant-Leadership: Essays* (San Francisco: Berrett-Koehler, 1998).

[10] Letty M. Russell, *Church in the Round: Feminist Interpretation of the Church* (Louisville: Westminster/John Knox 1993).

For Reflection and Conversation

- Why is servant leadership a practice of justice?

- What features of our society make it difficult to use the servant leadership image or interfere with efforts to model servant leadership?

- What are the most important aspects of servant leadership?

- Describe a servant leader with whom you are familiar. Similarly, describe a community of servant leaders.

- What is the relationship between servant leadership and evangelism?

Seasonal Practices

Introduction

> *[Mordecai enjoined them that] as the days on which the Jews gained relief from their enemies, and as the month that had been turned for them from sorrow into gladness and from mourning into a holiday; that they should make them days of feasting and gladness, days for sending gifts of food to one another and presents to the poor.* (Esther 9:20-22)

From Judaism, Christians inherit the practice of celebrating holidays and holy days. Holidays follow a secular calendar. In Judaism and Christianity, many are agricultural in origin or follow the rhythm of the seasons determined by the phases of the moon. Holy days follow a liturgical calendar. The Christian year begins in Western churches with Advent and in Eastern churches with Christmas and Epiphany. The cycle highlights the birth of Jesus, his baptism, his journey to the cross, his resurrection, the descent of the dove (symbol of the Holy Spirit), and the recognition of Christ as King and Lord.

The origins of many of the holy days of Judaism and Christianity were entirely secular. For example, in Judaism, Purim (during which the story of Esther is read) celebrated the Jews' ancient deliverance from a threatened persecution during the days of the Persians and Medes. Hanukkah may have been related at first to solar rites at the winter solstice. In Christianity, the fixing of the dates for Christmas and Epiphany was entirely arbitrary and represented an attempt to counter pagan rituals.

The distinction between ordinary time and sacred time is artificial. According to historian of religion Mircea Eliade, profane existence is never found in a pure state. However much people may live in a desacralized world, one who chooses in favor of secular life never succeeds in doing away completely with religious behavior. Even the most secular person preserves traces of giving life religious meaning.[1]

Religion tends to assimilate and sacralize secular days. A holiday may signify nothing more than a day off, yet many occasions such as national days or Labor Day are deemed suitable for religious observance. Many Christians organize watch-night services on New Year's Eve or draw attention to times of passage in the life cycle, such as the onset of puberty or the graduation of students, as revelatory of the creative design of God.

Just as religion valorizes the secular, secular society tends to mark the holy days. In Western countries, non-Christians enjoy a day off at Christmas and Easter. Inexorably, the religious significance of the holy days is diminished. Christmas becomes a time for parties or for the exchange of gifts. Easter becomes a time for showing off spring apparel.

In recent times, Christians have differed regarding the process of secularization. Some have welcomed the encroachment of the profane on the sacred. Others have called it a crisis. In 1965–1966, my first year at seminary, this difference made big news. A spate of authors examined the crisis in the church in books with titles such as *The Comfortable Pew: A Critical Look at the Church in the New Age, God's Frozen People,* and *The Secular City.* The 8 April 1966 issue of *Time Magazine* had a famous cover story, "Is God Dead?"[2]

God was not and is not dead, but reports of a pronounced disquiet in the church have proved prescient. While no symbol of human activity is more noticeable around the world than the presence of places where people worship, there are also signs of a profound malaise. We may call this malaise anxiety regarding the loss of meaning, the fading of moral horizons, or the loss of a secure sense of the future. Whatever its nature, this malaise calls for people of faith to respond.[3]

In his novel *Till We Have Faces*, C. S. Lewis observes that there are two ways by which we may respond to change, the tough line of attack and the brittle one. In terms of one classic study, these are the Christ against Culture and the Christ of Culture approaches. According to this analysis, we may stand firm, or we may bend. We may resist what is happening in the world, or we may accommodate.[4]

There is a third model, the way of paradox and transformation. This represents a fusion of the other two approaches. It allows the Christian to retain a sense of inner peace while adapting to external circumstances. The seasonal practices discussed in this concluding section attempt to chart a path along this third way.

Some years ago, several of us involved in the peace movement decided to form a group. We were Christians of different denominations. We wanted to root our participation in a social movement more deeply in Christian soil.

We met and agreed upon a set of practices. They included a weekly gathering for prayer and Bible study, a monthly meal to which we invited family and friends, and participation as a group in wider gatherings such as peace marches.

We also explored how to reclaim our holidays as holy days. We wanted to develop seasonal practices that gave common witness to our faith. We wanted to reclaim hope in dangerous times.

The writer of Hebrews makes clear the source Christians turn to for hope and strength. As surely as the times are troubled or changing, we have a certain anchor, Jesus Christ. *We have this hope, a sure and steadfast anchor of the soul, a hope that enters the inner shrine behind the curtain, where Jesus, a forerunner on our behalf, has entered . . .* (Heb 6:19-20).

---

[1] Mircea Eliade, *The Sacred and the Profane: The Nature of Religion*, trans. Willard R. Trask (New York: Harcourt, Brace and World, 1957), 23.

[2] Pierre Berton, *The Comfortable Pew: A Critical Look at the Church in the New Age* (Toronto: McClelland and Stewart, 1965); Mark Gibb, *God's Frozen People* (Philadelphia: Westminster, 1965); and Harvey Cox, *The Secular City: Secularization and Urbanization in Theological Perspective* (New York: Macmillan, 1965).

[3] Charles Taylor, *The Malaise of Modernity* (Toronto: Anansi, 1991).

[4] C. S. Lewis, *Till We Have Faces* (New York: Harcourt, Brace, 1956), 261. H. Richard Niebuhr, *Christ and Culture* (New York: Harper and Row, 1951).

Practices of Thanksgiving

> *. . . as you sing psalms and hymns and spiritual songs among yourselves, singing and making melody to the Lord in your hearts, giving thanks to God the Father at all times and for everything in the name of our Lord Jesus Christ.* (Ephesians 5:19-20)

The Spiritual Practice of Giving Thanks

The spiritual practice of giving thanks recovers the biblical themes of gratitude, praise, and rejoicing. Consider the variety of words authors use in the Bible to describe giving thanks to God. They include *acknowledge, adore, bless, boast in, declare the mighty works of, extol, fall on one's face, glorify, honor, invoke, kneel, magnify, offer gifts or sacrifices, praise, rejoice in, sanctify, sing hymns to, sing psalms, speak in tongues,* and *worship*! As well, there are special words of thanksgiving such as *hallelujah, hosanna,* and *amen.* The Scriptures also record outbursts of praise, like *Holy, Holy, Holy* (Isa 6:3), *Worthy is the Lamb* (Rev 5:12), and *thanks be to God, who gives us the victory through our Lord Jesus Christ* (1 Cor 15:57).

How shall we account for this great outpouring of praise? In both testaments, faithful people attributed to God the power to create, sustain life, and save. In worship, they reflected the experience of God. Worship in turn shaped practice and belief. In life, the knowledge of God was felt to be direct and intimate. This in turn contributed to their worship of God. The Latin tag *lex orandi, lex credendi* (the law of praying, the law of believing) was operative. That is, prayer was a norm for belief and vice versa. What was prayed indicated what may or must be believed and acted upon, while belief and action shaped what may or must be prayed.[1]

The Bible reveals a fundamental, human response to everything: to bless God for whatever that is. This is why we exist. *I sing your praises, O my God, and I will praise your name forever and ever, Every day will I bless you, and I will praise your name forever and ever* (Ps 145:1-2).[2] Psalm 145 is but one of many Psalms that express praise and thanksgiving. Many begin and end with expressions of gratefulness. Many originate in the worship of God.[3]

In ancient Israel, God's work of deliverance gave way to praise. Taking a tambourine in her hand, Aaron's sister, the prophet Miriam, celebrated deliverance of her people from bondage in Egypt. With other women playing instruments and dancing, she sang, *Sing to the* LORD, *for he has triumphed gloriously* (Exod 15:21). Hannah thanked God for Samuel's birth: *My heart exults in the* LORD; *my strength is exalted in my God* (1 Sam 2:1). Learning she was pregnant, Mary said, *My soul magnifies the Lord, and my spirit rejoices in God my Savior* (Luke 1:47).

In the immediate aftermath of their experience of the death and resurrection of Jesus, early Christians gathered in the temple and in homes where they broke bread and *ate their food with glad and generous hearts, praising God and having the goodwill of all the people. And day by day the Lord added to their number those who were being saved* (Acts 2:46-47). Joyful thanksgiving for the death and resurrection came to be the key act of worship.

In Greek the word for thanksgiving is *eucharist*. Christian eucharistic practices are diverse. Many adhere to some of the most ancient of customs. Among these is the exchange of the Peace of Christ. In the name of Christ, people greet each other warmly, shaking hands, embracing one another, and blessing others. In an atmosphere of openness and friendliness, passing the peace often takes a great deal of time. When appropriate, the worship leader calls the community to prayer and gives thanks for the bread and wine or juice. The congregation then partakes of the eucharistic elements. During this time of communion with God, the congregation generally sings songs that express gratitude for God's salvific work and ongoing presence.

This summary does not exhaust the significance of the Eucharist, or Lord's Supper. But its description points to several crucial principles. First, worship is oriented to actual experience. While the central ritual in worship for many Christians focuses specifically on the death and resurrection of Jesus, other moments to give thanks in worship lift up additional occasions for gratitude, such as the sharing of joys and concerns or giving offerings in money or kind. Second, giving thanks is a crucial dimension of all worship. Through music, prayer, preaching, teaching, and sacrament the church gives thanks for Jesus Christ and celebrates life. Third, we should not limit giving thanks to Sunday worship. A benediction marks the end of worship and passage from a gathered to a dispersed community. The worship leader calls upon the people to actualize their faith through the living out of the reality for which they have given thanks. Finally, freely offered, the spiritual practice of giving thanks is a daily occurrence. Perhaps the most common expression of giving thanks takes place when faithful people offer a mealtime grace. The word "grace" and cognates such as "gratitude" or "gratuity" have their source in the Latin word *gratia,* which can mean pleasure or favor. This suggests a dual meaning of giving thanks as a practice of an evangelistic lifestyle. Expressed in worship, daily living, and specific practices such as offering table grace, gratitude is an expression both of receiving and taking delight in God's gifts and of returning a favor in response.

We must sustain relationships between individuals and groups. It is more than a matter of courtesy to thank someone for something. In any relationship, gratitude expresses pleasure and favors exchanged in return. So it is with our relationship with the living God. Gratitude is not simply a mechanical transaction. We receive and express unrestrained delight in God's gifts. We also express our conviction that all life is a gift. To God we offer ourselves in return.[4]

The Religious Roots of Thanksgiving Day in North America

Thanksgiving Day draws upon three traditions. One is the harvest festival in ancient Israel. Celebrated in autumn, *Sukkot,* the Feast of Tabernacles, marks an end of the agricultural cycle culminating in the gathering of crops from the fields, orchards, and vineyards. The main practice is the construction of a hut or booth for use during the festival. Jews eat their meals in it. While we do not know the origin of this practice, it has been given both a historical context and theological significance. Historically, Jews recall the time when the slaves freed from Egypt wandered in the wilderness. They lived not in permanent dwellings, but in temporary booths. Theologically, Jews bear in mind their dependence on God's bounty.

Thanksgiving Day also draws on a second tradition, the harvest celebrations in European peasant societies. The key symbol is the cornucopia or horn of plenty.

Third, Thanksgiving Day recalls celebration by the Pilgrims in Massachusetts Bay Colony of their first harvest in 1621. The Pilgrims shared their harvest with the Indians around them. For three days the Pilgrims hosted Massasoit and ninety of his tribe, the Wampanoag, as well as a lone Patuxent Indian, Squanto. The presence of Squanto was especially significant. Years before the arrival of the Puritans in the Americas, first British

Captain George Weymouth and then the Spanish had held Squanto in captivity as a slave. Rescued by Spanish friars who converted him, Squanto returned to his homeland only six months before the Pilgrims. He found that his people had been killed four years earlier by a mysterious plague. Fear kept other Indians from staying on land associated with death. As a result, when the Pilgrims arrived, they discovered land available for a settlement and someone who could speak English. Squanto taught the Pilgrims many of the skills needed to survive in their new home such as use of local herbs for cooking and medicine, fishing, stalking deer, and planting corn or pumpkins.

The Pilgrims' first Thanksgiving Day celebrated abundance. Harsh conditions followed. The Pilgrims continued to look to God for sustenance but ultimately had to ration food. Each individual received five kernels of corn a day. To remind them of these hardships, the Pilgrims placed five kernels of corn on their plates during the second Thanksgiving Day in the Americas.

General days of blessing in Massachusetts began in 1674, when time was set aside to give thanks for divine goodness. Thanksgiving was beginning to serve secular and national as well as specifically religious purposes. Never intended to be a once-a-year event, the colonists set aside days for "public humiliation, fasting, and prayer." On these special days, they intentionally, gratefully, and willfully confessed dependence on God.

On 12 July 1775, the Continental Congress set aside a day for fasting, prayer, and thanksgiving. Recognizing the momentous nature of the circumstances, the proclamation called for observance by "the inhabitants of all the English colonies on this continent" of a day of prayer and fasting. Their goal was that "we may with united hearts and voices, unfeignedly confess and deplore our many sins and offer up our joint supplications to the all-wise, omnipotent, and merciful Disposer of All Events, humbly beseeching him to forgive our iniquities, to remove our present calamities, and to avert those desolating judgments with which we are threatened."[5]

The practice of appointing a day to thank God for bountiful harvests spread to Nova Scotia in Canada. In 1763 citizens of Halifax commemorated the end of the Seven Years' War with a day of thanksgiving.

The United States did not always celebrate Thanksgiving on the fourth Thursday in November. Through most of the country's history, the United States observed the holiday in early December. In 1863 President Abraham Lincoln turned the Christian practices of humiliation, fasting, and prayer into the national holiday we call Thanksgiving. He encouraged all citizens to express gratitude to God for all God's blessings. "We have been the recipients of the choicest bounties of Heaven. We have been preserved these many years in peace and prosperity. We have grown in numbers, wealth, and power as no other nation has ever grown. But we have forgotten God."

In 1939, the United States remained in a decade-long economic depression. Federated Department Stores chief Fred Lazarus Jr. recommended to President Franklin D. Roosevelt to move Thanksgiving Day a week earlier. Lazarus proposed this calendar shift in light of cultural trends. Advent and Christmas had ceased to be primarily a religious season, but rather the principal shopping season. Lazarus reasoned that lengthening the Christmas buying season would help the economy. President Roosevelt issued a proclamation. Within a few years, most states adopted laws recognizing the fourth Thursday in November as Thanksgiving Day. We were becoming a nation of buyers rather than believers, feasters instead of fasters, football fans instead of people focused on God.

In Canada, Parliament declared 6 November 1879 as a national Thanksgiving holiday. Subsequently, Canadians observed various dates, the most popular being the third Monday in October. On 31 January 1957, the Parliament of Canada moved the observance of Thanksgiving to the second Monday of October. Ernest Charles Drury, Ontario Premier from 1919–1923, lamented that, to give them a long weekend when the weather was better, townspeople had stolen a holiday owned by farmers. Other countries also have national days of thanksgiving.

Other Practices

Thanksgiving observances have recognized other events. The explorer Martin Frobisher celebrated God's care in the eastern Arctic in 1578. In our time, many nations have given thanks at the end of war. In the case of the First Great War, the guns fell silent at the eleventh minute of the eleventh hour of the eleventh day of the eleventh month in 1918. In the aftermath of the war, it was common that the victors plan parades. However, President Wilson of the United States and British Prime Minister David Lloyd George opposed proposals for national rejoicing that failed to pay tribute to the millions who had died. The United States designated 11 November Armistice Day or Veteran's Day, while Great Britain and commonwealth countries, including Canada, designated 11 November as Remembrance Day.

On 11 November 1919, a normal, busy weekday, all activity ceased throughout the British Empire and the United States. For two minutes of silent remembering, traffic stopped. Trains scheduled to leave at 11:11 departed two minutes late. Those already in motion halted. No one moved. Not a telephone rang. In London, England, one newspaper described a great awful silence that was almost pain. A deepening hush spread everywhere. It became pronounced and impressed observers with a sense of audibility. A spirit of memory brooded over all. Similarly, Australia and New Zealand set aside Anzac Day (25 April) to recall a specific battle, Gallipoli of World War I.

Recovery of the Spiritual Roots of Giving Thanks

We live in a consumer society. Greed has become a norm. Amid the noise of advertisers hawking their wares, it difficult to accept that there are any limits to commercialism. It takes a special consciousness to counter the many advertisements that tell us, "You cannot be happy unless you buy this" or "You are a nobody unless you own this." It is difficult to put things in the right perspective. What we are grateful for, we cherish. As a whole, North Americans are preoccupied with money. We are people in a rush. We are people who build religious edifices. Nonetheless, in the face of material prosperity, myriad choices of how to spend our money, and physical activity of a religious boom, we are witnessing the breakdown of community and a diminishment of the spiritual practice of thanksgiving that has shaped our common history. We would do well to recover the religious roots of thanksgiving in North America.

As evidenced by the television show *X-Files*, the idea of visitors from outer space fascinate some in our culture. Were an extraterrestrial to visit North America, what would it see? It might be struck by what friends from other countries notice when they visit us in Memphis, Tennessee. In recent months, my wife and I have entertained visitors from Australia, Cameroon, India, Japan, Liberia, Norway, and Zimbabwe. I have asked what they find most distinguishes North American culture. Friends comment on the availability of consumer goods and the size of church buildings. In some ways, these are related expressions of our material preoccupations.

Can we begin to restore to the season of Thanksgiving something of its earlier focus on God? Let me suggest three practices. The first is to retreat from consumption. There is evidence of such stirring even within our secular culture. Thanksgiving Friday is typically the busiest shopping day of the year. People flock to malls and Internet buying sites on their computers. In

1997, Kalle Lasn launched a counteroffensive. An Estonian by birth who fled to the West to avoid the Soviet takeover of that nation in the 1940s, Lasn called for would-be shoppers to treat Thanksgiving Friday as "Buy Nothing Day." In some circles, his appeal caught on and has become an international movement. Buy Nothing Day has become an annual day-after-Thanksgiving ritual of zero shopping.[6]

A second practice is fasting. The origins of fasting as a Christian and Jewish spiritual discipline are biblical. The Bible refers to fasting more than fifty times, including on festival days such as the Day of Atonement (Yom Kippur) and during times of distress, mourning, and thanksgiving.

In the Scriptures, the normal means of fasting consisted in abstaining from all food but not from water. During his forty-day fast in the Judean wilderness, Jesus "ate nothing" (Luke 4:2). The text did not say that Jesus refrained from drinking. It is reasonable to suppose Jesus could not have gone without water very long in the desert except as a supernatural act. Jesus taught fasting as an act of devotion to worship God in private (Matt 6:16-18) and as a form of focusing on the Holy One when Jesus would no longer be with his companions (Matt 9:14-15).[7]

Fasting became a crucial practice in early Christianity, notably during Lent, the season from Ash Wednesday until Holy Week. Historically, many Christians, including great reformers Martin Luther and John Wesley, have used it as a discipline of the Christian life, a holy exercise, a means of focusing on God, and a way of keeping balance in our lives.

Fasting expresses faith, dependence on God, and hope in God's providential care. The contemporary practice of fasting is not specifically spiritual or Christian. As a religious practice, Jews, Muslims, Hindus, North American Indians, and many others fast. Many people fast to lose weight, to attain healing, or to maintain fitness. If you desire to fast for physical reasons, you should seek medical advice.

A third practice is recovery of giving thanks daily. Can we consider each and every day as a gift gratefully received? Can we live with a new sense of vulnerability and trust in God? Is it even humanly possible to live out of a fundamental attitude of gratefulness?

In North America, especially, it is difficult to identify God as the source of life. Because of the phenomenal outpouring of human creativity and productivity, it is difficult for many modern people to think of God as the one to whom we should direct our sense of gratitude or to whom we should abandon ourselves willfully.

To acknowledge God as the source of life and giver of everything does not mean that we have to accept or try to forget what is not good. Nor does it mean that we ignore human accomplishments. Giving thanks expresses our sense that God is with us in everything, our times of sadness and sorrow as well as our times of gladness and joy. That is why the Eucharist, with its invitation to find hope even in death, is so crucial to the spirituality of giving thanks.

When we invite someone to our home for a cup of coffee, a meal, or some other purpose, we offer more than a meal. We offer conversation, friendship, and intimacy. As we invite someone to worship with us, especially for the celebration of the Lord's Supper, we are inviting them to share in the deepest mystery of faith, God's self-emptying and triumph. Among the four evangelists, Luke alone records the story of Jesus meeting two disciples on the road to Emmaus. They did not realize Jesus was with them until they shared the ordinary gesture of breaking bread. *Then their eyes were opened and they recognized him.* They said to each other, *Were not our hearts burning within us while he was talking to us on the road, while he was opening the scriptures to us?* They then returned to Jerusalem and told the others what had happened (Luke 24:31-35).

Jesus invites us to be open one to another. We are invited to see him in ordinary ways and places. A spirituality of gratitude calls us to live with a sense of trust that God is our companion even during our vulnerable times. Along the way, we discover God truly is with us and also with those with whom we share the gospel.

Recovery of giving thanks is indispensable for developing an evangelistic lifestyle. Genuine giving of thanks comes from the heart where we meet the God of love. As we express our oneness with God, we let others see and acknowledge the One from whom all gifts flow.

Prayer
God, thank you for bread, homes, health, loved ones, and peace. Thank you for Jesus. I pray for
bread for the hungry
homes for the homeless
healing for the sick
love for the disconsolate
peace for the those who fear
and knowledge of Jesus for all. Amen.

[1] John Koenig, "The Heartbeat of Praise and Thanksgiving," *Weavings* 7 (1992); David Steindl-Rast, *Gratefulness, the Heart of Prayer: An Approach to Life in Fullness* (Ramsey: Paulist, 1984); Geoffrey Wainwright, *Doxology—The Praise of God in Worship, Doctrine, and Life: A Systematic Theology* (New York: Oxford University Press, 1980).

[2] Nancy Schreck and Maureen Leach, *Psalms Anew in Inclusive Language* (Winona: Saint Mary's Press, 1986).

[3] Of 150 psalms in the canon, at least 40 are hymns of praise and thanksgiving. See Pius Drijvers, *The Psalms, Their Structure and Meaning* (London: Burns & Oats, 1965).

[4] Christina Georgina Rossetti (1830–1894) expresses this in a stanza of *In the Bleak Mid-Winter*: "What can I give him, poor as I am? If I were a shepherd, I would bring a lamb; if I were a wise man, I would do my part; yet what I can I give him—give my heart" (*Voices United: The Hymn and Worship Book of the United Church of Canada* [Toronto: United Church Publishing House, 1996], 55). A number of studies have noted the broader significance of giving thanks. See especially Lewis Hyde, *The Gift: Imagination and the Erotic Life of Property* (New York: Vintage, 1983) and Marcel Mauss, *The Gift*, trans. Ian Cunnison (New York: Norton Library, W. W. Norton, 1967).

[5] Winthrop S. Hudson, "Fast Days and Civil Religion," in *Theology in 16th and 17th Century England: Papers Read at a Clark Library Seminar February 6, 1971* (Los Angeles: William Andrews Clark Memorial Library, 1971). For the Jewish background, see A. Stanley Dreyfus, "Thanksgiving," *Oxford Dictionary of the Jewish Religion* ed. R. J. Zwi Werblowsky and Geoffrey Wigoder (New York: Oxford, 1997), 688-89. For general background on the United States, see "Thanksgiving Day," *The New Encyclopedia Britannica* vol. 11: Micropaedia (Chicago: Encyclopedia Britanica, 2002), 673. For general background on Canada, see David Mills, "Thanksgiving Day," *Canadian Encyclopedia* (Edmonton, Hertig, 1988) 4:2136. An Internet search resulted in hundreds of entries under Thanksgiving Day.

[6] See Juliet B. Schor, *The Overspent American: Upscaling, Downshifting, and the New Consumer* (New York: HarperPerennial, 1998), 144, for a typical Buy Nothing Day advertisement.

[7] Richard J. Foster, *Celebration of Discipline: The Path to Spiritual Growth* (rev. ed., San Francisco: Harper and Row, 1988), ch. 4: "Fasting." For the Jewish background, see "Fasts" in Philip Birnbaum, *Encyclopedia of Jewish Concepts* (New York: Hebrew Publishing Company, 1979).

For Reflection and Conversation

- How do you practice gratefulness and gratitude?

- What are some of the things for which you are grateful?

- Describe ways in which you might simplify your lifestyle.

- During what seasons is fasting appropriate?

- Can you express gratitude to God for everything?

- What is the relationship between thanksgiving and an evangelistic lifestyle?

Practices of Advent, Christmas, and Epiphany

. . . and laid Jesus in a manger, because there was no place for them in the inn. (Luke 2:7)

The Swirl of the Season

It is hard enough to focus on God at Thanksgiving, *a secular holiday.* Finding God at Christmas, *part of the Christian calendar,* poses even greater challenges. In North America, we are inundated by messages promising us beauty, happiness, and love, but only so long as it is procured through buying and selling, giving and getting.

As we saw with Thanksgiving, the season leading to Christmas presents opportunities boldly to share the gospel. I write in late 2000. The time for revelry and shopping is in full swing. Despite concerns about a downturn in the United States economy, merchants report that earnings are up, banks wind up another great year, and *Fortune 500* CEOs await fat bonuses. The decision United States politicians made seventy years ago to set the date for Thanksgiving at a time that would maximize the period for Christmas shopping has clearly proved successful.

My wife and I make an annual pilgrimage to some mall at the outset of the Christmas season. We go to watch and eavesdrop, not to buy. We pretend to be God's spies. We put on spectacles and a hearing aid by which we look and listen with God peeking over our shoulders.

Last year, I noticed a frantic shopper trying to find a Furby, a small, battery-driven fuzzball without which her six-year-old would not be able to survive Christmas. Attempting to be helpful, the merchant explained how to find one through searching newspaper ads or by computer online shopping. Even though such last-minute shopping might result in the mother paying a premium for the object of desire, she clearly was a participant in a cultural process that gauged the needs and wants of her child. She felt she had no choice.

This year I noted similar conversations or worse. At one store, a customer searched in vain for a popular item, the Sony PlayStation. I overheard another customer gloating *sotto voce* to her spouse that they had been wise enough to buy several and sell on eBay, which offers online computer bidding, the extra ones at twice the retail price.

My heart goes out to all caught in the swirl of the season. Words of Thomas Merton come to mind. "We live in the time of no room . . . . The time when everyone is obsessed with lack of time, lack of space, with saving time, conquering space, projecting into time and space the anguish produced within them by the technological furies of size, volume, quantity, speed, number, price, power and acceleration."[1]

From 1941 until his death in 1968, Merton lived as a monk at the Trappist Abbey of Gethsemani in Kentucky. He thought he was living in the time of no room. No room for nature. No room for quiet. No room for attention. No room for God. A generation ago, Merton seemed to anticipate the dilemmas of this season. We whirl about aimlessly through the malls of the modern city, thrown together, thrust and pitched out into an eddy. Amid all the parties, plenty, and preparation, it is no wonder that many feel isolated and lonely. Many people commit suicide because they are unable to find healing for the wounds of the heart or companionship.

Can we redeem the period in the church year between Thanksgiving and Christmas? With Madeleine L'Engle, a contemporary writer, I believe that it is possible. "There is nothing so secular that it cannot be sacred, and that is one of the deepest messages of the Incarnation."[2]

We name the season between Thanksgiving and Christmas Advent. In Advent, many take a journey that frees them from the swirl of the season and opens them to joy at a time to recall Jesus' birth. We live between the special events, growing and waiting for fulfillment of what will be. Just when we are almost ready to doze off, God breaks in. Life is never the same again.

Awakening to Unfolding Reality

Historically, the first Christian communities observed no feast of Jesus' birth. Only in the fourth century did Christmas and Epiphany come to be celebrated widely. Initially, the church highlighted Epiphany, a word that derived from *epiphaneia,* Greek for manifestation or appearance. Christians associated Epiphany with the baptism of Jesus when a voice came from heaven saying, *You are my Son, the Beloved; with you I am well pleased* (Luke 3:22), the visit of the Magi to the holy child (Matt 2), and the first miracle at Cana (John 2).

By the fourth century, celebration of the Nativity of Jesus was added to commemoration of the baptism of Jesus. Gradually, the festival grew into the twelve days between December 25 and January 6.

Why December 25 and January 6? This represented a Christianizing of a pagan festival honoring a sun deity, marked in the West on December 25 and in the East on January 6. The choice of these dates represented an attempt by the church to counter pagan festivities connected with the winter solstice. As well, the popularity of Christmas and Epiphany owed much to the contemporary theological controversies about the person of Christ.[3]

In part as a form of resistance to the secularization of time, Orthodox Christians continue to give emphasis to January 6 as the day of Christ's manifestation. In my Russian Orthodox upbringing, we tended to underemphasize December 25 and observe January 6 mainly as time for worship, family, and friends.

What about Advent? The Eastern Church never developed the tradition. In the fourth century the Western or Roman church began to observe a period of preparation for Christmas and Epiphany. Initially modeled on the season of Lent, the period of forty days (six Sundays) was reduced to four Sundays by the latter half of the sixth century. Advent was a season of preparation for the birth of Jesus through self-discipline, repentance, and, for some, pilgrimage to the Holy Land. It highlighted practices associated with the life of Jesus such as prayer and fasting.

Since the reformations of the sixteenth century, Advent has ceased to be principally a penitential season. It has become a period of preparation, reflection, and anticipation of Jesus' coming. Each Sunday receives a definite theological focus, such as the return of Christ and the establishment of God's ultimate reign of justice and peace; John the Baptist's announcement that God's promises will be fulfilled; John the Baptist's call to repentance; and ways in which the birth of Jesus takes place in our time.

The word *Advent* derives from the Medieval French *advenir*, suggesting an awakening to an unfolding reality. What does it mean to awaken to an unfolding reality? What is required to recover a sense of the unfolding reality of God?

The ancient Hebrews dreamed that God's redemptive work would come to completion. When John the Baptist was born, his father Zechariah stated that, by the tender mercy of God, a new day was dawning to give light to those who sit in darkness and in the shadow of death and to guide our feet into the way of peace (Luke 1:79). When Jesus was born, an angel announced to shepherds, *Do not be afraid, for see—I am bringing you good news of great joy for all the people.* A heavenly host praised God saying, *Glory to God in the highest heaven, and on earth peace among those whom he favors* (Luke 2:9, 14). Joseph and Mary presented the newborn in the temple. Simeon, known for piety and right living, took Jesus in his arms, praised God and said, *my eyes have seen your salvation, which you have prepared in the presence of all peoples, a light for revelation to the Gentiles and for glory to your people Israel* (Luke 2:30-32).

God has not ceased to enter human history. Sometimes it is hard to see God's salvation breaking in. Sometimes it is difficult to see God's reign of justice and peace unfolding. With patient preparation and confidence, we share good news during Advent. What Isaiah, John, and other prophets proclaimed in their time is true in ours. The Lord is with us, watching over us, challenging us to bear fruit worthy of repentance. Because the Lord is with us, we may pray with confidence that one day, justice and peace will dwell everywhere. God will see to it. Let the effect of our bold witness manifest in righteousness, peace, and trust forever (Isa 32:16-17).

By what practices can we share the good news of the birth of Jesus? Let me suggest using the "Christmas pledge."[4]

> Believing in the true spirit of Christmas, we can commit ourselves to remember those people who truly need our gifts; express our love in more direct ways than gifts; examine our holiday activities in the light of our deepest values; be a peacemaker within the circle of our family and friends; and rededicate ourselves to spiritual growth.

Remember Those Who Truly Need Our Gifts

According to Luke, the gospel of Jesus Christ began with a family for whom there was no room in the inn. Desperate and in labor, Mary took the first shelter she could find. Anxious Joseph must have been humiliated that his child would be born on a dirt floor among animals. Thus was Jesus born in a dark stable. There was no other place for him.

According to Matthew, three years of exile in Egypt awaited the family as they fled a tyrant who cared nothing for the weak and poor. They were a desperate family on the run and in hiding.

These stories make us aware of those who "live in the time of no room" in our countries. They include children who live on the streets of our cities, a doorway their bed; shack dwellers who struggle to keep privacy and dignity; women who hide in cupboards because of fear of the one who will report that they are undocumented, illegal aliens; communities facing forced removals due to toxic wastes; individuals who have had no money to insure homes now destroyed by flood, earthquake, or some other tragedy; domestic workers who care for children other their own; refugees whose only memory of family left behind is a handful of photographs; and teens at risk.

The birth narratives of the Evangelists parallel contemporary life circumstances of many. In a census year, imagine a decree has gone out that all should be registered at their favorite shopping mall. Everyone goes, except (initially) José, an undocumented refugee claimant, and his girlfriend María, who is great with child. Unwilling to be exposed in public, they think about an abortion, but a heavenly messenger appears to José in a dream saying, "José, do not be afraid to take María as your wife, for the child conceived in her is from the Holy Spirit. She will bear a son, and you are to name him *Jésus*, for he will save his people from their sins."

Since there is no public transportation, they walk to the shopping mall. While en route, the time comes for her delivery. María gives birth to her firstborn son in a boarded-up storefront. She wraps him in discarded rags and lays him in a box of empty whiskey bottles over a heating vent.

The worldwide web picks up the story. Soon wise folk from the east fax memos to malls: "We have heard of a child born in a storefront, cradled in a whiskey box, whose birth heralds the coming of a time when swords will be hammered into fishing hooks and nations shall study war no more, a time when the proud shall be scattered, the mighty pulled down, lowly ones exalted, and the hungry filled with good things, a time when death itself will be vanquished and creation set free from its bondage to decay. This is a great thing! Where can we see what has come to pass?"

Politicians hear all about this and summon consultants from the east to see how this birth can translate into a marketing bonanza. The mayor sends them to the malls saying, "Go find the child born in the shopping mall, then bring word that I too may worship him." Wise folk, the consultants find the child and worship him. Warned in a dream not to return to the mayor's office, they depart by another route.

The city could be Ottawa, Canada; Canberra, Australia; London, England; or another seat of power. Let us say Washington, District of

Columbia. The politicos go on a budget-cutting binge. Seven million children lose basic healthcare coverage. Fourteen million children endure food and nutrition program cuts. Over 150,000 children with disabilities lose their Supplemental Security Income. Cuts in Aid to Families with Dependent Children deny three million poor children benefits. Taxes on low-income working families increase, while non-needy citizens received $200 billion in benefits. The Pentagon receives $7 billion it did not request. The number of children living in poverty in the United States increases to more than 15 million while children in pariah countries such as Iraq and war-torn countries like Sierra Leone die in ever increasing numbers. Like Rachel, who wept in Ramah for her children, José and María weep because their beautiful child was born into a world of such suffering (Matt 2:18).

The story is not entirely fanciful. Bethlehem is a continuing event. Despite the hustle, bustle, and apparently boundless bounty of the season, for many individuals there seems to be no room anywhere for them. They are the healthless, homeless, hugless, and hopeless of our society. They are the street people, the mentally ill, and the addicted. They are the aged. They are the poor. They are people who feel abandoned and are without love, community, acceptance, or hope.

It is impossible to reconcile what is happening in the world with the gospel of Jesus. We live in times similar to those when John the Baptist said, *The time is fulfilled, and the kingdom of God has come near; repent, and believe in the good news* (Mark 1:14-15). During his life on earth, Jesus repeated this call to repent. He assured women and men that God forgave them and called them to discipleship. Jesus offered salvation, healing, and the possibility of a new creation.

One way to live into this gospel is to make our homes, congregations, and neighborhoods places of welcome for those who find no place in our society. In them we recognize the face of Jesus. We offer room at our table. With acceptance and friendship we nurture compassion, solidarity, and hope. Words of an African American spiritual proclaim:

> All kinds of people around that table
> One of these days! Hallelujah!
> All kinds of people round that table!
> Gonna sit at the welcome table one of these days.[5]

Express Our Love in More Direct Ways Than Gifts

Advent invites us to follow the magi to Bethlehem and reconsider its miracle. Bethlehem does not change. The miracle does not change. But we may change, and the eyes with which we are able to see the miracle may change. Practicing Advent thus becomes a special adventure rather than a routine pilgrimage.[6]

Developments in medical science and genetics have had a huge impact on how we view childbirth, and yet each birth is still a miracle. Do we have the capacity to marvel? Can we see God's beloved in each child? Nancy and I expected the birth of our first child on 25 December. The birthing extended beyond Christmas Day. Nonetheless, we called the newborn Nathaniel, a name that expressed and still conveys our deepest feeling that he is a gift from God. Just as joy enveloped us that season of Advent, Christmas, and Epiphany some thirty years ago, during each season we can again rejoice and make room for the Christ child.

My family has come to associate Advent with certain traditions. We cut a tree from a farm. We open a box that stores for eleven months a Nativity set purchased from Elias Mickel's family shop at Nativity Square in Bethlehem of the Holy Land. Dust and yellowed newsprint give way to a dozen magnificent olivewood carvings, the Christ child, Mary, Joseph, the shepherd, the animals, and a makeshift inn. Inexorably, we are drawn to the place where Jesus was born. We hum carols we have waited to sing these past months.

The following story illustrates that in a world of plenty, ways remain to take joy at the birth of Jesus and to love boldly. In 1994, two Christians from the United States traveled to Russia to serve as teachers in an orphanage. At Christmas, they shared the accounts of Jesus' birth to youth, many of whom had not heard the story before. They invited the orphans to draw a picture of what they had heard. Later when they were looking at the paintings, they noticed that one of the orphans had painted two infants in the manger. When asked about his drawing, the six-year-old explained that like Jesus, when he was born, there had been no room for him anywhere. In Jesus, he had now found a brother. He wanted to share something with the infant Jesus. The only thing that he could offer, the only gift he could give the infant Jesus, was his body warmth. He shared this freely with Jesus in the manger.

Examine Our Holiday Activities in the Light of Our Deepest Values

Many readers yearn to cut through the consumerism of Advent, Christmas, and Epiphany. Consider what joy there would be in heaven and on earth were our pockets to be filled to overflowing this season. What if we were to eliminate some of the frenzy of Christmas shopping by giving the most basic necessities to those in need?

One idea is to organize an alternative marketplace for giving to gospel priorities. Virginia Lee, my colleague in Christian education, tells of organizing such an event at a Richmond, Virginia, congregation. Along with members of the community, she began planning in May. As a contrast with gift-giving characteristic of North American society, the event was called "Glorious Gifts." Consumers purchased more than $17,000 at this alternative marketplace. The gifts translated into 43 days of food and shelter for the homeless at an emergency shelter; 51 meals feeding 250 people each at a food bank; 639 chicks and three heifers for hungry families served by Heifer Project International; 1,370 bricks to build affordable homes; 207 concrete blocks for building a community center.[7]

Be a Peacemaker within Our Circle of Family and Friends

In his *Christmas Carol*, Charles Dickens described freeing the ghost of Jacob Marley of his chains and moneyboxes. In much the same way, Advent, Christmas, and Epiphany offer a time to unburden ourselves of whatever prevents us from living into the mystery of divine love. We do so by building our common life together on the basis of the Christian love ideal expressed in the following story.

One of the great figures of medieval Europe was Jadwiga, youngest daughter of Louis I and Elisabeth of Bosnia. Queen of Poland from 1384 until 1399, she inspired a series of charters issued at Horodlo in 1413.

> Nor can that endure which has not its foundations upon love. For love alone diminishes not, but shines with its own light; makes an end of discord, softens the fires of hate, restores peace in the world, brings together the sundered, redresses wrong, aids all, injures none; who so invokes its aid will find peace and safety and have no fear of future ill.[8]

Rededicate Ourselves to Spiritual Growth

There are many ways to practice lifestyle evangelism during Advent, Christmas, and Epiphany. One is hospitality. In our household, for example, at times we have invited international students and refugees—those who might otherwise be alone—to our home each of the four Sundays of Advent. Another is service, looking for ways to let love permeate and flow through our daily living. We can, for example, visit the lonely in nursing homes or do a caroling service in their facilities. Another practice is to participate in commerce with conscience through alternative gift-giving, especially through organizations that empower the poor. Yet another practice is hospitality. We can extend a welcome to family and friends with whom we have not had sufficient time to nurture relationships.

Preeminently, the season of Advent, Christmas, and Epiphany is holy. We should sanctify time through simple gifts and ordinary service. In the seventeenth century, the Puritans in the United Kingdom and colonial North America ignored Advent, Christmas, and Epiphany because of the pagan trappings. Should we follow their example? Are we spoilsports, attacking core values of our culture? Perhaps. We *are* identifying areas of our lives for which gospel is countercultural!

If you read this chapter during the season of Advent, Christmas, and Epiphany, I ask you prayerfully to let gospel priorities help you to reorder your priorities, use of time, and giving. I ask you prayerfully to reflect on ways you can nurture in children the spirit of wonder and relation to the Holy Child. I ask you prayerfully to be sensitive to those most needful. Seek to understand and to express more than just the babe in the manger. For God has become one with us that we might become more like God. A Welsh carol I enjoy invites us into the Christ event:

> All poor men and humble,
> All lame men who stumble,
> Come haste ye nor feel ye afraid;
> For Jesus, our treasure,
> With love past all measure,
> In lowly poor manger was laid.
> Though wise men who found him
> Laid rich gifts around him,
> Yet oxen they gave him their hay;
> And Jesus in beauty
> Accepted their duty;

>Contented in manger he lay.
>Then haste we to show him,
>The praises we owe him,
>Our service he ne'er can despise:
>Whose love still is able
>To show us that stable
>Where softly in manger he lies.[9]

A seasonal prayer from T. S. Eliot's *"Choruses from 'The Rock'"*[10] begins, *Invisible Light, we thank Thee that darkness reminds us of light. O Light Invisible, we give Thee thanks for Thy great glory!* As the Holy Family found somewhere to stay in Bethlehem, so too may all who are homeless find a place of shelter; as the Holy Family found companionship in Bethlehem, so too may all who are alone find a place of welcome; as the Holy Family found safety in exile, so too may all refugees find a place of security. As we behold the glory of God in the Christ child, so too may we see the divine image in people around. Amen.

---

[1] Thomas Merton, *Raids on the Unspeakable* (New York: New Directions, 1966), 70-71; Thomas P. McDonnell, ed., *A Thomas Merton Reader* (rev. ed., Garden City: Image Books, 1974), 363.

[2] Madeleine L'Engle, *Walking on Water: Reflections on Faith and Art* (New York: North Point Press, 1980), 50.

[3] Peter G. Cobb, "The History of the Christian Year," in *The Study of Liturgy,* ed. Cheslyn Jones, Geoffrey Wainwright, and Edward Yarnold (London: SPCK, 1978), 414

[4] Jo Robinson and Jean Coppock Staeheli, *Unplug the Christmas Machine: A Complete Guide to Putting Love and Joy back into the Season* (rev. ed., New York: William Morrow, 1991), 13.

[5] "Welcome Table," in *An Advent Sourcebook,* ed. Thomas O'Gorman (Chicago: Liturgy Training Publications, 1988), 50.

[6] Douglas V. Steere, *Bethlehem Revisited*, Pendle Hill Pamphlet 144 (Wallingford: Pendle Hill, 1965), 5.

[7] Virginia Lee, "Glorious Gifts," *Virginia Advocate* (22 December 1994), 5; "Giving Good Gifts: Ideas and Resources for Avoiding the Malls," *Peacework* 4-5 (1999); <www.simpleliving.org>.

[8] Oscar Halecki, *Jadwiga of Anjou and the Rise of East Central Europe* (New York: Columbia University Press, 1991) and *Borderlands of Western Civilization: A History of East Central Europe* (New York: Ronald, 1952), 117-31. The Fellowship of Reconciliation has cited the Act of Horodlo on cards for the Christmas season.

[9] Percy Dearmer, R. Vaughan Williams, and Martin Shaw, *The Oxford Book of Carols* (London: Oxford University Press, 1928), 73 (#34).

[10] T. S. Eliot, "Choruses from 'The Rock,'" *The Complete Poems and Plays 1909–1950* (New York: Harcourt, Brace & World, 1952), 114.

For Reflection and Conversation

- How do you observe Advent?

- How do you resist some of the cultural trappings of the season?

- What role does community play in this season?

- How can you daily find room for the Christ child? Do you have the capacity to marvel at each birth? Can you see God's beloved in each child?

- What is the relationship between Advent, Christmas, Epiphany, and an evangelistic lifestyle?

Practices of an Easter People

He is not here. . . . He has been raised from the dead.
(Matthew 28:6, 7)

The Easter cycle is an ideal time to focus on Jesus' passion and resurrection relived in the power of the Holy Spirit. During Lent and Holy Week, we consider how God meets us within our humanity. We reflect on our individual sins and also the corporate ones that engender injustice and brokenness. For me, in light of my family history, it is a time to feel deeply the pain of division between Jews and Christians and between eastern and western Christians.

Good Friday gives way to Easter. God has saved us. The inherent power of the drama, reenacted in worship, transforms the barren places of our lives into a season of hope, joy, and peace. Jesus sends his Spirit to transform and empower us to witness to him in the world.

As with Thanksgiving and the Christmas cycle, the Easter season offers North American society a full measure of satiety.[1] Since the second century at least, the Easter liturgy has been the normal occasion for baptism. It constitutes a Christian Passover marking a passage from bondage to sin and death to freedom in Christ. Documenting the origins of seasons in the Christian calendar can be difficult. The Easter cycle is the only period that we can say with certainty goes back to first-century Judaism and the apostolic church. We become heirs of the apostles.[2]

Lent

To practice Lenten disciplines is a journey into discipleship. Lent is a time for repentance, amendment of life, and response to blatant forms of injustice. Lent is an appropriate time to recover foot-washing, a practice of humility, mutuality, service, and vulnerability. As followers of Jesus, we count the cost of discipleship. German theologian Dietrich Bonhoeffer writes, "Happy are the simple followers of Jesus Christ who have been overcome by his grace, and are able to sing the praises of the all-sufficient grace of Christ with humbleness of heart. Happy are they who, knowing that grace, can live in the world without being of it . . . ."[3]

Jesus' journey to Jerusalem was remarkable. In John 11 and 12, Jesus stopped in Bethany, where his friend Lazarus was ill and died. Jesus raised Lazarus. A sign of his own impending glorification, Jesus gave Lazarus life and presented a dramatic paradox: he who gives life must offer his life that all might have life. Jesus said, *I am the resurrection and the life. Those who believe in me, even though they die, will live* (John 11:25).

In this scene, Jesus affirmed Martha and Mary, sisters of Lazarus. According to customs of the day, Jesus had no reason to take the women seriously. Yet he confirmed the resurrection of the dead to Martha and accepted the adoration of Mary, who anointed his feet with costly perfume.

This act led to a crucial practice, foot-washing. During a family meal, almost certainly a Passover meal, Jesus took up towel and water. He washed the feet of his friends. He dismissed their objections and said, *I have set you an example, that you also should do as I have done to you* (John 13:15).

Easter Resurrection

Like many reared in North America, I celebrate a rich religious lineage that draws from Jewish, Russian Orthodox, and Protestant traditions. I find the Orthodox liturgy especially fertile.[4] Coming after weeks of fasting, the Easter service of worship starts around 11 P.M. Saturday night. Flowers and lights decorate the building. The Easter icon, the image of Christ the Victor risen from the dead, shows Christ destroying the gates of hell and freeing Adam and Eve from the captivity of death. At midnight, all lights go out. The priest leads congregants outside the sanctuary. Leaving, each person takes a candle and lights it from the Christ candle. "Come ye, take light from the Light that is never overtaken by night. Come, and glorify the Christ risen from the dead." With the Christ light illuminating the dark, the people process around the building three times. Arriving at the front door, the priest knocks and calls out, "Lift up your gates, O you princes; and be lifted up, you everlasting gates, and the King of glory shall enter in." A response from within asks, "Who is this King of glory?" The priest replies, "The Lord strong and mighty, the Lord mighty in war." This question is repeated until, on the third occasion, the priest responds, "The Lord of hosts, He is the King of glory." As though reenacting the ancient garden scene, the doors open. Words from the Bible are read. Bells ring. The people enter singing "Christ is risen from the dead, trampling down death by death and upon those in the tombs bestowing life."

The purpose of the elaborate ritual is to remind celebrants that Easter resurrection is now. Congregants witness to and join a living story. Embracing, they greet one another joyfully saying, "Christ is risen." Each responds, "Indeed, He is risen." Before the Divine Liturgy (Eucharist), the celebrant solemnly recites John Chrysostom's Easter sermon, first preached around AD 400. Easily the homily most read in Christian history, it invites the faithful to break their fast, forget their sins, and join in the feast of the resurrection. The celebrant invites members of the Church to partake of Christ, the Passover Lamb, whose table is set amid the congregation. They receive the Eucharistic gifts, as well as an Easter egg.

Easter proclaims the Day of the Commonwealth of God, a day that has no night for its light is the Lamb (Rev 21:22-25). Orthodox Christians call Easter *Pascha*. The word means Passover. It symbolizes the new and everlasting covenant foretold by the prophets. The imagery is clear: darkness and death give way to light and life. God has rolled away the rock blocking the sepulcher and opened the gates of heaven. Time past has become time present. As they enter mystically into New Jerusalem, the faithful celebrate the glory of the Lord showered upon them.

In some respects, the service follows Matthew's resurrection narrative, which differs significantly from the other three Gospels. In Matthew 27:62-66, one finds an episode the other Gospels do not include. Matthew states the chief priests and the Pharisees went to Pilate on Friday, the day of preparation for the Sabbath, to request that the tomb not only be sealed, but guarded as well. They wanted to ensure that no one could steal the body and then claim Jesus had been raised from the dead. Matthew makes it clear that no one could enter the tomb casually. So when the women arrive in accord with Jewish custom, after the Sabbath, they expect to be kept from entering the tomb by both the seals and the guard. In Mark and Luke, the women find the stone already rolled away. In John the scene is subdued and takes place in a corner of the garden.

In Matthew, Mary Magdalene and the other Mary come to tend the body as the first day of the week is dawning. An earthquake strikes with incredible force. An angel, looking like lightning in snow-white clothes, throws away the tombstone. The guards shake violently and become like death. The tomb opens. An inhabitant awakens. Jesus steps up to the guards, then the visiting women and tells them, "Do not be afraid." The women take hold of his feet and worship him. Finally, Jesus instructs the women to go to Galilee, where Jesus' other followers will see him.

With this account of an earthquake, guards overcome with fear, and the two Marys grasping the magnitude of what has taken place, Matthew makes clear that Jesus was really dead and truly raised. This news gives the followers of Jesus something to shout about. He who was buried is no longer in the tomb. He who was dead is alive. Christ is risen. Christ is risen indeed!

How can the fact of resurrection carry us beyond the festivity of the season? What is the message of the resurrection for us today? A verse from James Montgomery's "Go to Dark Gethsemane" offers a clue. Many readers will sing three verses of the hymn on Good Friday. Many do not get to sing the fourth verse that celebrates Easter: "Early hasten to the tomb, Where they laid His breathless clay: All is solitude and gloom; Who hath taken Him away? Christ is ris'n! He meets our eyes. Saviour, teach us so to rise."[5]

As we celebrate Easter resurrection, like the two Marys, we seek to let the risen Christ's love embrace and inspire us. But that is not all! In a poem titled *Manifesto: The Mad Farmer Liberation Front*, Kentucky theologian-farmer Wendell Berry offers further suggestions:

> . . . do something that won't compute. Love the Lord.
> Love the world. Work for nothing.
> Take all that you have and be poor.
> Love someone who does not deserve it . . . .
> Ask the questions that have no answers.
> Invest in the millennium. Plant sequoias.
> . . . put your ear close, and hear the faint chattering
> of the songs that are to come.
> Expect the end of the world. Laugh.
> Laughter is immeasurable. Be joyful . . . . Swear allegiance
> to what is highest in your thoughts . . . .
> Practice Resurrection.[6]

If ever there was something that doesn't compute, especially for modern folk like us, it is the resurrection. We adhere to a scientific worldview. We place our trust in technology. So how do we practice resurrection? Let me suggest several practices.

The Practice of Hope

The fact that Jesus is not in the grave gives us power for living. Think on it. That Jesus is not now in the grave is an ongoing fact. He was in the grave, but he is no longer. The words Orthodox believers sing on Easter morning sustain the hope by which I live. Especially present amid the Fridays of my life, I know that Christ is risen from the grave. God has trampled down death by death. Now raised from the dark tomb, Christ reigns and transforms our frailty to strength, our darkness to light, our tentative steps to discipleship and love.

In *Uncle Vanya* and the movie based on it, *Vanya on 42d Street*, the Russian playwright Chekhov has a scene that describes resurrection hope:

> Sonia to Voinitsky, who has been spurned in love: What's to be done, we must go on living! [Pause] We shall go on living, Uncle Vanya. We shall live through a long, long chain of days and endless evenings; we shall patiently bear the trials that fate sends us; we'll work for others, now and in our old age, without ever knowing rest, and when our time comes, we shall die submissively; and there, beyond the grave, we shall say that we have suffered, that we have wept, and have known bitterness, and God will have pity on us; and you and I, Uncle, dear Uncle, shall behold a life that is bright, beautiful, and fine. We shall rejoice and look back on our present troubles with tenderness, with a smile—and we shall have faith . . . . [Kneeling before him, lays her head on his hand; in a weary voice] We shall rest! [Telyegin softly plays the guitar] We shall rest! We shall hear the angels, and see the heavens all sparkling like jewels; we shall see all earthly evil, all our sufferings, drowned in a mercy that will fill the whole world, and our life will grow peaceful, gentle, sweet as a caress. I have faith, I have faith. [Wipes away his tears with a handkerchief.] . . . We shall rest.[7]

The living Christ, crucified and risen, gives us hope. Crucifixion and resurrection are a crucial duality. On the one hand, the cross counteracts overconfidence or triumphalism on the part of Christians. On the other hand, the resurrection lifts us from discouraged resignation. Following Jesus, we are led into the pain of the world. So we clothe the naked, feed the hungry, comfort the sorrowful, shelter the destitute, bind up the wounded, and speak words of salvation to sinners.

To practice resurrection, we manifest hope concretely in our lives. With faith grounded in the resurrection of Jesus, we share the liberation, healing, salvation, and eternal life Christ gives. In words of Australian Baptist pastor Thorwald Lorenzen, we demonstrate "a new commitment to holiness, to uncompromising justice, and to love for all humans, especially for those who lie bruised in the side streets of life."[8] Through it all, Christ is our friend for the journey.

The Practice of Dreaming

Dreaming new dreams is a second practice arising from the fact that Jesus is not in the grave but is risen. One dreamer inspired by resurrection hope was Martin Luther King Jr. who, like Jesus, took up his cross and died as a follower of Jesus. King said, "Darkness cannot drive out darkness; only light can do that."

King was a dreamer. At the heart of his dream were two potent symbols, the cross and empty tomb. In 1955 amid the Montgomery campaign, King wrote, "The cross is the eternal expression of the length to which God will go in order to restore broken community. The Resurrection is the symbol of God's triumph over all the forces that seek to block community." He went on to urge creation of the Beloved Community, his phrase for the Kingdom of God. In one of my favorite passages, King described realization of God's dream:

> One day, youngsters will learn words they will not understand. Children from India will ask: what is hunger? Children from Alabama will ask: what is racial segregation? Children from Hiroshima will ask: what is the atomic bomb? Children at school will ask: what is war? You will answer them. You will tell them: these words are not used any more. Like stage-coaches, galleys or slavery, words no longer meaningful. That is why they have been removed from dictionaries.[9]

At the time of King's death, many individuals inspired by King's courageous dream offered leadership to a city inflamed with anger, fear, and hopelessness. They helped bring healing and initiated efforts to create a different and better world, for example, through the creation of the Metropolitan Inter-Faith Association that offers a variety of programs to the city's marginalized.

Because of Easter, the world is fundamentally different now. Resurrection gives us hope. We have new places to go. We have new dreams to dream. The morning stars are singing together, and the children of God are shouting for joy. Already we see signs of that coming time when all God's children shall be free, when the glory of the Lord is revealed. Because Christ is risen, risen indeed, we celebrate resurrection in song.

Low Sunday: The Continual Practice of Celebration

Practicing resurrection extends beyond Easter Sunday. In particular, celebratory practices mark the worship of God's people through the entire Pascal season of fifty days leading up to Pentecost, a pilgrim festival that originated in Jewish practice. The English designation for the Sunday after Easter is Low Sunday. This may be a corruption of "laud" Sunday, a reminder that the early Christians believed Christ to be with them in the power of the Spirit before his ascension. In the Latin tradition, its name is *Dominica in Albis*, a reference to the custom of the newly baptized wearing their baptismal robes for seven days after Easter.[10]

On the Sundays following Easter, we, like the early Christians, celebrate the risen Christ with praise. It is a period to bear witness to the resurrection of Jesus. It is also a period to risk boldly in faith. In his account of the historic civil rights march from Selma to Montgomery in March 1965, Henri Nouwen recalls a particularly tense time. Viola Liuzzo, a mother of five children from Detroit, had been shot dead. Henri found himself at the table of the grandmother of Ronald, an African American friend. She fed everyone well. Then she said, "Let's pray together, that the Lord will protect you on this dangerous road and bring you safely home." They prayed and continued on the journey. As they approached the state line between Mississippi and Alabama, Ronald shared words that should mark our post-resurrection practice: "Risk in faith, decide in hope, and suffer the consequences."[11]

Pentecost: The Practice of Mission around the World

The fact that Jesus is raised from the dead gives us hope, generates dreams, and inspires celebration. The fact that Jesus is raised from the dead also gives us new places to go. Notice that according to Matthew, Jesus wanted to meet his followers in Galilee, the place of mission to Gentiles and other strangers.

He did not want his friends to hang around Jerusalem, but rather to go and make disciples of all nations.

Shortly thereafter, Peter preached the first sermon recorded in Acts. With certainty Peter stated, *God has made him both Lord and Messiah, this Jesus whom you crucified* (Acts 2:36). The awesome identity of Jesus as the Christ and Lord of the universe gave birth to the church and its mission. The enthroning of the crucified Jesus as Lord and Christ of all became and remains the basis for faith in the redemptive work of God and hope in life after death. Jesus' ministry did not end at the cross. Easter led to the formation of the early Christian community, formally marked at Pentecost. Now unhindered by limits of time and space, the risen Christ continues his earthly ministry through us. In his name and in his power, we forgive, grant reconciliation to believers, intercede, heal, and make known his saving and liberating presence on the earth throughout the world to the ends of time.

If you want to know someone who practices resurrection, do not check the car he or she drives, the cost of the clothes he or she wears, or how much he or she puts into the offering plate. Check for a life with prayerful gratitude, joy, and spontaneous, vibrant outreach. To discover a congregation that practices Resurrection, do not check for a carefully worded or theologically profound "Confession of Faith." Look for a grace-filled community known for its practices of love and compassion.

One contemporary hymn, "We Shall Go Out with Hope of Resurrection," sung to the traditional Irish melody "Londonderry Air," gives us encouragement to dream Easter dreams. I offer it as a closing prayer.

Prayer
    We shall go out with hope of resurrection;
    we shall go out, from strength to strength go on;
    we shall go out and tell our stories boldly;
        tales of a love that will not let us go.
    We'll sing our songs of wrongs that can be righted;
    we'll dream our dreams of hurts that can be healed;
    we'll weave a cloth of all the world united
        within the vision of a Christ who sets us free.
    We'll give a voice to those who have not spoken;
    we'll find the words for those whose lips are sealed;
    we'll make the tunes for those who sing no longer,
        expressive love alive in every heart.

We'll share our joy with those who still are weeping,
> raise hymns of strength for hearts that break in grief,
we'll leap and dance the Resurrection story,
> including all in circles of our love.[12]

May we, loving God, dance the resurrection story. With resurrection faith, hope, and love, may your presence lead us from strength unto strength. Through our dreaming and our living, we magnify the Holy One risen from the grave. Amen.

---

[1] With the sending of cards, Easter bunnies, new wardrobes, and the like, Easter manifests a commercial buildup in North America. Compared with Thanksgiving and Christmas, the scale may be reduced, but a cartoon in the 17 April 2000 issue of a cultural bellwether, *New Yorker*, suggests this may not continue to be the case. The setting is a department store. Kids line up behind a sign that reads, "Kids, tell the big bunny what you want for Easter!" With a somewhat sinister countenance, an executive comments, "I can't imagine why we didn't think of this before."

[2] Books on the nature and mission of the church frequently emphasize that, like unity, holiness, and catholicity, apostolicity is a mark of the church. Each believer must live it out. Two twentieth-century theologians accent this point. Hans Kung writes, "As an individual Christian, I must become a true successor of the apostles, I must hear their witness, believe their message, imitate their mission and ministry. I must be, and always become anew, a believing and living member of the apostolic community" (*The Church* [Garden City: Image, 1976], 460). Jürgen Moltman writes, "Unity in freedom, holiness in poverty, catholicity in partisan support for the weak, and apostolate in suffering are the marks by which it [the church of Jesus Christ] is known in the world" (*The Church in the Power of the Spirit: A Contribution to Messianic Ecclesiology*, trans. Margaret Kohl [London: SCM, 1975], 361).

[3] Dietrich Bonhoeffer, *The Cost of Discipleship*, trans. R. H. Fuller (London: SCM, 1959), 47.

[4] Presently I live in Memphis, Tennessee, where there are three Orthodox congregations. The Church of the Annunciation draws primarily from the Greek community. St. Seraphim Eastern Orthodox Church attracts mainly young converts from evangelical Protestantism and follows Russian practices. St. John Orthodox Church draws from the wider Orthodox world. The order of the service is uniform. There are cultural differences. For example, one sits in pews at St. John Orthodox Church and the Church of the Annunciation; if physically able, one stands during the liturgy at St. Seraphim Eastern Orthodox Church. See Cheslyn Jones, Geoffrey Wainwright, and Edward Yarnold, eds., *The Study of Liturgy* (London: SPCK, 1978) on liturgical history.

[5] "Go to Dark Gethsemane," in *The Hymnal* (Brantford: Baptist Federation of Canada, 1973), 80. *Voices United* (Etobicoke: United Church Publishing House, 1996) excludes verse four.

[6] Wendell Barry, *The Country of Marriage* (1973), reprinted in *Collected Poems* (1985) and *Baptist Peacemaker* 16/1 (spring 1996): 1.

[7] Anton Chekhov, "Uncle Vanya," *The Major Plays*, trans. Ann Dunnigan (New York: New American, 1964), 230-31.

[8] Thorwald Lorenzen, *Resurrection and Discipleship: Interpretative Models, Biblical Reflections, Theological Consequences* (Maryknoll: Orbis, 1995), 313.

[9] King quoted in *Reconciliation International* 6 (spring 1991): 2

[10] R. F. Buxton, "Low Sunday," in *The New Westminster Dictionary of Liturgy and Worship*, ed. J. G. Davies (Philadelphia: Westminster Press, 1986), 345.

[11] Henri Nouwen, *The Road to Peace: Writings on Peace and Justice*, ed. John Dear (Maryknoll: Orbis, 1998), 94-95.

[12] Words by June Boyce-Tillman, 1993, *Voices United*.

For Reflection and Conversation

- How do you celebrate the Easter season?

- How do you resist some of the cultural trappings of the season?

- What role does community play in this season?

- How do you practice hope?

- What is the relationship between Lent, Easter, Pentecost, and an evangelistic lifestyle?

Appendix

A Litany for Workers

Leader: O Lord, we give thanks this day for work: for work that sustains; for work that fulfills; for work that, however tiring, also satisfies and resonates with Your labor in creation.

People: As part of our thanks, we also intercede for those who have no work; who have too much or too little work; who work at jobs that demean or destroy, work that profits the few at the expense of the many.

Leader: Make us instruments of Your peace, advocates of Your justice, channels of Your blessing amid our daily labors.

People: Lord, hear our prayer.

Leader: To this end we renew our vows, begun in baptism, to extend Your redemptive purpose in the many and varied places of our work. In factory or field, in sheltered office or under open sky, using technical knowledge or physical strength, working with machines or with people or with the earth itself.

People: Together we promise

Leader: . . . to bring the full weight of our intelligence and strength and care to our work.

People: Together we promise

Leader: . . . to make our place of work a place of safety and respect for all with whom we labor.

People: Together we refuse

Leader: . . . to remain silent, even at the risk of our own security, when just relations are denied—when we or our coworkers are harassed or mistreated or discriminated against.

People: Together we refuse

Leader: . . . to engage in work that harms another, that promotes injustice or violence, that damages the earth or otherwise betrays the common good; or to resign ourselves to economic arrangements that widen the gap between rich and poor.

People: Together we refuse

Leader: . . . to allow our work to infringe on time with our families and friends, with our community of faith, with the rhythm of Sabbath rest.

People: Together we affirm

Leader: . . . the rights of all to work that both fulfills and sustains, to just wages, and to contentment.

People: Together we affirm

Leader: . . . that the redeeming and transforming power of the gospel, with all its demands for justice and its promises of mercy, is as relevant to the workplace as to the sanctuaries of faith and family.

All: We make these promises, we speak these refusals, and we offer these affirmations as offerings to You, O God, in response to Your ever-present grace, as symbols of our ongoing repentance and transformation, and in hope that one day all the world shall eat and be satisfied. AMEN.

Used by permission of Ken Sehested.